THE AUTOBIOGRAPHY OF CITIZENSHIP

THE AUTOBIOGRAPHY OF CITIZENSHIP

Assimilation and Resistance in US Education

TOVA COOPER

Rutgers University Press

NEW BRUNSWICK, NEW JERSEY, AND LONDON

LIBRARY OF CONGRESS CATALOGING-IN-PUBLICATION DATA

Cooper, Tova, 1969–
    The autobiography of citizenship : assimilation and resistance in US education
/ Tova Cooper.
        pages   cm. — (The American literatures initiative)
    Includes bibliographical references and index.
    ISBN 978-0-8135-7015-0 (hardback)
    ISBN 978-0-8135-7014-3 (pbk.)
    ISBN 978-0-8135-7016-7 (e-book)
    1. Citizenship—Study and teaching—United States. 2. Immigrants—Education—
United States—History—20th century. 3. Minorities—Education—United States—
History—20th century. 4. Assimilation (Sociology)—United States—History—20th
century. 5. Education—Demographic aspects—United States—History—20th century.
6. Americanization—History—20th century. I. Title.
LC1091.C59 2015
372.83'0440973—dc23

                                                                2014016471

A British Cataloging-in-Publication record for this book is available
from the British Library.

Visit our website: http://rutgerspress.rutgers.edu

Manufactured in the United States of America

THE
AMERICAN
LITERATURES
INITIATIVE

A book in the American Literatures Initiative (ALI), a collaborative
publishing project of NYU Press, Fordham University Press, Rutgers
University Press, Temple University Press, and the University of Virginia
Press. The Initiative is supported by The Andrew W. Mellon Foundation.
For more information, please visit www.americanliteratures.org.

For Stan

CONTENTS

Illustrations

ACKNOWLEDGMENTS

This project has gone through many phases since 2004, when I first began researching it. I could not have gotten this far without the intellectual, practical, financial, and emotional support of many people. John Carlos Rowe has been a never-ending source of advice and support. Sarah Abramowicz ceaselessly read my chapters, shared her brilliant insights, and made suggestions that always bore fruit. Several of the chapters also benefited from feedback provided by members of the Works in Progress group at the University of South Florida, including Michael Clune, Maria Cizmic, and John Lennon, who were especially generous with their time. Toward the end, the excellent and detailed advice from the anonymous reader at Rutgers University Press, as well as from Sarah Wilson, was invaluable in bringing this project to fruition. I am also indebted to the editorial support of Lee Davidson and Katie Keeran, and to some late-night research assistance from Cory Barrows.

Financial support provided by the University of California and the University of South Florida helped make this book possible, as did a host of librarians at the Library of Congress, the National Archives, the New York Public Library, the Huntington Library, and Special Collections, Rutgers University Libraries. This book certainly benefited from the open-ended financial support of my parents, Janet and Barry Cooper, who, with my sister, Jill Terrell, have offered me a particularly dependable form of unconditional love and encouragement.

If there were something better than a superlative, then I would use it to describe how Stan Apps—my husband, best friend, and intellectual compatriot—made it possible for me to write this book. Stan didn't just read every chapter of the dissertation, and then the book, several times; he read some sentences and paragraphs over and over again, always providing exactly what I needed at any given moment—whether that was comforting praise, incisive editorial suggestions, a sounding board for my emerging ideas, or the occasional truthful confession that a particular idea simply wasn't any good. Finally, my superhuman boy Leo and my superadorable baby August have provided me with something to look forward to after the long days of writing and revising this book.

The Autobiography of Citizenship

Introduction

In his 1867 poem "When I heard the Learn'd Astronomer," Walt Whitman rejects the academic structure of American education, which was undergoing a sea change in the period following the Civil War. The poem's speaker becomes "tired and sick" after hearing a popular lecture on astronomy and leaves the lecture hall for the great outdoors, where he can learn by gazing "in perfect silence at the stars."[1] Emily Dickinson similarly rejects a hierarchical educational model in "If the foolish call them 'flowers,'" a poem whose speaker suggests that educated people—mere "Stars, amid profound Galaxies"—should not assume that their ostensibly superior terminology is the only way to identify truth.[2] These poems about education speak to the student-centered perspective and the spirit of "hands-on" learning that were emerging alongside rote education in late nineteenth-century America.

Beginning in the 1830s, nineteenth-century educators began to consider what type of moral and religious education common schools should provide to American children, a development that became increasingly urgent as the US population expanded, urbanized, and diversified during the second half of the nineteenth century. Most early common-school reformers agreed that schools should give "all children of whatever origin a basic education to form them into good Americans, which meant civically moral, patriotic, English-speaking Protestants."[3] Beginning in the mid-1850s, common-school reformers responded to an increasingly diverse US population by developing the "one best system," which would impose a "uniform course of study," "standard examinations," and a "systematic plan of gradation" on urban public schools.[4]

By the early twentieth century, *educational progressivism* had become an umbrella term for a number of groups with varying and sometimes incompatible ideologies, objectives, and methods. Though the "one best system" was relatively successful, it came under attack by administrative progressives who wanted public schools to tailor their curricula to the various socioeconomic levels, rather than to impose uniformity. For instance, figures such as Edward Cubberley and William Dooley promoted the testing and classification of children to facilitate their channeling into academic or vocational tracks.[5] While the administrative progressives advocated for schools that promoted "social efficiency and social control," libertarians and social constructionists rejected this use of school and instead envisioned school as a platform for radical social change.[6] Another group—pedagogical progressives such as John Dewey and his followers—sought to institutionalize "cooperative, democratic schooling" but found it difficult to realize their program in public schools that were dominated by a "hierarchical structure of differentiated schooling."[7] As a result, the pedagogical progressives realized their objectives in small private schools or tried to inspire individual public school teachers "to change [their] philosophy . . . curriculum, and . . . methods."[8]

At the turn of the twentieth century, public conversations about the role of education began to change as a result of demographic shifts that followed the passage of the Thirteenth and Fourteenth Amendments, the breakup of Indian reservations facilitated by the 1887 Dawes Act, and a vast increase in immigration from southern Europe, eastern Europe, and the Asia-Pacific triangle between 1880 and 1924. During this period, progressive activists, philanthropists, government agents, and teachers actively debated what kind of training best suited new US citizens. Though education officials rhetorically promoted full civic, or political, membership, in reality citizenship education programs usually trained new citizens for life in the civil rather than the civic sphere—that is, in the world of work rather than the world of political participation.[9] Educational institutions that prepared nonwhite and non-Protestant students for US citizenship regulated the bodies, time, clothing, and ideas of their predominantly working-class students in ways that helped solidify their positioning on the bottom rungs of a hierarchical class structure once they entered mainstream US life.[10] Schools instituted rhythmic and repetitive physical activities to produce conformity through habituation and trained future laborers in the Taylorist mode. During this period, photography became an apt medium for documenting everyday experiences. As a result, citizenship educators published photographs of student life in school publications as another means through which to regulate the bodies of new citizens.

The US legal landscape at the turn of the twentieth century further belied the quality of civic membership that educators had promised to American Indians, African Americans, and a variety of immigrant groups.[11] African Americans suffered from Black Codes and state-sanctioned violence in the aftermath of Reconstruction. American Indians were denied the citizenship that had been guaranteed to them by the 1887 Dawes Act. And politically radical immigrants were subject to revocation of their naturalization status, and subsequent deportation, as a result of the 1917 Immigration Act's criminalization of "unpatriotic" activities. Moreover, members of these groups who faced economic hardship and legal discrimination often became alienated from their families, languages, and cultures as a result of their education. In many cases, these older forms of community no longer provided citizens relief from the disappointing realities of Americanization.

Social Darwinism also affected the economic, legal, and cultural realities of new citizens. The public sphere was dominated by anxiety that immigrants, as well as nonwhite, native-born Americans, would sully the future of the United States with inferior physical and cultural traits, bloodlines, and temperaments.[12] Such anxieties were expressed by academics educated at Harvard, Yale, and Princeton, supported by Presidents Theodore Roosevelt, Woodrow Wilson, and Calvin Coolidge, and transformed into law by legislators and Supreme Court justices (especially Oliver Wendell Holmes Jr.). Popular but misguided scientific ideas about evolution, and later genetics, informed the curricular realities of most citizenship education programs, even those that adopted progressive ideas and methodologies such as hands-on learning and student-centered classrooms.

As the cultural historian Carl Degler has argued, social Darwinism was a conservative movement intended to preserve the status quo through its promotion of laissez-faire government policies and reliance on a "survival of the fittest" ideology.[13] However, social Darwinist ideology not only informed conservative educational institutions but also pervaded the philosophies and practices of progressive educators with more liberal agendas. At one end of this spectrum stood conservative educators such as Captain Richard Henry Pratt and Booker T. Washington, who promoted hands-on learning to shape the cultural identities of new US citizens in an assimilationist mode or to train laborers for maximum efficiency in the capitalist marketplace.[14] At the other end of this spectrum were figures such as John Dewey and Emma Goldman, who incorporated the educational philosophies of Johann Pestalozzi, Friedrich Froebel, and others into child-centered programs that championed individualism and resisted the prepackaged transfer of knowledge from teacher to student.

The evolution of US cultural identity at the turn of the twentieth century, represented by practices at citizenship education institutions and autobiographical writing by new citizens, is the subject of this book.[15] Between the Civil War and the First World War, "learning by doing" operated as a flexible technology through which educators inculcated competing conceptions of national identity into new citizens. Whereas many studies of citizenship education focus on the experiences of particular ethnic or racial minorities, this book instead *compares* the educational experiences of the largest groups of new US citizens from this period: European immigrants, African Americans, and American Indians.[16] While individual histories of these groups have demonstrated how citizenship education programs undermined the new citizen's civil, political, and legal equality, this book's comparative approach emphasizes the experiences shared by members of non-Anglo or non-Protestant groups.[17] It also focuses on archival materials—such as student essays and letters, photographs, and curricular records—to illustrate precisely *how* citizenship education programs sought to reproduce a socially and economically stratified citizenry through the adoption of embodied practices.

With its examination of embodied education, this book offers a series of insights about visual, political, and educational culture in the United States. It argues that educational photography helped cultivate a national sensibility; that liberalism, republicanism, and cosmopolitanism coexisted as models of national belonging; that varying manifestations of social Darwinism shaped progressive education; and that an inclusive rhetoric of citizenship was belied by the material and legal experiences of new citizens. The book foregrounds three central types of evidence: public conversations and written documents in which educators expressed their views on citizenship education; repetitive, embodied practices through which educators transmitted their concepts of US democracy; and competing visions of education and national identity that new citizens articulated in their autobiographical writing.

Unpublished letters, stories and essays from school newspapers, and published memoirs and novels also showcase a range of responses to citizenship education programs. Each chapter juxtaposes archival materials that recreate school life with literary texts by students and educators, such as W. E. B. Du Bois's "Diary of My Steerage Trip across the Atlantic" (1895); Jane Addams's *Twenty Years at Hull-House* (1910); Charles Eastman's boarding school autobiography, *From the Deep Woods to Civilization* (1916); Abraham Cahan's autobiographical novel, *The Rise of David Levinsky* (1916), and his Yiddish-language autobiography, *The Education of Abraham Cahan* (1926); and Emma Goldman's autobiography, *Living My Life* (1931). Some of these texts illustrate how new citizens reproduced school lessons uncritically; others challenge dominant conceptions of national membership; and still others express ethnically specific visions of national belonging. All of these books evidence how new citizens internalized aspects of the dominant culture as a result of embodied learning. Yet they also articulate alternatives to the dominant US culture with educational theories, practices, and autobiographical narratives influenced by extranational or international perspectives.

Much of the archival material presented here either illustrates how embodied practices were central to the objectives of citizenship educators or adds complexity to the historical record with the first-person perspectives of new citizens and their teachers. At the New York Public Library, I discovered Estelle Reel's 1901 curriculum for the Indian boarding schools; at the National Archives, I read through dozens of letters and questionnaires completed by former Carlisle students; at the YIVO Institute for Jewish Research, I encountered photos of student life and letters from Jewish immigrants who attended citizenship education classes; at the Dorot Jewish Division of the New York Public Library, I read through unpublished autobiographies of Jewish students who underwent citizenship training at the Hebrew Orphan Asylum; at the University of California, Irvine, I uncovered W. E. B. Du Bois's unpublished transatlantic diary while reading through his papers; and at the Huntington Library and the Rutgers Special Collections, I found photos, student magazines, unpublished diaries, and other evidence of life at the libertarian Modern School. My encounter with these archives resulted in chapters that balance historical and literary elements differently. Some chapters detail the quotidian experience of life at particular schools; others emphasize writing by educators associated with new-citizen groups; and still others focus more on autobiographical interpretations of education and national belonging by new citizens.

"Learning by Doing" across the Educational Spectrum

Between 1880 and 1930, citizenship education programs drew on both traditional and progressive educational practices as they encouraged new citizens to identify with a mainstream national identity. Despite the success that many institutions had with this endeavor, some new citizens maintained the cultural or ethnic identities they had held prior to their nationalist education. Others articulated revisionary portraits of US identity made possible by their education. Some even influenced mainstream US culture as a result of their revisionist writing and activism. Many new-citizen writings dramatize a dialectical interplay between the nationalist agenda promoted by citizenship education programs and the culturally specific identities that these citizens articulated through autobiography.

This book identifies the circumstances that helped determine whether a new citizen would embrace a mainstream identity or choose to cultivate a hybrid one. When a particular educational program adopted conservative educational practices such as rote learning and a hierarchical classroom structure, new citizens were more likely to express satisfaction with their experience of education and citizenship and to express a sense of belonging to mainstream US culture. In other cases where schools adopted progressive methods such as hands-on learning, the outcomes were more varied. When progressive methods were imbued with a nationalist bias, new citizens were more likely to articulate mainstream, nationalist identities. Conversely, when schools offered hands-on learning but also allowed students to engage actively with the curriculum, new citizens were more likely to adapt the school's lessons to their preexisting beliefs, practices, or identities. In this respect, hands-on learning did not in itself operate to realize any particular agenda; rather, its effects depended on the framework into which it was incorporated. In other words, hands-on learning was not itself ideologically charged; rather, it operated as a flexible technology that educators adapted to achieve contradictory objectives.

Up through the late nineteenth century, neither hands-on learning nor compulsory schooling was widespread in the United States. Between 1852 and 1918, compulsory schooling laws were passed on a state-by-state basis and enforced unevenly.[18] Existing schools were resistant to change, and by the turn of the century many still relied on the antebellum methods of "whole-group instruction, drill, and recitation."[19] A minority of schools, however, benefited from the influence of European reformers, including Pestalozzi and Froebel, and their American counterparts, such as Francis Parker and John Dewey. These educators not only rejected the idea that academic training should be limited to the leisure class but also disagreed with the use of physical discipline for punishment.

As John Dewey and his daughter Evelyn argue in their 1915 book, *Schools of To-morrow*, "learning by doing" was an antidote to an outdated system of education that saw manual work of any kind as unthinkable. According to this older model, "The less the body in general, and the hands and senses in particular, were employed, the higher grade of intellectual activity. True thought resulting in true knowledge was to be carried on wholly within the mind without the body taking any part at all."[20] When traditional educators did focus on the body, they did so to dole out punishment for nonconformist behavior. By contrast, progressive educators began to cultivate students' minds by emphasizing "muscular and sense training."[21] Progressive educators believed not only that people could learn more successfully through embodied training but also that such training could help them adapt more successfully to a range of life circumstances.

Most of the progressive schools that the Deweys admired objected to "a rote system of learning that emphasize[d] obedience to authority, memorization of facts, and disciplinary punishment for disobedience."[22] Such traditional models were usually organized around two central figures, the "Intellectual Overseer" and the "Drillmaster."[23] While the "Overseer" "assigned work, punished errors, and made students memorize," the "Drillmaster" "[led] students in unison through lessons requiring them to repeat content aloud."[24] The demand that students learn material by rote, combined with a disregard for individuals' learning styles, interests, and special capacities, was central to traditional education. Traditional schools often combined rote-teaching methods with lessons in patriotism and morality, promoting the conformism central to civic republican ideology. For instance, as early as 1789, the Massachusetts Legislature passed a law requiring towns with over fifty families to have a schoolmaster who, in addition to offering instruction in English, would teach students a "love of their country, humanity, and universal benevolence; sobriety, industry, and frugality; chastity, moderation, and temperance," so they might "preserve and perfect a republican constitution."[25] As this list of objectives suggests, institutions that promoted civic republicanism deemphasized individual differences in the service of a nationalist agenda.

The conservative educator's disregard for individuality was precisely what motivated John Dewey and his contemporaries to develop a progressive approach to education. Innovators such as Dewey and Parker envisioned schools as democratic communities where students would learn most effectively through immersive methods such as experiments and field trips.[26] At the same time, both progressive and conservative educators shared Dewey's objection to "traditional education" because it presented "knowledge that had no foothold in experience or demanded rigid habitual responses."[27] Educators across the political spectrum adopted Dewey's approach, which resulted in some programs that focused on promoting individual diversity, and others that chose to emphasize manual training, physical education, and instruction in personal hygiene.

Depending on their political affiliations, progressive educators influenced by Dewey also envisioned the aims of education differently. At the leftist end of this spectrum, educators cultivated students' individuality in the service of reforming a "hierarchical, fragmented society incapable of understanding diverse points of view."[28] These educators hoped to help US society realize its democratic principles more effectively.[29] One such example was Marietta Pierce Johnson, whose Organic School in Fairhope, Alabama, eschewed competition and extrinsic rewards in favor of developing the child's "spontaneity, initiative, interest, and sincerity."[30] Whereas liberals used Dewey's inspiration to promote a diverse democracy, conservatives invoked his ideas in the hopes of increasing the efficiency of capitalist laborers.

This contradictory development may have been influenced by a contradiction within Dewey's own philosophy. While Dewey encouraged schools to embrace students' diverse points of view, he nonetheless sanctioned efforts to train students for optimum efficiency in the capitalist workforce. It is therefore not surprising that conservative educators influenced by Dewey thought that "fully developed individuals" trained by progressive methods would "make for the best workers in the postwar division of labor."[31] Nonetheless, Dewey disliked having his ideas invoked to realize social Darwinist aims; as a result, he increasingly "sought to distance himself from the practical changes being implemented in US schools (going so far as to refuse membership in the Progressive Education Association in 1919)."[32]

The progressive embrace of individuality was an important, but not sole, factor in contributing to the expansion of hands-on learning. The rapid expansion of industrialization, urbanization, and immigration at the turn of the twentieth century led to increased school attendance and a proliferation of views about the role of public education in US life. One central debate—about whether to include manual and vocational training in the schools—intensified after the Philadelphia Centennial Exposition of 1876. This exposition showcased the manual instruction shops popularized by Victor Della Vos in Moscow; in turn, manual instruction was adopted by university presidents John Runkle (of MIT) and Calvin Woodward (of Washington University), and later by public school educators across the United States.[33] Other educators, such as Emerson White of Purdue, vociferously opposed the increasing influence of manual training in the schools; White thought it was "ridiculous for public schools to devote their energies to handicraft training at a time when the machine was assuming an ever-greater burden of production." White wrongly judged the influence that manual training would come to hold over public education. As its popularity increased, however, manual training ceased to represent the idealism inspired by the Philadelphia Exposition, which had caused educators such as Woodward to set up "shop teaching *with no immediate vocational goal.*" By the early twentieth century, public schools wholeheartedly had adopted manual and vocational training in the service of producing laborers for the capitalist marketplace.[34]

William Wirt's Gary Plan perfectly exemplifies this shift. Wirt initially developed his plan for the public schools of Gary, Indiana, which served a largely working-class, immigrant population. At the Gary schools, students split their time between "shop, laboratory, playground, and auditorium," were given the flexibility and freedom to work at their own pace, and learned skills that served the industrial needs of the school and the community.[35] Progressive educators, who believed schools should increase workers' adaptability to the conditions of industrial capitalism, supported the Wirt system.[36] As educational historians Ronald Cohen and Raymond Mohl explain, John Dewey, alongside William Wirt and Alice Barrows (who worked together to promote the Gary Plan), "accepted technology as a given and viewed the school as a mediating institution between the individual and technological society."[37]

Unlike the progressives who supported vocational education, Samuel Gompers and the union movement opposed both its inclusion in public schools and efforts to secure federal funding for it—at least until 1910, when they were compelled to accept its inevitability. The unions believed that public schools were working together with businessmen to increase vocational education as a way of threatening unions with cheap scab labor.[38] While Wirt was not colluding with businessmen as some believed he was, the Wirt schools were "essentially turning out workers for the city's mills and factories and consumers for their products."[39] While some immigrants and migrants surely benefited from vocational education, others opposed it, evidenced, for example, by the vocal and successful campaign to remove the Gary Plan from the New York City public schools, a campaign actively supported by parents who "conceived of vocational education as a method of forcing children into factory jobs."[40]

William James, Social Darwinism, and the Tradition of the Remembering Body

At the same time that John Dewey was objecting to the production of "rigid habitual responses" in educational institutions, William James was philosophizing about the nature of habit and its ability to ingrain itself deeply within the structures of the brain.[41] James's theory of habit prefigures a contemporary trend in cognitive psychology, which emphasizes our ability to reprogram the brain's neural pathways by replacing habitual thoughts or actions with new ones. Whether or not nineteenth-century citizenship educators read James's work, they did seek to inculcate "American" habits of thought and action into new citizens by instituting repetitive activities. Even though James was critical of social Darwinism, his views about individual mutability were compatible with some social Darwinist educational practices. Situating himself at the intersection of philosophy, psychology, and physiology, James argued that habitual actions had a lasting impact on the human mind. In his 1890 work *Principles of Psychology* James writes that habits acquired at an early age, when our brains are most plastic, may reappear effortlessly later in life: "The period below twenty is more important still for the fixing of *personal* habits, properly so called, such as vocalization and pronunciation, gesture, motion, and address."[42] If James is correct, his theory might help explain this book's argument that students who came to citizenship education programs at an older age, or with more developed identities, were less likely to undergo Americanization without also experiencing doubt or resistance.

By 1906, James had considered his theory of habit more fully, in concert with his development of pragmatism as a theory of action.[43] In his 1906 lecture "The Energies of Men," presented to the American Philosophical Association at Columbia University, he explains that a shift in ideas could precipitate new habits, which might in turn affect an individual's physiological processes.[44] In the lecture, James shares the story of a friend who was cured of a prolonged case of nervous prostration after spending a long period practicing yoga, meditation, and asceticism. Though James locates the source of this man's transformation in the ideas that motivated his new behaviors, this example testifies to James's belief that "mental disciplines . . . shaped the minds and bodies of those who were trained in them by inscribing habits in their nervous systems."[45] Though during this period there was no solid scientific evidence that embodied training resulted in physiological change, educators nonetheless sought to cultivate new practices and beliefs through embodied activities.

James was not alone in considering the physiological repercussions of noninstinctual habits. Similar concerns mark the philosophical traditions initiated by Jean-Baptiste Lamarck, Herbert Spencer, and Charles Darwin. In his 1872 book *The Expression of the Emotions in Man and Animals*, Darwin identifies a link between repetitive, embodied behaviors and mental structures. In this book, he strongly asserts that "some physical change is produced in the nerve-cells or nerves which are habitually used."[46] Darwin also accepted Lamarck's principle of "acquired characters," which held that social habits or moral attitudes acquired during an animal's lifetime could be transferred hereditarily to its offspring.[47] One important difference between Darwin and Lamarck, however, is that Darwin refused to attach a moral or political agenda to this theory.[48] William James also objected to the adoption of Lamarck's theories to promote a nationalist agenda—vocally criticizing Herbert Spencer, for instance, for justifying his laissez-faire theory of government with reference to natural selection.[49]

In spite of their varying beliefs, James, Darwin, and the social Darwinists all viewed social practices and physiological change as interconnected phenomena. Darwin and James noted the embodied effects of habitual action, whereas social Darwinist educators subscribed both to the idea that training influenced physiology and to Lamarck's theory of acquired characteristics. At a time when citizenship education programs and social Darwinism were equally prominent, many citizenship educators justified their efforts to reshape the identities of new citizens by referencing the heritability of habits. Thus their training would be doubly effective, influencing present and future generations of new Americans.[50]

Ultimately, the theory of acquired characteristics was a short-lived phenomenon, which dissipated with the shift from evolutionary biology to genetics. As Carl Degler explains, once August Weismann made his 1892 discovery that acquired habits could not be passed on without the alteration of genetic material, social scientists and educators despaired that "no amount of education or improvement in the social environment over time could either eradicate anti-social behavior or foster socially desirable actions."[51] Once differences in race were seen as immutable, the popularity of citizenship education programs began to wane.

During their period of dominance, however, these programs were shaped not only by the social Darwinist idea that individual habits were influenced by one's ethnic, racial, or national identity but also by the belief that curricular choices could alter habits and identities. Citizenship educators instituted work practices, reading programs, and physical activities that would, in their view, facilitate nationalization. School curricula taught students to engage in physical activities in unison, to articulate their experiences with similar narrative structures, and to envision themselves as members of the nation. Educators hoped that such practices would encourage students to cross-identify with each other *and* with mainstream US ideologies such as patriotism, capitalism, and consumerism.[52]

This book explores how individuals might acquire new beliefs through repetitive practices. Though William James's physiological theory of habit offers insight into this issue, work by more contemporary theorists, such as Pierre Bourdieu, Henri Bergson, and Marcel Mauss, has influenced my consideration of habitual actions and the cultural beliefs that may result from them. William James was ahead of his time in locating the neurological basis of habit in the "electrophysiological currents" that "underlie conscious awareness, emotional feeling, and behavioral actions."[53] Henri Bergson's work usefully builds on this idea through its attention to the significance of unconscious actions that can reveal an individual's feelings, ideas, and beliefs. As Edward Casey explains, Bergson carefully distinguishes skilled actions, which require a "remembering-how," from embodied memories.[54] In Bergson's view, an individual's character is best revealed through habitual actions that are performed unconsciously: "unskilled and unuseful actions, such as slouching in a certain way, gesturing excessively when speaking, drooling unselfconsciously, or grimacing at insects."[55] Paying attention to these unconscious movements allows us to focus on the phenomenological question of who we are when we are simply existing, performing our identities with motions and gestures that embody our unconscious way of moving through the world.

The ideas of Marcel Mauss and Pierre Bourdieu are also useful for considering the cultural implications of habit. For Mauss, "even the most mundane and routine activity is a cultural technique, whose form varies both historically and culturally."[56] In a similar vein, Bourdieu focuses on the effects of an individual's performance of verbal and nonverbal language. As Bourdieu's work shows, both verbal and nonverbal language can reveal an individual's internalization of social, economic, and cultural norms. By focusing on the dialectical interplay between an individual and his or her environment, Bourdieu and his interpreters usefully build on William James's observation that lived culture is not static. As Sue Ellen Henry insightfully explains, Bourdieu reveals not only how culture informs habit but also how culture can shift in response to individuals who incorporate and then reshape cultural norms. According to this schema, individuals harbor "cognitive aspirations and expectations," which the body either "achieve[s] or avoid[s]" in response to the demands of the social world; as a result of the internalization and reworking of social demands, an individual may effect social change.[57] This book shows how, on the one hand, curricular practices taught new citizens to adopt particular mental structures and physical styles, yet how, on the other hand, new citizens ironized or revised the nationalist principles embedded in these styles.

Coexisting Conceptions of Citizenship

In the late nineteenth century, the United States experienced a conservative trend in which citizenship came to be understood in assimilationist terms. Before this, "an enlightened minority of Americans [had] supported a fairly cosmopolitan and hopeful view of our national identity" and had viewed assimilation "as a process of mutual engagement and common adjustment."[58] By the late nineteenth century, however, the dominant understanding of citizenship had shifted to a civic republican one that demanded total adaptation to a homogenous national culture. Educational historian Stephen Macedo attributes this shift to increased immigration, poverty, crime, and political radicalism, alongside declining church attendance—demographic shifts that united the "early progressives" in their "desire to promote a more nationalized vision of citizenship."[59] As Macedo explains, by the early decades of the twentieth century, "unhyphenated Americanism was available to all, but as an imperative, not merely an option."[60] This view had become widespread by the end of the First World War, exemplified, for instance, by a postwar editorial Theodore Roosevelt wrote for the *Kansas City Star* in April 1918. In the article, Roosevelt promoted an ultranationalist vision by insisting that only English should be taught and used in public schools; that newspapers should be prohibited from publishing in any language other than English; and that immigrants who did not learn English within five years of their arrival should "leave the country."[61]

Despite the increasing dominance of republican citizenship (or civic republicanism), liberal and cosmopolitan theories of national belonging also gained prominence at the turn of the twentieth century. In various configurations, these three forms of citizenship informed the day-to-day operations at the educational institutions examined in this book. Assimilationist educational programs that sought to erase cultural difference were influenced by civic republican ideology, whereas educational institutions that validated the "voices, experiences, and perspectives" of minority subjects sought to realize liberal or cosmopolitan ideas about citizenship.[62] While all of these institutions promoted "learning by doing," their differing objectives were often informed by educators' diverse views about the citizen's role in the public sphere.

Educators often adopted positions that reflected citizenship traditions informed by the ideas of either John Locke or Jean-Jacques Rousseau. The demand for a uniform citizenry central to republican citizenship and assimilationist education is grounded in Rousseau's vision of the social contract. Rousseau stressed that citizens were bound to uphold a unique conception of "right" that emerged only after their formation as citizens.[63] Unlike Locke, who prioritized the "natural" rights that preexisted the social contract, Rousseau thought that a particular community's conception of "right" depended on its members' shared characteristics. Once formed, the community would become a homogenous entity bound to protect this consensual vision of right. Rousseau believed this approach was necessary to ensure the citizen's "security (of property and person)" and to preserve his freedom.[64]

By prioritizing the cultivation of obligations over rights, assimilationist education programs were influenced by Rousseau's vision of republican citizenship.[65] Civic republican ideology holds that because the citizen's primary membership is in the nation-state, she or he should embrace patriotism, consensus, unity, and loyalty to nationalist symbols and icons.[66] Traditionally, however, the civic republican conception of citizenship also has been associated with political activity, either referring to "the degree and nature of public involvement by members of a polity," or presenting "active engagement in political life" as a normative ideal.[67] In late nineteenth-century America, educational institutions emphasized either conformity or political action and in some cases embraced civic republicanism in a contradictory fashion. For instance, conservative institutions like Carlisle and Tuskegee sought to form a homogeneous citizenry while simultaneously deemphasizing political engagement: Carlisle was a boarding school that sought to "Americanize" American Indians by eradicating their tribal identities, and Tuskegee was a normal school that improved on (rather than rejected) an agricultural lifestyle for African Americans. By promoting a depoliticized vision of civic republicanism, these assimilationist institutions undermined the multiple affiliations, practices, and viewpoints of minority subjects;[68] with this approach, they hoped to prevent the articulation of nonconformist views in the civic sphere.[69]

The assimilationist model of citizenship education competed for dominance with liberal and cosmopolitan models. The latter two were influenced by John Locke's view that a state's legitimacy depends on its ability to institutionalize respect for man's natural rights and to codify them in its political and legal structures.[70] The radical potential of Locke's vision derives from its inclusiveness and its malleability. In other words, if all individuals do not see their natural rights represented by the state, then the state should be subject to "critique and transformation."[71] French and American revolutionaries invoked this aspect of Locke to "challenge existing political structures . . . and to expand the range of individuals recognized as citizens within the state."[72] Linda Bosniak describes this liberal, or liberal-democratic, understanding of citizenship in terms of its concern with "standing," as well as its demand for equal civil or social rights for all citizens.[73] As my book illustrates, new-citizen autobiographers also invoked this logic as they challenged the civic republicanism reproduced by mainstream educational institutions.

Educators such as Charles Eastman and Abraham Cahan worked within the liberal tradition as they championed a unified political culture that nonetheless respected cultural and political difference. This liberal model of citizenship has three central tenets: it represents the rights of oppressed groups to exercise political freedom; it expects all members of the community to recognize and respect the rights of others; and it promotes critical thinking and consensus building.[74] Renato Rosaldo and Juan Flores have used the term *cultural citizenship* to describe this approach to belonging; it demands "the right to be different (in terms of race, ethnicity, or native language) with respect to the norms of the dominant national community, without compromising one's right to belong, in the sense of participating in the nation-state's democratic processes."[75] Figures such as Eastman and Cahan were ahead of their time in promoting a culturally pluralist approach to citizenship that validated difference within unity—an approach that predated the cultural relativism of Franz Boas and other cultural anthropologists whose ideas did not become popular until the 1920s.[76]

Traditionally, both liberal and cosmopolitan theories of citizenship have demonstrated a commitment to "a universalist, humanitarian value system" that upholds the "values of empathy, care, compassion, and other humanistic traits as central to one's civic education."[77] One important difference between liberalism and cosmopolitanism, however, is that the latter promotes a more global interpretation of Locke's ideas. Though Eastman and Cahan invoke pan-Indian and Yiddish influences as they advocate for more inclusive public and political spheres, these figures nonetheless remain committed to expanding the parameters of national belonging, rather than reimagining them with an alternative structure, as do cosmopolitan thinkers such as W. E. B. Du Bois, Jane Addams, and Emma Goldman.

This book represents Du Bois, Addams, and Goldman as cosmopolitan thinkers: Du Bois and Addams articulate a vision of citizenship informed by Immanuel Kant's theory of global morality; they also shared Goldman's tendency to cross national boundaries in her life, politics, and philosophy. In assuming that a common humanity united individuals across and beyond national boundaries, Du Bois and Addams shared Kant's view that because humans are united by a "moral commonality," the creation of global institutions might ensure the realization of a "universal or cosmopolitan standard of judgment."[78] Goldman is not traditionally associated with Kantian cosmopolitanism, primarily because the antistatist position of traditional anarchism is not compatible with Kant's vision of an international political order (he theorized about a federation of nations in his 1795 text *Perpetual Peace: A Philosophical Sketch*). Nonetheless, we can view Goldman as a cosmopolitan anarchist if we adopt the perspective of Carl Levy, who argues—citing recent work by Richard Falk and Alex Prichard—that "philosophical anarchism's traditions of cooperation, nonviolence, community, small-scale social organization and local solutions can be applied to practices in cosmopolitics."[79]

In expressing a global sensibility, the educational autobiographies of Du Bois, Addams, and Goldman prefigure the radical ethics of a twenty-first-century cosmopolitanism that Gavin Kendall, Ian Woodward, and Zlatko Skrbis define in *The Sociology of Cosmopolitanism*. According to Kendall and his coauthors, the ideal cosmopolitan subject "looks outward to see difference as an opportunity for connection rather than as a pretext for separation."[80] This "requires putting oneself in the place of the other" to achieve, in Bryan Turner's words, a "critical recognition ethics" through which the individual can practice "recognition of the other, respect for difference, critical mutual evaluation, and finally care for the other."[81] Du Bois's and Addams's active pursuit of this ideal has led Jonathan Hansen to identify them as cosmopolitan patriots who "embrace a social-democratic ethic that reflected the interconnected and mutually dependent nature of life in the modern world." Applying Hansen's insight to Emma Goldman as well, we can see how these educational autobiographers demonstrated a primary loyalty not to the "American nation-state" but rather to the "ideal of democratic social reciprocity for which the nation-state was [merely] a vehicle."[82]

Du Bois, Addams, and Goldman use their educational autobiographies to validate the multiple experiences and points of view of a US citizenry that varied in age, gender, ethnicity, and race. They imagine an ideal democratic sphere that is welcoming to citizens who maintain "overlapping affiliations"—a term Hansen uses to describe John Dewey's similar vision.[83] These figures pursue their reform of US democracy by employing *reconstructionist discourse*, which allows them to "question, rethink, and confront, when necessary, the ways in which democratic institutions are not working on behalf of all citizens."[84] In so doing, Du Bois, Addams, and Goldman pay special attention to the circumscribed material horizons of the cultural "others" whom they observe, theorize about, and teach. In this respect, they consider the material and economic realities of postcolonial subjects who are "tied to the earth."[85] On the one hand, Du Bois, Addams, and Goldman evoke ideal forms of citizenship in autobiographies that exist as forms of curricula. On the other hand, however, they share a weakness with the Enlightenment humanists who inspired them. In particular, Addams and Du Bois sometimes express elitist sensibilities in their educational autobiographies, and in so doing qualify the revolutionary scope of their ideas.[86]

Crossing Genres: Educational Autobiography, the Bildungsroman, and the Secular Jeremiad

Assimilationist, liberal, and cosmopolitan theories of citizenship not only influenced day-to-day life in citizenship education programs but also appear as discourses in educational autobiographies produced by new citizens. This book defines educational autobiographies as texts through which members of new-citizen groups interpret, shape, and occasionally resist the conceptions of US citizenship that they have acquired in educational institutions. Whether the autobiographers are students or educators associated with new-citizen groups, many of their texts intertwine narratives about lived experience with ruminations on national belonging and the role of education in cultivating it.

No single genre classification could encompass the collection of texts examined in this book, which includes essays by American Indian students, photographic records of student life, fiction and poetry documenting the Americanization process, and autobiographies that double as educational philosophies. Nonetheless, most of these texts evidence the process by which new citizens, both as individuals and as members of different cultures, experienced nationalist education. Likewise, most feature protagonists who not only demand inclusion in the nation but also critique the nation's failure to realize its democratic ideals.

The educational autobiographies examined in this book variously adopt genre characteristics of the bildungsroman, the autobiography, and the secular jeremiad. In so doing, they offer insight into forms of self-making that emerged out of a dialectic between the autobiographer's particular ethnic, racial, or cultural background and the educational institution's distinctive vision of national identity. Whether it is an essay in a school newspaper or a published novel, the educational autobiography continually confronts dominant conceptions of national membership with an extranational perspective such as pan-Indianism, cosmopolitanism, or libertarianism.

New citizens did not simply accept their qualified inclusion in the idealized form of US citizenship that they encountered at educational institutions. Many felt conflicted about adopting American values and practices. These students, and sometimes educators who identified with them, exposed the contradictions between educational ideology and practice, often by invoking the same outsider perspectives that mainstream institutions sought to eradicate. No matter how religiously students internalized and reproduced their nationalist lessons, they often expressed at least a kernel of ambivalence in their narratives of national belonging. New citizens may have adopted assimilationist language that would allow them to be heard in the public sphere, but they often manipulated it to reshape the terms of the conversation. This book examines the figurative and rhetorical dimensions of educational autobiographies as they articulate forms of cultural particularity that survived processes of ethnic disidentification. These autobiographies expose contradictions in the assumptions, beliefs, and narrative tropes promoted by educational programs that attempted to reproduce forms of economic selfhood complicit with the demands of industrialization and modernization in capitalist America.

The educational autobiographies examined here can also be understood in terms of the differences between civic republican, liberal, and cosmopolitan theories of citizenship. While some educational autobiographies illustrate a correspondence between conservative educational practices and civic republicanism, others highlight resistance to civic republicanism from within assimilationist institutions. Other educational autobiographies testify to the existence of liberal or cosmopolitan ideas about national belonging during this period. Both students and educators who articulate resistance to assimilationist discourse and practice do so by creatively invoking the genre conventions of the bildungsroman.

Though most critics define the bildungsroman as a genre specific to the novel, others note that the bildungsroman, like the autobiography, can hover "on the border between confession and re-creation."[87] In this respect, the bildungsroman form can be a useful lens through which to examine educational autobiographies. Invoking Stephen Greenblatt's discussion of "self-fashioning," Todd Kontje defines the bildungsroman as a literary mode that challenges the "sharp distinction between literature and social life."[88] Because bildungsroman authors have sought to "reinvent the self in fiction," the genre, Kontje argues, is primarily metafictional.[89] It not only transforms literature through its self-reflexivity but also "examines this transformation."[90] We can align the educational autobiography with the bildungsroman by showing how the protagonists of both forms narrate their development self-reflexively, while also seeking to reshape the terms and contexts that frame that development.

While Kontje has defined the bildungsroman as metafictional, critics of autobiography also have emphasized the metafictional qualities of that genre. In his poststructuralist examination of autobiography, for instance, Paul Jay challenges "the easy opposition between referential and fictional."[91] Channeling De Man, Jay explains, "Since the 'life' in an autobiographical work is produced and determined by the technical demands of self-portraiture, its referential qualities are too highly mediated by those demands to be deemed reflective in any simple or pure way of a 'life' outside of or prior to the 'life' produced in and by the text embodying it."[92] Jay insists that the autobiographical text reshapes the real by mediating it and filtering it through a set of genre conventions. From this perspective, it makes sense to challenge the binary categorization of autobiography and bildungsroman and to focus instead on the shared genre conventions through which educational autobiographers and bildungsroman authors self-consciously examine their protagonists' adaptation (successful or not) to the demands of the social world.

Another reason for examining the educational autobiography within the context of the bildungsroman has to do with the concept of *Bildung* that predated the bildungsroman and gave rise to it. In *Human Rights, Inc.*, Joseph Slaughter reminds the reader that the bildungsroman originally emerged in response to the concept of *Bildung* that German idealists (particularly Humboldt) defined as "a civic course of acculturation by which the individual's impulses for self-expression and fulfillment are rationalized, modernized, conventionalized, and normalized within the social parameters, cultural patterns, and public institutions of the modern nation-state."[93] This process of acculturation precisely describes the function of citizenship education programs and the subject matter of the educational autobiographies examined in this book. Though German philosophers originally envisioned *Bildung* as a process limited to the upper classes, Slaughter points out that challenges to its elitism existed as early as 1780, when Johann Pestalozzi warned, in "Education for Citizenship" (1780), that revolutionary consequences might ensue if the German "ruling classes continued to deny the advantages of *Bildung* to the masses."[94] By the early twentieth century, Pestalozzi's demand that the state offer *Bildung* to the masses was being realized in US institutions. In this respect, *Bildung* is a useful concept with which to understand both US citizenship education and the educational autobiography.

Critics of the bildungsroman have debated whether an ironic sensibility informs the genre's urtext, *Wilhelm Meister's Apprenticeship*. For these critics, the question of whether Goethe ironizes his protagonist's experience of assimilating to the social world has important consequences for the genre's development. Kontje argues that beginning with Blanckenburg's 1774 essay on the bildungsroman, critics have misread the genre as portraying the protagonist's complete or satisfied adjustment to the social world.[95] In contrast, Kontje insists, canonical examples of the genre refuse to offer an easy, unironic resolution to the conflict between the individual's inner life and the demands of society.[96] Like Kontje's history of the bildungsroman, this book emphasizes moments of narrative irony that illustrate the protagonist's ability to negotiate authoritatively with the demands of mainstream culture.

Kontje rightly describes the bildungsroman as a genre that emphasizes the individual's difficult adjustment to social institutions. Another bildungsroman critic, Joseph Slaughter, offers insight into the degree and nature of psychological compliance accompanying such adaptation. Slaughter identifies a spectrum of narrative responses to the social order, ranging from affirmation to revision; in this respect, his work is useful for examining educational autobiographies that promote, critique, or reimagine received models of national belonging. Slaughter's typology of the bildungsroman maps onto the educational autobiographies discussed in this book. Slaughter distinguishes the realist and idealist bildungsromane from the more ironic forms of the genre, the antibildungsroman and the dissensual bildungsroman. According to Slaughter, the realist bildungsroman portrays an intractable social order that demands total conformity from the individual assimilating to it.[97] Frances Johnston's highly formal photos of Native American and African American boarding school students, discussed in chapter 2, fit into this category. The idealist bildungsroman, exemplified by *Wilhelm Meister's Apprenticeship*, instead narrates a "dialectical process" of mutual consent between the individual and society, one that nonetheless results in the individual's solid grounding as a citizen.[98] Autobiographical writing by Charles Eastman and Abraham Cahan echo the central terms of the idealist bildungsroman. In stark contrast with these two models, the antibildungsroman represents a total refusal to be incorporated into a "deformed and insular" society.[99] Frances Johnston's self-portraits and Emma Goldman's autobiography align most closely with the antibildungsroman.

Slaughter's last category—the dissensual bildungsroman—deserves particular attention, because this subgenre perfectly characterizes Eastman's *Deep Woods*, Du Bois's "Diary," and Jane Addams's *Twenty Years*. The dissensual bildungsroman foregrounds the gradual incorporation into society of individuals who have been excluded from the universalist categories of liberal democracy. Whereas Kontje usefully points out that the bildungsroman exposes the citizen's problematic adaptation to the social order, Slaughter, through his discussion of the dissensual bildungsroman, explains how and why certain types of citizens cannot adapt. In part, he argues, they cannot adapt because the public sphere is riddled with "biases and exclusions" based on gender, race, ethnic, religious, and class differences; the dissensual bildungsroman exposes how such exclusions are "constitutive of, rather than incidental to, the liberal public sphere's hegemonic functioning."[100] The dissensual bildungsroman also challenges the idea of a "singular national public" by emphasizing the "presence of competing publics within the domain of the nation-state."[101]

The dissensual bildungsroman recalls the genre of the American jeremiad that Sacvan Bercovitch describes in his eponymously titled book. According to Slaughter, the dissensual bildungsroman "[publicizes] the discrepancy between the rhetoric of liberty, equality, and fraternity and the inegalitarian social formations and relations in which that rhetoric is put into historical practice."[102] Likewise, the American jeremiad exposes how developments in US history have failed to represent the nation's democratic ideals. The American jeremiad, however, also seeks to rectify this trend; it insists on reforming the social field rather than rejecting it completely.

The nineteenth-century Jeremiahs whom Bercovitch discusses imitate the prophetic structure of the book of Jeremiah by aligning the decline of US society with its failure to maintain a commitment to its founding ideals. American Jeremiahs reimagine the religious mission of the original Jeremiah by transferring it onto a nationalist scenario. In the book of Jeremiah, God—speaking through Jeremiah—informs the Israelites that the degraded state of their society has resulted from their disloyalty to its founding tenets. Jeremiah prophesies a positive future that depends on the reformation of Israelites themselves: "If you really mend your ways and your actions; if you execute justice between one man and another; if you do not oppress the stranger, the orphan, and the widow; if you do not shed the blood of the innocent in this place; if you do not follow other gods, to your own hurt—then only will I let you dwell in this place, in the land that I gave to your fathers for all time."[103] Jeremiah recalls a time when God was more present in the people's lives, and he lists the misconduct and sinful behaviors that ended that period. As a prophet, however, Jeremiah promises that once the people restore their covenant with God they can recover the former state of goodness that characterized their world.

In keeping with its religious precursor, the American jeremiad invokes a lost covenant; however, it defines that lost covenant in terms of US democratic institutions. Bercovitch praises the reparative impulses of nineteenth-century Jeremiahs such as Ralph Waldo Emerson and Henry David Thoreau, who take the nation to task for losing touch with its founding principles. At the same time, however, he faults these authors for failing to challenge inequalities written into the nation's founding documents. In a description that seems to inveigh against civic republicanism from a liberal viewpoint, Bercovitch writes,

> The jeremiad has always restricted the ritual of consensus to a certain group within the culture. . . . The American consensus could also absorb feminism, so long as that would lead into the middle-class American way. Blacks and Indians too could learn to be True Americans, when in the fullness of time they would adopt the tenets of black and red capitalism. John Brown could join Adams, Franklin, and Jefferson in the pantheon of Revolutionary heroes when it was understood that he wanted to fulfill (rather than undermine) the American dream. On that provision, Jews and even Catholics could eventually become sons and daughters of the American Revolution.[104]

This passage critiques nineteenth-century authors for placing the burden of belonging to the nation on the shoulders of new citizens. These newcomers must, according to this logic, adapt to mainstream, middle-class norms or find themselves unjustly excluded from the benefits of national membership.

In contrast, the educational autobiographers examined in this book avoid the mistake made by Bercovitch's nineteenth-century Jeremiahs. Unlike the transcendentalist authors with whom Bercovitch finds fault, these educational autobiographers critique the normative understanding of national membership as outsiders who see themselves as Americans. These authors naturalize their claims to national belonging by restipulating US democracy in terms of their cultures' contributions, whether historical or contemporary. Likewise, they argue that their exclusion from US institutions constitutes a central inadequacy of US democracy, and they seek to reform those institutions so as to institute a more ideal form of nationalism. These autobiographers produce jeremiads that employ reconstructionist discourse or invoke the genre characteristics of the dissensual bildungsroman. As a result, they invent what Nancy Fraser calls "subaltern counterpublics"—spaces in which "members of subordinated social groups invent and circulate counterdiscourses, so as to formulate oppositional interpretations of their identities, interests, and needs."[105] Invoking extranational and international contexts as they identify the failures of US democratic institutions (including the citizenship education programs they attended or taught at), these educational autobiographers expose inequality in the public and political spheres that they not only occupied but also sought to redefine.

The authors examined here differ from Bercovitch's nineteenth-century Jeremiahs in several important ways. Instead of validating middle-class values, these authors critique the capitalist sensibility of mainstream US culture. Furthermore, they seek to revive America's founding ideals by invoking extranational sources of inspiration. Charles Eastman draws on a pan-Indian, tribal discourse that allows him to name the Indian as the true American, while he works simultaneously to "nativize" public culture in the United States. Jane Addams and W. E. B. Du Bois call for a culturally relativist corrective to the social Darwinist model of assimilation. And Abraham Cahan and Emma Goldman draw on transnational Jewish and anarchist sources, respectively, to challenge the mainstream culture's expectation of conformist identity.

The False Promise of Economic Subjectivity

Economic subjectivity is a discourse common to the autobiographies analyzed in this book. In *National Manhood*, Dana Nelson describes economic subjectivity as a central feature of white, middle-class identity in the nineteenth-century United States. As Nelson demonstrates, white, middle-class men forged a shared national identity in the face of racial, ethnic, and national difference by unifying around the trope of civic entitlement.[106] Though economic subjectivity was an identity shared primarily by an elite group of white men, this book demonstrates how this ideal also circulated across boundaries of race and class.

Horatio Alger's popular 1868 novel *Ragged Dick* perfectly exemplifies the central role that economic subjectivity played in cultivating a national identity across class divisions. The novel's protagonist, Dick Hunter, undergoes an education in saving that propels him from his position as an uneducated bootblack to one as a respectable clerk. After following a wealthy acquaintance's advice to save his meager earnings in a bank account, Dick is able to track his ever-increasing balance in the bankbook that comes to symbolize his newly acquired economic identity. As the narrator explains, Dick finally "felt himself a capitalist" only after he was able to gaze upon his bankbook's ever-increasing balance.[107]

As Michael Moon argues, *Ragged Dick* relies most heavily on the "lucky break" to advance Dick's fortunes, thus coding as magical the idea that a working-class boy might rise out of his station as a manual laborer.[108] It is true that Dick's continuous accumulation of money hinges in part on his industry and frugality. Yet Dick ultimately escapes a life of manual labor because of his good luck rather than good character. Because Dick happens to be on the Staten Island Ferry when a rich man's child falls overboard, he is able to save the child from drowning; in turn, the grateful father offers Dick a job as a counting-house clerk. In contrast with Dick's experience, most street children in the late nineteenth century did not easily escape from the economic underclass.[109] At the same time, however, they were like Dick in that they regularly encountered an economic ideology that defined success in capitalist terms of work, desire, and consumption.

Dick's trajectory is unlike the one traversed by many of the new citizens whom I discuss in this book. At the conclusion of *Ragged Dick*, Dick has just begun an upwardly mobile journey that will lead, so the narrator implies, to his ever-increasing status and success. On the contrary, working-class children who attended citizenship education programs usually learned to identify with and function as members of the working class. Officially, educators argued that their programs would help new citizens achieve full belonging in the civic sphere. In reality, however, curricular practices contributed to a stratified public sphere in which nonwhite and non-Protestant Americans were to live out their lives in the civil realm as producers and consumers. In this respect, educators rhetorically invoked the two central features of civic republicanism—the emphasis on unity and demand for political participation—but their programs cultivated only the first.

Place, Space, and Visuality

Many citizenship educators documented their programs through school newspapers, detailed student records, and photographs. Whether informal or professional, photographs of school life not only represent ideological and practical realities but also capture significant developments in the culture of photography. Photography was a relatively new medium in the early twentieth century, and photographers of various stripes were eager to use photos to do more than simply record what stood in front of the camera. In one arena, documentary photographers such as Jacob Riis and Lewis Hine captured the rapidly changing American scene and then used their photographs to promote social change. In another arena, Alfred Stieglitz championed pictorialism in his effort to raise the status of photography to an art form, arguing that photographs could serve as a medium for artists' unique perspectives.[110]

The photos examined in this book offer particular insight into the intersection of photography, curricula, and autobiography in citizenship education programs. Chapter 2 compares Frances Benjamin Johnston's photos of white students at Washington, D.C., public schools with her photos of Native American and African American students at Carlisle and Hampton. Chapter 5 analyzes libertarian education at the Modern School, examining several photos of life at the school, which may have been taken by the school's unofficial photographer, Oscar Steckbardt.[111] These two sets of photos represent citizenship education at opposite ends of the political spectrum. With their stiff formality and institutionalized distance, many of Johnston's photos mimic the assimilationist ideology directed at nonwhite students. At the same time, her less formal photos point to the progressive practices shared by educational institutions across the color line. As chapter 2 illustrates, the fact that Johnston portrays both black and white students kinesthetically points to the ideological flexibility of progressive educational practices. Chapter 4 also addresses these practices by discussing how German Jewish educational institutions used photography to promote ritualistic movement and the resulting embodiment of assimilationist ideology. Conversely, the Modern School photographs examined in chapter 5 feature a quality of movement that testifies to the radical possibilities of progressive methods. These photos evidence a curriculum that was always subject to change, depending on the whims or interests of students and teachers. In spite of ideological differences among these photographs, they share the quality of being texts that challenge the binary between documentary and pictorialist photography. All of the photos that this book discusses exist simultaneously as works of art that capture the photographer's vision and as records of the progressive methods common to citizenship education institutions across the political spectrum.

A Map for Reading

In examining educational autobiographies, this book argues that the more a particular text challenges both assimilationist education and civic republicanism, the further it diverges formally from the structure of the idealist bildungsroman. The manuscript begins by analyzing texts that adhere most closely to paradigms of realist and idealist bildungsromane and shifts increasingly toward texts that invoke elements of the dissensual bildungsroman. The move away from the realist and idealist models of the bildungsroman correlates with the authors' critiques of the dominant, assimilationist model of citizenship education.

Chapter 1, "On Autobiography, Boy Scouts, and Citizenship: Revisiting Charles Eastman's *Deep Woods*," suggests that Charles Eastman offers a subtle critique of assimilationist rhetoric while still reproducing its basic presumptions. After examining the rhetorical and material history of American Indian education, this chapter challenges the critical consensus about Eastman. It does so by drawing on a wider range of his work than previously has been examined, for example by locating Eastman's critique of assimilationist rhetoric in his writing for the Boy Scouts and his late work with the Society of American Indians. The latter part of the chapter adopts this broadened perspective to reexamine Eastman's canonical autobiographical text, *From the Deep Woods to Civilization* (1916), which many critics mistakenly have represented as an endorsement of assimilationist ideology.

Chapter 2, "The Scenes of Seeing: Frances Benjamin Johnston and Visualizations of the 'Indian' in Black, White, and Native Educational Contexts," echoes my approach to Eastman in that it examines a wider range of Johnston's citizenship education photos than those about which critics usually write. In so doing, it reveals Johnston's ambivalent visual representation of assimilationist rhetoric. The chapter explores this ambivalence by demonstrating how Johnston's educational photography tells a series of contradictory stories that mirror contradictions in progressive educational ideology and practice. The chapter juxtaposes Johnston's visual presentation of the "Indian" with archival letters and essays in which American Indian boarding school students critically reimagine the "Indian" to challenge the dominant culture's bifurcated structure of citizenship and political representation.

Chapter 3, "Curricular Cosmopolitans: W. E. B. Du Bois and Jane Addams," compares Du Bois's unpublished 1895 text, "Diary of My Steerage Trip across the Atlantic," as well as sections of his 1968 *Autobiography*, with Addams's *Twenty Years at Hull-House* (1910). This chapter argues that both Addams and Du Bois viewed cosmopolitan internationalism as an ideal model for citizenship education. Even though both authors rely to some degree on evolutionary paradigms, they also choose formal strategies that reflect their embrace of cultural relativism and a pragmatist educational philosophy. Both also model nonrestrictive embodiment and international influence as alternatives to nationalism, Addams by creating a space of international exchange in her Chicago settlement house, and Du Bois by invoking the Middle Passage to describe his transatlantic ship journey and to critique the race and class inequalities that qualified democratic citizenship at the turn of the twentieth century. Comparing work by these educators, this chapter emphasizes how the cosmopolitan perspective that Addams and Du Bois shared allowed them to challenge the nationalist and assimilationist ideologies that undergirded dominant developments in citizenship education.

Chapter 4, "Educating the *Ostjuden*: Abraham Cahan and Gestures of Resistance," compares Abraham Cahan's mock-bildungsroman, *The Rise of David Levinsky* (1916), with his Yiddish-language autobiography, *Bleter fun Mein Leben*, translated variously as *Pages from My Life* and *The Education of Abraham Cahan* (1926). The analysis of Cahan is situated within the history of German Jewish efforts to Americanize eastern European Jews through rhythmic, regimented movement and English-language education. The chapter then turns to Cahan's fictional and nonfictional autobiographies, which offer a satirical portrait of German Jewish educators and businessmen who funded educational institutions that worked to assimilate and depoliticize a newer generation of eastern European Jews. The chapter argues that German Jewish institutions such as the Educational Alliance and the Hebrew Orphan Asylum achieved only qualified success because their programs could not replace immigrant identities;

as Cahan's work demonstrates, these identities are situated in the embodied memories and habits that individuals develop as a result of their early educational experiences. Chapter 3 also illustrates how Cahan's attention to the multiple and sometimes conflicting sets of embodied memories that individuals acquire prefigures Pierre Bourdieu's theory of embodiment.

Chapter 5, "Emma Goldman, the Modern School, and the Politics of Reproduction," demonstrates how Goldman's opposition to reproductive ideology affected not only her educational ideals and the anarchist school she helped to found but also her attempts to live, and narrate, a life outside the confines of motherhood and the nuclear family. This chapter situates Goldman's autobiography, *Living My Life* (1931), in the context of the libertarian school that not only realized her cosmopolitan politics but also embodied her critique of reproduction. The chapter shows that Goldman experienced and articulated her opposition to the repressions of conventional citizenship discourse as a resistance to biological reproduction. Alongside other educators associated with the Modern School, Goldman viewed the family and the school as institutions limited by their immersion in reproductive ideology. Rejecting the hollow rhetoric of democratic equality, she envisioned a transformation of US life based on an international, anarchist political vision. This chapter reads *Living My Life* as an antibildungsroman that violates genre conventions to express Goldman's simultaneous rejection of a normative nationalism and a normative gender identity. It draws parallels between *Living My Life* and the Modern School, whose libertarian educators provided an alternative to dominant educational institutions, which they viewed as being complicit with the capitalist norms of US nationalism.

On the whole, this study interprets archival evidence of educational practices and their contexts to reveal how citizenship education actually operated. By attending to the unique configurations between texts (or educational practices) and contexts (such as curricular documents), this book exposes subtle contradictions in the multiple ideologies of progressive education, social Darwinism, and US citizenship. Calling attention to the unstable territory between texts and contexts, the book identifies the source of the freedom with which new US citizens participated in inventing their own identities. The autobiographical narratives examined represent a wide range of visions articulated by citizens who participated in their self-invention, despite economic, generic, or other limitations. Each chapter analyzes both autobiography and curricula, sometimes showing how new citizens created curricula with the intention of reforming the inadequacies of their own education; sometimes showing how an autobiographer's work directly challenged dominant curricular formations; and sometimes showing how autobiographers produced narratives of their own education that also capture the ideals they pursued in their work as educators.

1 / On Autobiography, Boy Scouts, and Citizenship: Revisiting Charles Eastman's *Deep Woods*

Educational efforts to assimilate American Indians took place roughly between 1879--when Captain Richard Henry Pratt opened the Carlisle Indian Industrial School—and 1924, when the US government finally granted them citizenship rights. Carlisle was the first of many boarding schools that operated as total institutions, regulating and transforming the bodies and identities of native students.[1] These Americanization efforts were relatively successful as a result of a multipronged approach that included the replacement of tribal dress with American dress, the prohibition of native languages, the subjection of students to a culture of surveillance, and the institution of a curriculum that focused on eradicating native practices and beliefs. These educational policies helped to materialize an ideology that presumed the superiority of white, Protestant culture.[2]

Of all the citizenship education programs examined in this book, the American Indian boarding school movement most exemplifies the process by which educators adopted both traditional and progressive educational methodologies to enact civic republican objectives. These schools not only removed native students from their families and tribes but also instituted curricular policies intended to infiltrate and reprogram every aspect of students' lives and minds. Though these schools were not always successful in achieving their objectives, some boarding school memoirs testify to the enormous impact of assimilationist schooling. In spite of their moments of resistance, memoirs by Zitkala-Ša, Luther Standing Bear, Charles Eastman, and others employ formal structures that echo the realist bildungsroman—the most restrictive embodiment of this form—by portraying an intractable social order that demands total conformity from its subjects.[3]

Though most boarding school memoirs acknowledge this demand for total conformity, some of them also recall Todd Kontje's argument that the bildungsroman is self-reflexive about its use of genre formulations. This self-reflexivity is often accompanied by expressions of resistance to boarding school ideology.[4] This chapter illustrates how autobiographical writing by the Dakota/Santee Sioux author Charles Eastman—particularly his book *From the Deep Woods to Civilization: Chapters in the Autobiography of an Indian* (1916)—expresses an insincere conformity with the tenets of US colonial education. As Diana Fuss explains, insincere expressions of conformity are characteristic of postcolonial writing: "When situated within the context of colonial politics, the psychoanalytic *assumption* that every conscious imitation conceals an unconscious identification needs to be carefully questioned, read for the signs of its own colonizing impulses... [because] not all forms of imitation are identifications."[5] In keeping with Fuss's exhortation, this chapter challenges the critical consensus that Eastman's autobiography testifies to his embrace of assimilationist ideology. Rather, it exemplifies the idealist bildungsroman: a genre that narrates a "dialectical process" of mutual consent between the individual and society, one that nonetheless results in the individual's solid grounding as a citizen.[6]

In both *Deep Woods* and other texts through which he engages with mainstream US culture, Eastman invokes embodied metaphors and practices to portray a "dialectical process" of mutual consent. In *Deep Woods*, Eastman invents metaphors of bodily transformation to justify his belonging as a US citizen. In his later, more overtly political writing, Eastman literalizes the idea of mutual consent by arguing that the ideal American is the product of intermarriage between natives and whites. Intermarriage is not the only vector through which Eastman articulates this cultural interdependence; he also draws attention to native influences on US democratic traditions. Moreover, he seeks to extend this influence by creating a Boy Scouts' curriculum, which asks middle-class, white American boys to act out native practices that represent a Sioux epistemology.

Eastman's memoir has an inarguably assimilationist framework. Like many other late nineteenth- and early twentieth-century autobiographers, Eastman wanted to claim belonging to the United States but had to do so in an atmosphere replete with nativist and racist attitudes. New citizens who wanted to critique mainstream US culture or politics had to do so from behind a veil of belonging. Many critics have cited *Deep Woods*, as well as an earlier memoir, *Indian Boyhood* (1902), as examples of Eastman's immersion in a social Darwinist mind-set and his complicity with, or, at best, ambivalence about, the ideology of assimilation.[7] Eastman has been particularly controversial in recent years because American Indian literary critics who have embraced native struggles for political sovereignty and cultural autonomy (Craig Womack and Robert Allen Warrior, for example) view Eastman's acculturation to mainstream US culture and his rejection of reservation life as evidence of his antipathy to Indian tribes' ongoing struggles to be recognized as nations. In *Red Matters* (2002), Arnold Krupat contrasts "nationalist" critics such as Womack and Warrior with an approach that he terms "cosmopolitan comparativism"; Krupat recognizes the influence of Western intellectual culture on native authors and attempts to establish a productive dialogue not only between Indian nations and the United States but also between Indian nations and other ethnic groups within the United States.[8] Krupat's model makes sense as a lens through which to situate aspects of Eastman's writing that reveal the influence of mainstream US culture. As this chapter also emphasizes, Eastman made concrete and fruitful efforts to bring "Indian" (and, particularly, Sioux) values to US life. Eastman's success is particularly impressive, given the immersive methods with which assimilationist educators sought to undermine his tribal identity.

Eastman's critics correctly suggest that in his autobiographical texts he represents his adoption of "civilization" as progress; this chapter focuses instead on how the assimilationist rhetoric of *Deep Woods* functions as a genre convention through which Eastman offers a veiled critique of the violent and dramatic transformations effected by his education in US institutions. Using Gerald Vizenor's terms, we can interpret Eastman's assimilationist persona as a set of "manifest manners" through which he enacted his survival. From this perspective, Eastman was a "warrior of survivance" who simulated the language and values of the dominant culture self-consciously, in order to "undermine the simulations of the unreal in the literature of dominance."[9] In other words, Eastman emphasized his assimilation to the dominant culture because this was his only means to achieve power. From this position of dominance, Eastman could then critique the rhetorical structures and corresponding ideologies of mainstream US culture.

Many critics have dismissed Eastman as an assimilationist not only because they have treated *Indian Boyhood* and *Deep Woods* as representative texts but also because they have not identified these texts' simulations of survivance. Moreover, they have overlooked other texts through which Eastman conveyed his increasing skepticism about US culture and policies. Because of these omissions, Eastman's critics have missed the opportunity to see Eastman as a figure who adapted his pan-Indian sensibility to reimagine civic culture in the United States. Whereas the surface narrative of *Deep Woods* represents Eastman's identity as multilayered, with his "Indian" qualities subsumed by the white American ones, his other texts highlight the centrality of "Indian" values to US culture and promote recognition of native contributions to historical and contemporary life in the United States. By situating *Deep Woods* as one in a series of texts (published between 1914 and 1919) through which Eastman critiqued the ideology and exclusionary citizenship policies of the United States, this chapter emphasizes the productive elements of Eastman's ambivalence.[10]

Because Eastman relied on the general category of the "Indian" (an effect of his boarding school education, and common usage during his time), I adopt Eastman's use of this term when discussing his work and context; however, I follow Raymond Wilson in assuming that in many cases Eastman is really writing about his tribe. As Wilson points out in his biography of Eastman, because Eastman "seemed to draw little distinction between being an Indian and being a Sioux, his works tend to emphasize the similarities rather than the marked differences among Indian cultures." Wilson admits that Eastman's use of the term *Indian* "helped to influence the contemporary stereotyped image of Native Americans," but he also points out that "most of what [Eastman] wrote applied to his kinsmen."[11]

Charles Eastman (1858–1939) was a doctor, an autobiographer, a children's book writer, and a political activist who, at the age of fifteen, began years of schooling that would distance him increasingly from the Sioux upbringing of his childhood. Eastman had good reason to be critical of the US government, whose policies not only separated him from his father at the age of four but also resulted in his father's transformation into a Christian homesteader. In 1862 the Santee Sioux violently protested against the corrupt and destitute conditions on their reservation. To avoid repercussions for the uprising, Eastman's grandmother and uncle fled with the four-year-old Charles to Canada, where they lived with the Canadian Sioux and raised Eastman to be a hunter. Eastman also underwent training as a warrior to avenge the death of his father, whom he mistakenly believed was killed as punishment for the uprising. At fifteen, Eastman was uprooted again when his father suddenly

appeared in Canada to bring him back to Dakota Territory. Once Eastman returned to the United States, his father encouraged him to begin
his American schooling.[12] During his eighteen years of education in US
schools, Eastman received ample training in the ideologies of assimilation, capitalism, and individualism.[13] His American education cut him
off linguistically, culturally, and geographically from his tribe and taught
him to think of himself as an "Indian."

Eastman excelled in the schools he attended, became acculturated
to life in the United States, and lauded US citizenship as an antidote
to the corruption of reservation life. Eastman's embrace of US citizenship—which posed a direct threat to Indian sovereignty—was a sign of
his immersion in assimilationist ideology. This ideology intensified during the early decades of the twentieth century, when rapid population
growth, urbanization, and the growing centrality of consumerism to US
culture led many white Americans to increase their demand for natural resources, particularly land. One way the US government responded
to this greater demand for land was through its campaign to assimilate
Indian tribes into mainstream US culture by simultaneously educating
them, transforming them into farmers, and making their land available
to white settlers.

Although—or perhaps because—boarding school education inter-
rupted his tribal education, Eastman enacted a reversal of sorts in his
adult life, teaching young white children (and adults) some of the very
values and practices characteristic of his Sioux upbringing. Whereas the
US government's assimilation policy systematically undermined tribal
cultures and demanded that Indians assimilate fully into mainstream
US life, Eastman promoted a space in white America for values he
viewed as common to many tribes (including his own), such as communal organization, a respect for the natural world, and an economy of the
gift. Even though some aspects of Eastman's life, including his early support for the Dawes Act and his marriage to a white woman, attest to his
complicity with assimilationism, both his writing and his political work
illustrate his commitment to recuperating characteristics of tribal life
that US educators hoped to eradicate.[14] Eastman did not abandon Indian
communities, as some critics have suggested; not only did he advocate
for the Sioux in land claims cases against the US government, but in his
writing he promoted a dual-directional assimilation, offering up native
values and practices as antidotes to the ills of mainstream US culture.[15]

Eastman spent much of his life retelling Sioux (and other tribal) myths
and histories, publishing articles for the Boy Scouts and the out-of-doors

movement, and penning speeches through which he advocated Indian citizenship.[16] In these texts, Eastman strategically manipulates images of the Indian to reshape US culture so it might benefit from the ideals of his early childhood. In *Indian Scout Talks: A Guide for Boy Scouts and Campfire Girls* (1914) and *The Indian To-Day: The Past and Future of the First American* (1915), Eastman expresses his disappointment with individualism and wastefulness in American life. In articles he wrote for the *American Indian Magazine* in 1918 and 1919, Eastman addresses inequalities resulting from US educational and citizenship policies. Critics of *Deep Woods* often overlook these texts, but the broad perspective they offer on Eastman's lifework provides a context for nuancing our understanding of the assimilationist elements of his autobiography.

A Curriculum for Consent: American Indians and Boarding School Education

Historians refer to the years between 1879 and 1924 as the Assimilation Era because, during this period, the US government coerced American Indian adults into abdicating communal land ownership and its attendant social structures, while simultaneously isolating and Americanizing Indian children in government schools.[17] Education, as a central component of the government's ongoing policy to reduce and nationalize reservations, was supposed to "civilize" the declining populations of native peoples who continued to survive as foreign nationals within the borders of the United States. Twenty-five off-reservation boarding schools were built between 1879 and 1902, and, with the exception of Carlisle, all were located in the Midwest, Southwest, or West.[18] In 1891, Congress made Indian education compulsory, and in 1893, it authorized the Indian Office to "withhold rations, clothing, and other annuities from Indian parents" who refused to send their children to school.[19] Funding for the schools came from three main sources: treaty agreements with particular tribes, monies from Indian land sales, and annual funds from Congress.[20] The earliest schools were run somewhat haphazardly, without any particular curricular standards, and often were marked by infighting among agents and school superintendents vying for power in an atmosphere practically unregulated by the federal government. By the mid-1890s, Thomas J. Morgan, the commissioner of Indian affairs (1889–93), had brought a degree of systemization to the boarding schools, both by instituting a uniform course of study in 1890 and by creating a hierarchy by which reservation schools would serve as "feeders" for the more advanced off-reservation schools.[21]

Government officials, educators, and ostensibly pro-Indian policy reformers justified the education campaign by arguing that assimilation would prevent American Indians from becoming extinct.[22] Ironically, however, their good intentions effected American Indians' ethnic dis-identification without ensuring easy assimilation into, or legal equality within, mainstream US culture.[23] A brief look at the form of citizenship imagined and institutionalized by legal and educational reformers in the late nineteenth century offers a useful prologue to this chapter's discussion of Eastman and his critics. The 1887 Dawes Act (also known as the General Allotment Act) improved the legal status of assimilated American Indians and helped them protect some of their lands in the face of the government's failure to curb the rapid advance of white settlers; however, it also led to white settlers' seizure of valuable Indian lands and set the stage for the government's heavy emphasis on Americanizing and "civilizing" the Indian. The Dawes Act promised US citizenship and its attendant "rights, privileges, and immunities" to all Indians "born within the territorial limits of the United States" but qualified this promise by arguing that it would grant citizenship only to an Indian who had "voluntarily taken up, within said limits, his residence separate and apart from any tribe of Indians therein, and [who had] adopted the habits of civilized life."[24] Not only did the Dawes Act exclude reservation Indians from its provisions, but it also delayed the allotment process for those who had abdicated tribal membership.[25] Promising full citizenship only in name, the Dawes Act legalized popular sentiments that Indians should be "civilized" before becoming citizens. It also facilitated the government's aim to break up Indian reservations.

With its stated (but unrealized) objective of rapidly assimilating Indians into US society, the Dawes Act consolidated an educational policy that caused the destruction of tribal communities and the loss of much Indian land. Moreover, it failed to make good on its promise of equality through education. The logic behind the Dawes Act rested on a fundamental contradiction: while official discourse promised educated American Indians all the benefits of civic (or political) membership in exchange for their identification with mainstream US culture, school curricula regularly undermined this promise by offering mostly practical training intended to transform American Indians into a permanent underclass within civil, not civic, society. According to the consensual version of birthright citizenship theoretically offered to American Indians in the late nineteenth century, Indians born in the United States only had to consent to US political ideology in order to become citizens. However, the legal landscape belied this expectation.[26] Although European immigrants and African Americans automatically were becoming citizens during this period, a series of nineteenth-century legal cases reveals that American Indians were able to attain citizenship only on a case-by-case basis.

Justice John Marshall had set the stage for inconsistencies in Indian citizenship law with his 1831 decision in *Cherokee Nation v. Georgia*.[27] In this influential case, Marshall denied the Cherokee Nation's "motion for an injunction" against the state of Georgia because, he argued, it was not a foreign nation. Despite having an "unquestionable, and, heretofore, unquestioned right to the lands they occupy," he writes, Indians are rather "domestic dependent nations . . . in a state of pupilage . . . [whose] relation to the United States resembles that of a ward to his guardian."[28] By creating the nondefinitive legal category of the domestic-dependent, by which Indians acquired the indeterminate status of being neither citizens nor sovereigns, Marshall sowed confusion for future legal decisions pertaining to Indian citizenship; for if Indians weren't citizens and weren't foreigners, what were they?[29]

Even after passage of the 1866 Civil Rights Act and the Fourteenth Amendment (1868), the ambiguous status of American Indians that Marshall had written into law continued to reverberate in contemporary assumptions that Indians maintained divided loyalties. The Civil Rights Act declared that "all persons born in the United States and not subject to any foreign power, excluding Indians not taxed, are hereby declared to be citizens of the United States" who "shall have the same right[s] . . . as [those] enjoyed by white citizens."[30] However, many American Indians *were* subject to tribal governments. The Fourteenth Amendment improved Indians' chances for citizenship by subtly rewording the Civil Rights Act's language: "and not subject to any foreign power" became "subject to the jurisdiction of the United States," while the proviso "Indians not taxed" was removed altogether.[31] The problem with these ostensibly beneficial changes, as Rogers Smith argues, was that Trumbull and Howard, the proponents of this new clause, wanted to institute the government's "limited *but ultimate* . . . sovereignty over the tribes, while also denying that the tribes were members of the American political community."[32] Trumbull and Howard reworded the jurisdiction clause ambiguously, making it easier for later judges to rule that Indians were loyal to two governments and therefore were not under the "full and complete" jurisdiction of the United States.[33]

Later decisions held that American Indians would not be subject to the jurisdiction of the United States unless the US government had formally dissolved their tribe. The 1883 case *Ex parte Crow Dog*, for example, held that a federal court did not have jurisdiction to try one Indian (Crow Dog) for killing another one when the matter had already been adjudicated by tribal council. In his majority decision, Judge Stanley Matthews argued that while the Sioux "were to be urged, as far as it could successfully be done, into the practice of agriculture, and whose children were to be taught the arts and industry of civilized life," they were not currently to be judged by standards that were not their own. Judge Matthews further opined that "it was no part of the design to treat the individuals as separately responsible and amenable, in all their personal and domestic relations with each other, to the general laws of the United States."[34] As Rogers Smith explains, Matthews's statement assumes that the "civilization" of Indian communities needed to happen on reservations *before* individual Indians could be treated as citizens.[35]

The majority decision in the 1884 *Elk v. Wilkins* case ruled that not even individual Indians who had relinquished tribal affiliation and had been assimilated into white society were necessarily eligible for citizenship rights. As the ruling judge (Gray) on that case concluded, citing a previous opinion by the Oregon district court judge, "An Indian cannot make himself a citizen of the United States without the consent and cooperation of the government. The fact that he has abandoned his nomadic life or tribal relations, and adopted the habits and manners of civilized people, may be a good reason why he should be made a citizen of the United States, but does not itself make him one."[36] Even though Elk had met city and state residency requirements, and had relinquished his tribal affiliation, the decision in this case made the granting of Indian citizenship rights a case-by-case matter. As Smith explains, the decision in *Elk v. Wilkins* produced "a despised and rejected class of persons, with no nationality whatever."[37] Along with other legal developments, this decision limited American Indians' eligibility to participate in politics, voting, and other civic activities once they left the tribal setting. It was not until passage of the Major Crimes Act of 1885 that the government's hands-off policy began to change. This law allowed the federal government to hold "criminal jurisdiction over Indians for seven major crimes, and paved the way for the US government's increasing, and ultimately unlimited, sovereignty over Indian affairs."[38]

Legal limitations on the civic membership of American Indians were no doubt influenced by public debates about their preparedness for cultural membership in US society. These debates revolved around whether Indians should become legal citizens before or after becoming

Americanized. One vocal reformer, Justice William Harsha, argued that the Indian could be transformed into a laborer, a private landowner, and an educated citizen (the reformers' central goals) only if he first became "a *person* before the law."[39] In an 1882 *North American Review* article, "Law for the Indians," Harsha states that only "when his possessions are secure" will the Indian's labor "be both profitable and attractive; when he feels himself a man, he will desire his own and his children's education; when he can be protected by law, the granting of land to him in severalty will be something more than a pretentious form."[40] Invoking the same logic that Du Bois would later use when he demanded the immediate legal equality of African Americans, Harsha questions the assumption that Indians would adopt American work practices when the law would not protect the fruits of their labor. Others, such as James Bradley Thayer, shared Harsha's sentiments and faulted Dawes for privileging cultural over legal citizenship in his law, which ultimately was meant to eclipse Thayer's more pro-Indian bill.[41]

While the incipient years of the education campaign (1879–83) incited a plethora of opinions on its methodology and goals, many educational bureaucrats shared the conviction that education and land privatization should be prerequisites for citizenship.[42] To assimilate, the Indian would have to choose sedentary over nomadic living, practice agriculture rather than hunting, and embrace private property instead of communal land and living arrangements. Educators often articulated their beliefs about these practices using a symbology of clothing. As Secretary of the Interior Samuel Kirkwood argued in 1881, during the first session of the Forty-seventh Congress of the United States, "The end to be attained is the civilization of the Indians and their final absorption into the mass of our citizens, clothed with all the rights and instructed in performing all the duties of citizenship."[43] Kirkwood's clothing metaphor crystallizes a contradiction central to the assimilation campaign: even as he speaks of *absorbing* the American Indian into US society, his metaphor implies awareness of the difficulties of eradicating one culture and replacing it with another. One is not absorbed into clothing; rather, one puts it on and takes it off.

Clothing became a central symbol through which proeducation spokespeople stressed the role that government schools would play in teaching American Indian children how to desire and acquire material things.[44] This priority is evident in official discussions of Indians' civic rights and responsibilities, which often shifted into valorizations of economic subjectivity. For instance, in *Land and Law as Agents in Educating*

Indians, Merrill Gates, a writer and president of the Lake Mohonk Conference of Friends of the Indian, questions, "The problem before us is, how shall we educate these men-children in to that great conception of the reign of law, moral, civil, and political, to which they are now strangers?"[45] A moment later, Gates stresses the importance of "awaken[ing] in an Indian the desire for the acquisition of property of his own, and by his own honest labor."[46] He states, "We need to *awaken in him wants.* In his dull savagery he must be touched by the wings of the divine angel of discontent. Then he begins to look forward, to reach out. The desire for property of his own may become an intense educating force. . . . Discontent with the tepee and the starving rations of the Indian camp in winter is needed to get the Indian out of the blanket and into trousers,— and trousers with a pocket in them, and with a *pocket that aches to be filled with dollars!*"[47] Gates abandons his purported goal of educating the Indian in law, politics, and other aspects of civil society and instead says that the Indian should be educated in desire, or rather discontent—the motor of desire. This passage recommends incorporating the Indian into the civil sphere as a subject whose discontent is central to the reproduction of consumer capitalism.[48] Not only does this "pocket" symbolize the imbrication of capitalism, education, and citizenship, but it also enacts a metonymic reduction that conflates the Indian's identity with his clothing. In the passage, Gates imagines the Indian not only wearing new clothes but also becoming one with them, thus achieving the fantasy of absorption that Samuel Kirkwood, in the passage cited earlier, invoked but abandoned. Here, the Indian does not put clothing on and take it off but becomes one with the clothing itself.[49] In this vein, boarding schools literally replaced indigenous with "American" clothing and documented these transformations with before-and-after photos that they circulated as propaganda to advertise the schools' successes.[50]

Whereas educational officials and politicians used metaphors to imagine the Indian's embodiment of American identity, the boarding schools themselves imposed physical and psychological discipline with the intention of cultivating new, embodied identities in boarding school students. Enforcing assimilationist ideology with a combination of hands-on learning and corporal punishment, citizenship educators institutionalized a process of *Bildung* that Joseph Slaughter describes as "a civic course of acculturation by which the individual's impulses for self-expression and fulfillment are rationalized, modernized, conventionalized, and normalized within the social parameters, cultural patterns, and public institutions of the modern nation-state."[51] As a result of the thorough nature of cultural normalization practiced at such programs, autobiographical accounts of it often took the form of the realist or idealist bildungsroman, which evidenced the narrators' desire to identify with and incorporate into the dominant social world.

Memoirs by boarding school teachers also offer insight into the process of *Bildung*. In *Girl from Williamsburg*, for example, Minnie Braithwaite Jenkins narrates her experience teaching at the Fort Mojave boarding school after she was "refused admittance to William and Mary College."[52] While many boarding schools adopted progressive educational methods to Americanize students, some teachers, like Jenkins, nevertheless drew on old-fashioned disciplinary techniques. Jenkins was like many other boarding school teachers: middle-class white women who found that teaching with the Indian Service offered them more independence, authority, and pay than they could earn as local public school teachers.[53] This independence was intensified by the women's isolation from their families and communities, as well as from a lack of oversight on the part of school authorities.[54]

In her memoir, Jenkins confesses that she used corporal punishment and dramatizes the literal embodiment of assimilationist policy in the classroom. This narrative offers insight into how the pressures of enforcing school policies, such as the requirement to speak only English or the demand for bodily conformity, could lead teachers to justify the use of corporal punishment even when they knew it was wrong. By representing her confession with shifting perspectives, Jenkins reveals her belief that her behavior was simultaneously inappropriate and justifiable. In so doing, she attests to the multiple loyalties that teachers may have had, and to the challenge of upholding policies that the children could not or would not abide. Recreating a conversation between herself and her students, Jenkins writes,

> "Well, I have done everything I could to make you stop speaking Mojave. Now you tell me what I can do?"
> The five little ones crossed their legs in quite a bored man-of-the-world air and as one they pronounced, "why, *spank—of course.*"
> *So spank I did.*[55]

In this exchange, Jenkins abdicates responsibility by attributing her methods to the students' desire. On another occasion, however, Jenkins admits that her approach to corporal punishment is misguided. In a moment of desperation, she interrupts a dance lesson to punish a clumsy student: "I drew off and slapped her—with all my might. She fell in a heap on the floor and lay there—blinking up at me. My terrible temper! See what it had done to me! Tears of shame and embarrassment filled my eyes." Jenkins immediately retracts this confession of responsibility, however, explaining that Lu "was always an exasperating pupil"; moreover, Jenkins describes the other students as being complicit with her: they expressed a "thrilled surprise... as much as to say, 'Just see what our little one [Miss Jenkins] can do.'"[56] Here, Jenkins fantasizes that her students view her as the childlike (and thus innocent) party—their "little one." Though Jenkins feels ashamed that she resorted to corporal punishment, her story also reveals that shame was not always a strong enough motivator for teachers like her, whose authority and independence were further intensified by a dominant ideology that viewed ill-treatment as a justified response to (perceived) native inferiority.

Whereas Fort Mojave experienced disciplinary extremism and widespread insubordination—a sign that corporal punishment was ineffective in maintaining order and promoting assimilation—other boarding schools, such as Carlisle, used psychological discipline to control students and enact an assimilationist agenda.[57] What Fort Mojave and Carlisle did share was a prohibition against speaking tribal languages. One venue through which Carlisle realized this English-only policy was its student-run printing press. The role that the printing press played in cultivating citizenship perfectly exemplifies William James's argument that repeated physical actions will result in the creation of new neural pathways. Carlisle students who ran the printing press participated in the slow, methodical work of printing the school paper while also gaining expertise in English sentence structure and imbibing the school's ideology, which was expressed in its publications. Given what James and his successors have discovered about cognitive neuroscience, we can surmise that operating the press likely intensified students' internalization of the assimilationist ideology memorialized by newspapers such as the *Indian Helper*.

The *Indian Helper* was a four-page newsletter about school life, which Pratt conceived as propaganda for school supporters, government agents, and the students themselves. As a newsletter that students printed but did not write, the *Indian Helper* enhanced Carlisle's efforts to define the students' future membership in US society in civil rather than civic terms.[58] This newsletter actually called attention to the students' roles as mere recorders. As its motto read, "The *Indian Helper* is PRINTED by Indian boys, but EDITED by the-man-on-the-band-stand [MOTBS], who is NOT an Indian."[59]

The MOTBS, who was likely the alter ego of the newsletter's editor, Marianna Burgess, not only functioned as the newspaper's editorial figurehead but also symbolizes Carlisle's success at intertwining embodied and psychological training.[60] The MOTBS existed as an imaginary persona who had his own column in the *Indian Helper* and used it to advertise his ability to see all violations of school policy: "His surveillance was not confined to a single, central viewing point. He could mingle unseen amongst the children on the grounds, prowl through the classrooms and dormitories, or gate-crash a school picnic undetected."[61] By claiming to be everywhere and to see everything, the MOTBS exacted students' compliance with school policies and likely inspired them to experience guilt if they were disobedient. As Jacqueline Fear-Segal writes in her discussion of the MOTBS, "Few things about their dress, deportment, manners, physical appearance, or behavior escaped his comment. . . . Interspersed amongst commonplace school news, the minutiae of children's lives were described and placed on public display."[62] The MOTBS's column was somewhat addictive, probably because readers were eager to find out what circumstances would define each new visitation of this mysterious and charismatic figure.[63] Yet the MOTBS was not merely an imaginary or narrative figure; he also existed as the "physical figure of the Man-on-the-band-stand . . . directly in the center of Carlisle's campus . . . [who] had a full view of all students' and teachers' activities."[64] The MOTBS thus existed simultaneously on two fronts: as a fictional narrator who commented on student activities in the school paper and as a statue memorializing his living presence.

One way the MOTBS enacted psychological discipline was through his omnipresent and seemingly omniscient persona. In one of his weekly editorials, the MOTBS warns students that from his perch he can

> see all the quarters, the printing office, the chapel, the grounds, everything and everybody, all the girls and the boys on the walks, at the windows, everywhere. Nothing escapes the Man-on-the-band-stand. . . . Don't be too secure. There may be a flag staff on the Bandstand some day and the man may buy himself a spy glass. It is not safe to predict that one day his vision may not extend much farther. Already he sees into the homes of the boys and girls who go out upon the farms; and—but let us wait until that "someday" comes.[65]

As "the NEWS personified," the MOTBS functions as a panopticon. His gaze is both invisible and material: on the one hand he exists as the idea of being watched, and on the other hand he is embodied both by the school newspaper and by the statue.[66] Carlisle forbade students to speak their native languages and required them to adopt the habits and values of mainstream US culture. They were supposed to speak English and act "American" as they built the school's buildings, laundered its clothes, and washed its dishes. By mythologizing his simultaneous omniscience and omnipotence, the MOTBS could enforce compliance under the guise of providing entertainment. Students who printed the *Indian Helper*, or read it regularly—and evidence suggests they did—might well have internalized his watchful gaze.[67]

Charles Eastman and American Indian Activism: From the SAI to the Boy Scouts

One central purpose of boarding schools such as Carlisle was to teach American Indians to exchange a tribal consciousness for an individualist one and to take up professions—such as farming individually owned plots of land—that were consistent with the individualism of mainstream US culture. In this respect, the boarding school movement was one arm of a broader policy that involved the breakup of reservations and the devaluation of native cultures. Nonassimilated American Indians who lived in communal (and, as some argued, communist) societies constituted a symbolic threat to America's capitalist ideology. Anxiety about commun(al)ism arose in public debates about whether American Indians should be assimilated fully on tribal lands before being granted citizenship.[68] In his 1881 report to Congress, Samuel Kirkwood argues that the teaching of "civilized" practices should precede the dissolution of reservations, not only because the tribal relation "interferes with the administration of both civil and criminal law among members of the tribe," but also because it "is a hinderance [sic] to individual progress. It means communism so far at least as land is concerned."[69] As Kirkwood's comment illustrates, the practice of sharing land or other commodities among American Indians greatly disturbed Euro-Americans.

Euro-Americans also objected to tribal attitudes toward wealth characterized by the economy of the gift, which focused less on acquisition than on "the dissipation of useful wealth."[70] One manifestation of this noncapitalistic economy that troubled Euro-Americans involved the practice "of giving away . . . the property of a man who died."[71] Objections to this practice followed a Lockean logic. John Locke believed that if an individual used his property productively, he would then be its rightful owner. Giving away, burying, or burning a dead person's property was wasteful and inappropriate according to the conception of value in a capitalist market economy. As Christopher Bracken explains, wastefulness was the only restriction to John Locke's conception of "the right to private property: you may own as much as you can use before it spoils. What limits the right to own what is one's own, then, is the act of waste."[72] The distribution of property among Indian communities, or its destruction after a person's death, was more consistent with the economy of the gift, which, as Bracken argues, "sits at the very limit of the Western European economy. The gift is the sign of this outer boundary. A pure loss without return, the gift marks the zone where civilization ends and barbarism begins."[73] The idea of giving without necessarily receiving something in return challenged the assumptions about ownership and exchange on which capitalism rested.

Many government officials objected to Indians' communal ownership of property, and their perception that Indians were failing to "use" their lands appropriately influenced government policy. This discomfort with Indian land-use patterns also reflected the Lockean view that "as much land as a man tills, plants, improves, cultivates, and can use the product of, so much is his property."[74] Many tribes did not till the soil, and the US government sometimes invalidated native land claims by referencing this unwillingness. Francis Paul Prucha elucidates the reasoning behind this policy when he rhetorically asks, "If the lands were not profitably used by the Indians, should they not be utilized by others who would pay for the use and provide funds for the benefit of the Indians?"[75] The problem was not simply that the settlers wanted to take American Indian lands; as long as the tribes existed, the economy of the gift and communal organization that characterized some American Indian attitudes toward property would represent a symbolic "[violation of] the principle of classical utility, which . . . forms the basis of bourgeois reasoning."[76] As Michael Rogin explains, "Indians were a symbolic demon to emergent liberal society in the new nation. Liberalism insisted upon work, instinctual repression and acquisitive behavior; men had to conquer and separate themselves from nature. Indians were seen as playful, violent, improvident, wild and in harmony with nature. Private property underlay liberal society; Indians held land in common."[77] Given the public anxiety that American Indians might import a commun(al)ist sensibility with them into the United States, it makes sense that government programs would encourage them to acquire private property and attend boarding schools, where they could learn skills and values that would enhance their adaptation to capitalist society.

As a writer and activist, Charles Eastman did disseminate a communal sensibility within US culture. Nonetheless, he also embraced the United States and enjoyed being an "acculturated" American, as he described himself.[78] Eastman's involvement with the Society of American Indians (SAI) has led various critics to view him as complicit with US assimilation policy—a conclusion dependent on a flattened perception of the SAI's complex history. The SAI was a pan-Indian organization that became a means for contact and cooperation among boarding school graduates who did not return to reservations but who wanted to be connected with other English-speaking natives despite widely varying linguistic and tribal origins.[79] Many of the organization's founding and active members were Carlisle or Hampton graduates who self-identified as Americans, believed in "self-help," and became successful financially in their professions as doctors, lawyers, educators, and government employees.[80] The organization worked to convince white Americans that Indians could assimilate successfully without abdicating traits and values common to many tribes, such as a love of nature, communalism, and Indian art forms.[81] Some SAI members worked to nativize public culture in the United States, unifying around the concept of an Indian race and attempting to orchestrate control over their symbolic inclusion in the public sphere.

Scholars such as Robert Warrior and Sean Teuton have denounced the SAI—and Eastman's complicity with its agenda—for "redirect[ing] Native political goals from national independence to cultural dismantling and Christian, capitalist assimilation."[82] In *Tribal Secrets*, Warrior claims that the SAI was "the educational arm of federal policy that during that time was concerned with individually allotting communally held Native lands, abrogating traditional forms of government, and undermining all efforts to maintain community integrity."[83] Lucy Maddox, in her revisionist history of the SAI, instead argues that through the SAI American Indian intellectuals maintained some control over their representation in public conversations about their future. In her discussion of Eastman's political and spiritual writing, as well as his involvement with the YMCA and the Boy Scouts, Maddox applauds Eastman's efforts to transform civic culture in the United States, even as he represents his Sioux experiences and beliefs as a set of "idealized, generic, detribalized" Indian values.[84] Maddox insightfully argues that Eastman's political writings emblematize his attempts to find agency within US culture.[85] However, she also claims that Eastman's writing "reflects or echoes the published statements coming from the SAI."[86] By aligning Eastman unequivocally with the SAI, Maddox inadvertently validates the positions of critics such as Warrior. Eastman's critics argue that his membership in the SAI emblematizes his alignment with US educational policies; they also criticize his attempts to preserve traditional Indian values "in the context of attempting to live out the ideals of white Western civilization."[87]

In his misguided assessment of Eastman as an apologist for assimilation, Warrior decontextualizes Eastman's statements, overlooks his shifting politics, and disregards his ambivalent relationship with the SAI. Warrior is correct to point out that Eastman was influenced by assimilationist ideology. We can see this, for instance, in Eastman's comment at the SAI's founding meeting in 1911 that "no prejudice [from the US government] has existed as far as the American Indian is concerned."[88] Nonetheless, Warrior emphasizes the most egregious aspects of Eastman's alignment with US policy by taking his statements out of context— arguing, for instance, that the statement cited above conveys Eastman's naive belief that "the history of Native to non-Native relationships of his time had nothing to do with prejudice."[89] In fact, Eastman made this remark in response to his colleague Hiram Chase, who claimed that US educational institutions such as Hampton and Carlisle failed to teach the Indian "the history of his country . . . and of his own race, and of his rights as a citizen."[90] Eastman objected to Chase's conclusion because it echoed the dependent attitude that Eastman associated with reservation life; Eastman sought to convince Chase that "it lies within us to show the paleface what we can do."[91] Warrior's critique of Eastman does merit our attention; Eastman invokes an ideology of self-reliance that prevents him from faulting government schools for providing native students with an inadequate education. Nonetheless, Warrior analyzes Eastman's contributions to US culture too narrowly. He not only bases his conclusions on Eastman's early association with the SAI but also fails to acknowledge the diverse agendas of SAI members and their varying degrees of support for assimilation.[92]

Even though Eastman was one of the SAI's founding members and remained on its membership rolls throughout its existence, he was critical of it for failing to recognize and promote the multiplicity of tribal cultures. Eastman's simultaneous membership in and critique of this assimilationist organization echoes the "cosmopolitan comparativism" theorized by Arnold Krupat, as well as the concept of "cultural citizenship" articulated by Rosaldo and Flores.[93] Krupat insists that we recognize the inevitable influence that mainstream US culture had on figures such as Eastman, while Rosaldo and Flores call for a form of citizenship that will preserve the Native/American dialectic. These theories help explain Eastman's overdetermined position, which in turn helps us understand his shifting relationship to the SAI. According to SAI historian Hazel Hertzberg, Eastman was only sporadically involved with the SAI from its inception in 1911 through the early 1920s.[94] As Hertzberg points out, Eastman did not even attend the SAI's second meeting, ostensibly because he believed the organization was not taking shape as an "intertribal body, an Indian congress of official tribal delegates."[95] Eastman remained an inactive member of the SAI in part because he believed it was not sufficiently involved with the "moral and social welfare" of Indian communities.[96]

Elizabeth Hutchinson's discussion of Eastman in *The Indian Craze* further suggests that Eastman was more committed to tribal specificity than many critics acknowledge. As evidence, Hutchinson cites Eastman's response to Angel de Cora's promotion of a pan-Indian aesthetic in her art curriculum. In the executive report on the SAI's first annual conference, Eastman complains, "We have been drifting away from our old distinctive art. . . . Our teachers who are white people have mixed the different characteristics of different tribes, so that you cannot tell an Arapaho from a Sioux now, and cannot tell a Cheyenne from a Crow. I hope that in this gathering we will come to some realization of these things in a proper sense; that we may take a backward step, if you please, in art, not in the sense of lowering our standard, but returning to the old ideas that are really uplifting."[97] Hutchinson reads these comments as evidence of Eastman's antipathy to a pan-Indian aesthetic, at least in matters of art instruction. However, the comments also evidence Eastman's promotion of "cultural citizenship": his demand that American Indians have the right "to be different (in terms of race, ethnicity, or native language) with respect to the norms of the dominant national community, without compromising [their right to participate] in the nation-state's democratic processes."[98] From this perspective, it makes sense for Eastman to have articulated awareness of tribal differences even as he promoted a pan-Indian organization through which natives would be able to achieve equal political representation in the civic sphere.[99]

Eastman continued to promote tribal particularity and pan-Indianism as he sought to realize his political aims more overtly. It was not until 1918 that Eastman renewed his active involvement with the SAI; at this point, he surmised that he might achieve some of his political goals through the organization. Eastman had long been a critic of the paternalistic Indian Office (also known as the Indian Bureau), which "carried out government policies regarding Indian education, health, and resources."[100] When he became SAI president, Eastman not only tried to use the organization to abolish the Indian Office but also worked with Zitkala Ša and Carlos Montezuma (other SAI members) to help Indians achieve legal citizenship, fight for control over their property, and master English.[101] Eastman and his cohorts ultimately failed to achieve their goals within the SAI. Even though other SAI members agreed with them that the Indian Office exercised too much control over Indian life, most were not willing to reject "the protective hand of the government."[102] In 1919, the organization's membership began to decline rapidly, and, as Peter Iverson argues in his biography of Carlos Montezuma, by the early 1920s the SAI began "backing away from its strong stance against the Bureau. People now talked of reorganization rather than abolition."[103] In 1919, when Eastman discovered that the SAI was abandoning its quest for Indian citizenship, he relinquished his involvement with it.[104]

Eastman's history with the SAI provides a useful context for reconsidering his marginalized body of work, in which he critiques US culture and attempts to reform it by promoting "Indian" (and particularly Sioux) values. Eastman's 1914 *Indian Scout Talks*, for example, illustrates his attempt to create an educational apparatus for young white children under the aegis of the Boy Scouts.[105] As early as 1910, Ernest Thompson Seton, one of the Boy Scouts' founding members, solicited Eastman's contributions to the organization's official magazine, *Boys' Life*. Seton used the articles—which were eventually collected in *Indian Scout Talks*—as a guide and a reference for the Boy Scouts' activities and programs. Eastman also gave lectures to groups of Boy Scouts and Campfire Girls and served as a camp director and national councilman for the organization.[106]

As a writer of Boy Scouts literature, Eastman relished the opportunity to teach non-Indian children some of the Sioux values that had survived his immersion in almost two decades of US schooling. Eastman took advantage of his new position as an educator to reverse his own educational experience. In *Indian Scout Talks*, he refers ironically to this reversal when he suggests that white children should undergo an education in "savagery" to remedy white America's failures.[107] The scouting ideal that Eastman develops in *Indian Scout Talks* illustrates his objection to the individualism and selfishness that he encountered in mainstream US culture. Describing his own culture, he writes, "Every boy, from the very beginning of his training, is an embryo public servant. He puts into daily practice the lessons that in this way become part of himself. There are no salaries, no 'tips,' no prizes to work for. He takes his pay in the recognition of the community and the consciousness of unselfish service. Let us have more of this spirit of the American Indian, the Boy Scout's prototype, to leaven the brilliant selfishness of our modern civilization!"[108] This passage articulates Eastman's awareness that education is a form of citizenship training, "every boy . . . an embryo public servant." Eastman's ideal citizen does not embody the central characteristics of individualism and capitalism: he works for the community and takes pleasure in this knowledge.

Though Eastman's comments echo Rousseau's theory of an obligation-based citizenship, his Boy Scouts writing, as well as his other arguments in favor of American Indian citizenship, also illustrate the Lockean elements of his thought. As this book's introduction explains, Locke tied a state's legitimacy to its ability to codify man's natural rights in its political and legal structures; states unable to do this should, Locke believed, be subject to "critique and transformation."[109] According to this schema, a state might transform to include a broader range of individuals as citizens.[110] We can identify the Lockean elements of Eastman's thought in his simultaneous effort to gain citizenship rights for American Indians and critique of how capitalism and Christianity undermine US political structures.

Eastman sought to transform the quality of civil membership and to expand the parameters of civic membership in the United States by invoking American Indian ideas about spirituality and community. At times, however, he relies on an evolutionary framework as he calls for a return to native practices and perspectives. In *Indian Scout Talks*, for example, Eastman occasionally invokes the stereotype of the noble savage, thus relegating the Indian to a superior but inescapable earthy realm. In a passage from "Wood Craft and Weather Wisdom," Eastman aligns the Indian with intuition and nature: "[The Indian] keeps his soul at one with the world about him. . . . The wild man has no chronometer, no yardstick, no unit of weight, no field-glass. He is himself a natural being in touch with nature. Some things he does, he scarcely knows why: certainly he could not explain them. His calculations are as swift as a flash of lightning; best of all, they come out right!"[111] The Indian of this passage echoes the primitivism embraced by upper-class boys' camps at the turn of the twentieth century. As Philip Deloria explains in *Playing Indian*, these camps often emphasized "holistic experience over the fragmentation of the city and [insisted] that to feel nature one had to journey back in time to a simpler life, return, richer but unable to articulate what this pseudomystical encounter had been all about."[112] In Eastman's passage, he adopts this vague mysticism as he portrays the modern Indian.[113]

Here and elsewhere, Eastman engages in strategic essentialism; he repeats stereotypes as he voices his objections to US culture.[114] The previous passage critiques US culture's obsession with acquisition and details; after all, chronometers, yardsticks, and field-glasses are all instruments with which human beings measure and dissect their experiences. According to Eastman, these tools inhibit the development of spirituality and rob a person of his soul. Eastman goes on to explain that the "over-civilized man is trained to depend on artificial means. He winds his watch, pins his thought to a chronometer, and disconnects himself from the world-current; then starts off on the well-beaten road."[115] Eastman invokes the "primitive" Indian, but only as a means to an end, which is the reform of US culture and political life. Eastman seems to be saying, "We American Indians seek to participate in US institutions once they are revived by their contact with native cultures." In this respect, Eastman becomes an American Indian Jeremiah, who calls for a return not to original American values but to American Indian ones.

Not only does Eastman call for a transformation of US culture, but through his Boy Scouts writing he offers up a program for enacting this change. Many boys' camps from this period required white children to participate in "Indian" rituals as training for adaptation to capitalist life; their curriculum was based on the evolutionary ideology that children had to experience primitive conditions in order to advance through the stages of civilization. By contrast, Eastman's curriculum promotes Indian values and practices as an alternative to capitalism. Philip Deloria argues that during this period most boys' camps appeared antimodern but "invariably pointed back to the modern city. Camps frequently set up miniature economies, campers earning money for chores, subcontracting their work to others, forming companies to handle such contracts, hiring, firing, banking, and loaning money across the camp network."[116] Conversely, in *Indian Scout Talks*, Eastman instructs his projected audience to engage in "primitive" activities so that they may acquire a vantage point from which to question the values that US culture has instilled in them.

At Eastman's imaginary school, the white child does not acquire training in the qualities of selfishness, individualism, and acquisitiveness that are central to modern capitalism. Neither does his student "play Indian" so as to reaffirm the interests of the dominant culture. Eastman instead exhorts his students to "follow the trail of the Indian in his search for an earthly paradise."[117] This metaphor evokes an open-ended journey that the student ideally will continue to follow after completing his formal education. Thus, even though Eastman evokes a stereotypical Indian in *Indian Scout Talks*, his curriculum participates in his ongoing critique of US culture and prefigures the revisionary portrait of US citizenship that he articulated more forcefully toward the end of his publishing career.

As a boarding school student, Eastman underwent a combination of ideological reprogramming and practical training. As an educator, Eastman enacted a reversal of sorts, creating a Boy Scouts' curriculum that required campers to act out Sioux values. Throughout *Indian Scout Talks*, Eastman provides instructions for the white child who wants to imitate Indian practices. In turn, Eastman promises the child entry into the superior culture of the "out-of-door man." In "The Language of Footprints," for example, Eastman promises that a "faithful study of the language of footprints in all its details will be certain to develop your insight as well as your powers of observation." In "Hunting with Sling-shot and Bow and Arrow," he assures the assiduous student, "You can learn it, too."[118] Eastman even encourages Boy Scouts and Campfire Girls (to whom the book is dedicated) to take on Sioux "honor names" and provides an extensive list of these names, along with their translations and connotations. In chapters titled "Indian Ceremonies for Boy Scouts" and "The Maidens' Feast: A Ceremony for Girls," Eastman explains that Indian ceremonies "are always in demand" and gives instructions for the performance of "several which have been adapted to your use from the ancient rites of the Sioux nation."[119] These examples illustrate how East-man's popularization of Sioux practices outside their original contexts resulted in their inevitable distortion. Nonetheless, Eastman may have believed that incorporating Sioux culture into mainstream US life was his only means of preserving his culture. Therefore, while his instruc-tions for the reification of Sioux ceremonies may seem painfully cheer-ful, we should also see his curriculum for what it is: an attempt to reverse his own experience by assimilating the dominant culture to his own through the education of white boys.

Like Tayo in Leslie Marmon Silko's *Ceremony*, Eastman seems to understand that his traditions will not survive unless he adapts them to changing circumstances. Knowing that the "ancient rites of the Sioux nation" have lost their traditional context, Eastman incorporates them into his pedagogical efforts. In "A Winter Masque," Eastman addresses the "unfortunate" white boy who "has no hill or pond or river near for coasting and skating" during the winter months. Eastman's own early childhood, he informs his readers, had no such limitations; it was like a boy's adventure story made real: "In my day we were independent of all save natural features; no policeman to interfere with our fun, no fences or trespass signs,—and no shops or indulgent fathers to purchase our equipment!"[120] With a goading tone, Eastman urges the white boy to adopt Indian practices; he appeals to a "boy's instinct" (in this case, the desire for freedom from the rules) that is identical in white "outdoor boy[s]" and "Indian boy[s]."[121] In drawing equivalencies between white and Indian children, Eastman not only challenges an ideology of presumed, innate racial difference but also justifies his promotion of an American/Indian identity.

By the time he published *Indian Scout Talks*, Eastman already had become comfortable with the pragmatic route that allowed him to focus his energies on a two-tiered solution to the enforced transformation of native peoples. On the one hand, he tried to influence the dominant culture with his articulation of "Indianness"; on the other hand, hoping for a literal transformation of American bodies, Eastman promoted a complete racial "amalgamation" of natives with white people, which he saw as the "solution" to a process of cultural dilution over which he had little control.[122] By this time, Eastman had accepted the impossibility "for the Indian to continue to exist as a separate race, with his proper racial characteristics and customs, within the limits of the United States," as he stated in his 1911 presentation at the Universal Races Congress.[123]

It is in this broader context of Eastman's shifting politics that we return to *Deep Woods*. Two years after he published this memoir, Eastman reversed his earlier belief that the American Indian was "a 'dying race.'"[124] In 1918, as president of the SAI, Eastman emphatically exclaimed, "[We] are not a dying race. . . . We are alive and asking for our share of the LIBERTY AND DEMOCRACY THAT WE HAVE FOUGHT FOR."[125] This comment demonstrates that Eastman increasingly aligned himself with the interests of American Indians; it also belies the argument that *Deep Woods* evidences his unequivocal capitulation to assimilationist ideology.

Reading between the Lines of *Deep Woods*

Some critics of Eastman's work recognize his challenges to assimilationist ideology in *Deep Woods*. Focusing on the second half of his memoir, writers such as Hertha Wong, Malea Powell, and Erik Peterson emphasize the ambivalence marking Eastman's rhetoric of assimilation. These critics note that even though Eastman aligns himself with white, Christian culture, he also establishes equivalencies between Christian and Sioux values. The same critics also suggest, however, that Eastman undermines his denunciation of selfish individualism in "civilized" Christians by imposing an evolutionary framework on his autobiography, presenting his development from an "Indian" to an "American" as a progressive one. Because Eastman persistently reaffirms his belief in the ideals of Christianity and civilization, his critics read *Deep Woods* as evidence that his struggle between traditionalism and assimilationism ends with his promotion of the latter.[126] On the contrary, I argue that *Deep Woods* questions the sincerity of its assimilationist framework; in so doing, it suggests that Eastman's "conscious imitation" does not necessarily reveal his "unconscious identification."[127]

In his preface to *Deep Woods*, Eastman provides the reader with a guide for detecting the critique of US life embedded in his assimilationist narrative. He explains that his life story concludes with only a "partial reaction" in favor of the Sioux philosophy; yet, a moment later, he alerts the reader to his unreliability as a narrator: "It is clearly impossible to tell the whole story, but much that cannot be told may be read 'between the lines.'"[128] Later in the autobiography, as he discusses his own reading practices, Eastman clarifies this advice when he confesses that he made a "great mistake" in taking "civilization and Christianity at their face value."[129] With these comments, Eastman urges his readers not to make the mistake of reading his book as literally as he read US culture when he was a student. Eastman's explicit reference to the things he cannot say in *Deep Woods* points to his awareness that the genre in which he is writing—the citizenship autobiography—has its own limitations.

In *Autobiographical Transactions in Modernist America*, William Boelhower explains that the strategic employment of tropes of belonging is a technique characteristic of immigrant, or ethnic, autobiographies from the early twentieth century. Although Eastman was not an immigrant to the United States, both American Indians and immigrants experienced pressure to relinquish aspects of their culture in order to become American. European immigrants easily became citizens and maintained ties to their ethnic communities during this period, but the law required American Indians to abandon their communities if they wanted to acquire citizenship. Despite this historical difference between immigrants and American Indians, Boelhower's comments on the autobiography of citizenship apply to Eastman's text.[130]

The autobiography of citizenship is, in Boelhower's terms, a "schooling genre" through which the autobiographer narrates his or her struggle to claim belonging as a US citizen.[131] Ethnic autobiographies often retain traces of ambivalence that emerge as part of the process of consent required by one's adaptation to the dominant culture. As Boelhower explains, the ethnic autobiographer of the early twentieth century may have claimed "100% Americanness," but he was always "doubling back."[132] In other words, the autobiographer's consent was not absolutely transparent and sincere; rather, "It was due to xenophobic pressure and the consequent need to allay spreading nativist fears that most immigrant/ethnic autobiographers sought to pass themselves off as Americans by didactically copying and promoting officially acceptable behavioral codes."[133] If the autobiographer harbored doubts about the dominant culture, he had to express them subtly because of "the strong ritual requirements of American behavioral codes in these early, nativist decades."[134] The doctrine of consensual citizenship required Eastman to demonstrate consent to US political ideals if he wanted to become a citizen. Eastman thus mimics the "acceptable behavioral codes" of ethnic autobiography when he depicts his transformation into an American as an entry into "civilization." Eastman consents, but his professions of allegiance to mainstream US culture function as a generic convention of the new-citizen autobiography. Eastman's new-citizen autobiography also echoes the idealist bildungsroman. Eastman promotes dual-directional assimilation as a preferred form of cultural adaptation, echoing the mutual consent traditionally tracked by the idealist bildungsroman. Moreover, Eastman manipulates the trope of ambivalence to emphasize the uneasiness of adapting to dominant social norms.

In *Deep Woods*, Eastman asks the reader to judge between competing rhetorics—national and native—by dramatizing a conflict between the nation's idealistic narratives about itself and the actual events that belie such ideals. *Deep Woods* ultimately suggests that white America's endless attempts to reimagine itself as a democracy are sullied by its insistence on efficiency and materialism. In turn, these qualities threaten the spiritual ideals and social well-being of Native America. As in his earlier texts, in *Deep Woods* Eastman rejects the capitalist concept of exchange that infuses all aspects of US culture. He also exposes the hypocrisy of "thrift" by juxtaposing it with the excesses marking US policies toward Indian tribes and their lands. Such critiques undermine the complimentary evaluation of mainstream US culture that appears as a surface narrative of *Deep Woods*. Reading "between the lines" of this text allows us to recast Eastman's ardent expressions of belonging as elements of a genre convention deployed by new-citizen autobiographers who hoped, as Eastman did, to find a means of surviving within mainstream US society. *Deep Woods*'s continually resurfacing indictment of white culture hollows out its moments of laudatory identification, emphasizing the (literary) conventionality of Eastman's claims of belonging.

Throughout *Deep Woods*, Eastman's laudatory depiction of "Indian" ideals supersedes his moments of identification with an ostensibly superior white culture. It may at first seem difficult to reconcile Eastman's 1914 exhortation from *Indian Scout Talks*—"Let us follow the trail of the Indian in his search for an earthly paradise!"—with his praise for Christianity and civilization just two years later in *Deep Woods*. Eastman's critics are correct to point out that in key moments of *Deep Woods* he represents himself as an apologist for the government schools; Eastman writes that he is "an example of the benefits of education for the Indian" (148) and depicts a narrative of his assimilation as progress. Eastman assures the reader that he has abandoned the Sioux lifestyle, dramatizes his strong identification with white, Protestant culture, and presents even his incisive challenges to this culture within an evolutionary framework. In the first part of the book, Eastman describes his transformation from a traditional Sioux warrior and hunter to a student, then an educated doctor, and then a lobbyist for American Indian rights. Eastman repeatedly attributes his education to his identification with the white man. It was at Beloit College, Eastman tells us, that he first allowed himself to "think and act as a white man" (57). The positive tone of such passages is unmistakable; Eastman assures us that at school his "eyes were opened intelligently to the greatness of Christian civilization, the ideal civilization, as it unfolded itself before [him]" (56).[135] Representing his degree of civilization in terms of its remoteness from his tribal childhood defined by hunting and gathering, Eastman echoes the social Darwinist position that Lewis Henry Morgan articulates in his 1877 book, *Ancient Society*. Morgan argues that a culture's movement along a savagery-barbarism-civilization continuum depends on its means of accessing food. According to Morgan, hunting-gathering societies remain underdeveloped because cultural sophistication results from "control over the production of food."[136] If we were to judge *Deep Woods* according to the surface narrative that evokes Morgan's theory, we could categorize it as a realist bildungsroman that embraces assimilation and promotes civic republican ideology.

At other moments in *Deep Woods*, however, Eastman interrogates the ostensible superiority of the whiteness with which he claims to identify. Though he aligns himself with mainstream US culture, he simultaneously critiques it. For example, Eastman speaks with relish of his visit to a Sac and Fox village because it has given him the opportunity to have contact with the "racial mind" (150). Here, Eastman seems sincere in describing his alienation from the Sac and Foxes. His meeting with them has not exactly been successful, for the Sac and Fox chief has rejected the educational and religious ideologies that Eastman is promoting.[137] Eastman's professed alienation from the "racial mind" recalls Dana Nelson's analysis of the projective techniques by which late nineteenth-century white men formed and maintained their identities by distinguishing themselves from the ostensibly savage American Indian.[138] By invoking the "racial mind," Eastman reveals his alignment with the white man. Significantly, however, Eastman's comment appears only as a concluding frame to his description—perhaps as an afterthought, perhaps to soften his critique for a mainstream reader.

In the preceding scene, Eastman challenges the biological grounding of race as he discusses his visit to the Sac and Foxes. Identifying himself as both Indian and white, Eastman suggests that it is not one's race but one's practices (in this case, of Christian values) that constitute one's identity. Eastman recounts how one of the Sac and Foxes returned his lost wallet even before he had discovered it was lost, and he uses this to exemplify how Indians are truer Christians than white men. After receiving the wallet, which still had in it his "railway tickets and a considerable sum of money," Eastman tells the "state missionary" that they had "better let these Indians alone!" He justifies himself by setting the Indians' Christian behavior against the Christian hypocrisy he has encountered in mainstream US culture. Addressing the missionaries, Eastman exclaims, "If I had lost my money in the streets of *your* Christian city, I should probably have never seen it again" (149, emphasis added). In light of his pronoun shift (through which he calls attention to his native self), we can interpret Eastman's earlier, condescending reference to the "racial mind" as ironic rather than sincere.

As the discussion above illustrates, Eastman engages in racial mimicry so as to reshape the contours of whiteness. By appearing to identify with the white man but representing native values as superior, Eastman attempts to rescue "civilization" from its practitioners. After the wallet incident, Eastman "freely admitted [to the Sac and Fox, and to the reader] that this nation is not Christian, but . . . the Christians in it are trying to make it so" (150). According to the logic of this passage, when these Christians succeed, they will be emulating behaviors already practiced by the Sac and Foxes, as well as by other Indians who have not been corrupted by white men. As early as 1911, in *The Soul of the Indian*, Eastman suggests, "There is no such thing as 'Christian Civilization.' I

believe that Christianity and modern civilization are opposed and irrec-
oncilable, and that the spirit of Christianity and of our ancient religion
is essentially the same."[139] Eastman continued to make such claims until
as late as 1918; in "The Indian's Plea for Freedom," a speech he made to
the SAI, Eastman argues that Indian values are "nearer the Christ principle than the common standards of civilization."[140] Through depicting
his visit to the Sac and Foxes, Eastman inhabits his role as an American
Indian Jeremiah. He asks us to imagine a country where nativized white
subjects might live together with Indians, embodying values that are
Christian in name but Indian in origin. With this vision, he challenges
the binary thinking that definitively distinguishes white from Indian.

Just as Eastman subsumes his critique of the white man beneath his
professed distance from the "racial mind," elsewhere in *Deep Woods*
Eastman explains that his Sioux philosophy has not disappeared completely but merely has been "overlaid and superseded by a college education" (150). The image of a mind overlaid with education evokes the
palimpsest-like nature of this text itself, whose submerged layers might
surface at any time. Probing the surface narrative of *Deep Woods* (in
which Eastman recounts the lessons of his white education with abstrac-
tions), we encounter the sincerity of detail with which he describes his
Sioux education. When, for example, he depicts white men whose corrupt economic behaviors belie their status as good Christians, Eastman's
repeated mantra of "Christian civilization [as] the ideal civilization" (57)
begins to read falsely. Eastman invokes the convention of the Christian
confessional (he was saved from savagery by Christianity) but exposes
it as an artificial form by juxtaposing it with detailed and laudatory
accounts of his encounters with the Sioux. As Eastman illustrates the
incompatibility of Christianity and capitalism, his invocation of the
superior lessons of "civilization" begins to appear insincere, as though
it merely had been a strategy for justifying his claim to US citizenship.

As he continues to describe his education in *Deep Woods*, Eastman
continues to compare white culture unfavorably with his own. At other
moments, he challenges the white-native binary altogether. Recalling
one of his first math lessons, Eastman emphatically critiques the white
man's acquisitive practices: "Aside from repeating and spelling words,
we had to count and add imaginary amounts. We never had any money
to count, nor potatoes, turnips, nor bricks. Why we *valued* nothing
except honor; that cannot be purchased!" (47, emphasis added). Here,
"we" takes on an overdetermined meaning, referring first to boarding
school students and then to Indians. While this pronoun choice asserts

Eastman's commitment to a native concept of honor, a later shift into the third-person allows Eastman to abandon the binary terms of this debate altogether. Contrasting the white man's focus on acquisition with his own culture's failure to improve itself, Eastman asks, "What is the great difference between these people and my own? I asked myself. Is it not that *one* keeps the old things and continually adds to them new improvements, while *the other* is too well contented with the old, and will not change his ways nor seek to improve them?" (64, emphasis added). Eastman's use of a question here undermines his ostensible valorization of white culture. At the same time, his shift from referencing Indians as his "own" people to describing them as "the other" emblematizes his discomfort with a clear-cut perception of his own identity.

Though Eastman's discussion of his math lesson conveys his "native" dissatisfaction with counting and purchasing, he goes on to articulate praise for the capitalist economy, this time aligning himself with the school's head teacher, Dr. Riggs: "Later on, when Dr. Riggs explained to us the industries of the white man, his thrift and forethought, we could see the reasonableness of it all. Economy is the able assistant of labor, and the two together produce great results. The systems and methods of business were of great interest to us, and especially the adoption of a medium of exchange." Eastman's praise might result from the fact that Riggs functioned as a surrogate father and teacher-mentor to him; as he claims, Dr. Riggs was the man who had "[made] it possible for [him] to grasp the principles of true civilization" (48). However, Eastman's reaction is not unusual, given that American Indian boarding schools replaced parents with teachers, presenting children with an impossible choice: to cathect to their educators (and the ideology they represented) or to exist without attachments.

Eastman's further discussion of the math lesson in this scene reveals his ambivalence about the value of capitalism. Whereas at first Eastman complains, as a student and a Sioux, about learning to count things his people did not have, he later expresses satisfaction with capitalism. However, the rote manner in which Eastman expresses this satisfaction, combined with his indeterminate use of the pronoun *it,* belies his sincerity. Eastman claims to "see the reasonableness of it all" (48). But what is "it all" that he claims is so reasonable? Is he referring to the white man's "thrift and forethought"? His "economy" and "labor"? A capitalist "medium of exchange"? Because Eastman unapologetically critiques these characteristics elsewhere in his writing, we might consider the distanced and rational consideration of the passage to be a ruse, rather than an indication of Eastman's belief in the superiority of capitalist values.

Perhaps the most convincing evidence of this text's artificially assimilationist framework comes at its conclusion, when Eastman explains why he has been compelled to continue embracing his American education. He writes, "When I reduce civilization to its lowest terms, it becomes a system of life based on trade. The dollar is the measure of value, and *might* still spells *right*; otherwise, why war? Yet even in deep jungles God's own sunlight penetrates, and I stand before my own people still as an advocate of civilization. Why? First, because there is no chance for our simple life any more; and second, because I realize that the white man's religion is not responsible for his mistakes" (194–95).[141] With this passage, Eastman admits that his adoption of white civilization and US identity is a matter of "might" over which he has had little choice. Even so, he has managed to exercise some control over his identity within the confines of "civilization." In the very last words of *Deep Woods*, Eastman writes, "I am for development and progress along social and spiritual lines, rather than those of commerce, nationalism, or material efficiency. Nevertheless, so long as I live, I am an American" (195). Eastman's use of the word *nevertheless* here is central to our understanding of both this comment and his project as a whole. Eastman sees himself as an American despite the fact that, to him, US culture is a system in which efficiency eclipses social and spiritual responsibility. By simultaneously identifying as American and rejecting capitalist values that he associates with mainstream US culture, Eastman suggests that being American necessarily requires one to transform and improve the culture.[142]

Indian and American: Eastman's Politics of Citizenship

This chapter has suggested that Eastman claimed for himself an Americanism even truer than that of the founders themselves and that he was deeply critical of US capitalism and individualism. Eastman's pan-Indian stance, as well as his self-figuration as a Jeremiah, allowed him to claim an authentic "Americanism" without simultaneously validating the ideology of capitalism. Eastman's procitizenship writing most clearly reveals the nature of his status as an American Indian Jeremiah, one who occupies the special category of the insider-outsider and therefore is able to avoid the pitfalls that Sacvan Bercovitch associates with nineteenth-century Jeremiahs (which I discuss in this book's introduction).

In a speech advocating Indian citizenship that he presented at the SAI's 1919 conference, Eastman proposes, "We Indians started the whole basis of Americanism. . . . [We] laid the foundation of freedom and equality and democracy long before any white people came here and those who took it up, but they do not give us credit."[143] Eastman also suggests that while Indian tribes did fight with each other, they never went so far in their violation of American ideals as to steal land and enslave others (elsewhere, Eastman attributes the increasing violence of intertribal fighting to the presence of white traders). Concluding his speech, Eastman exhorts Indians to "keep [their] old characteristics that [they] have contributed to the country—those characteristics that have been put into the Constitution of the United States itself."[144] Here, one can usefully distinguish Eastman's jeremiad from the form Bercovitch describes.[145] If Bercovitch faults the "classic" American authors for being complicit with middle-class values, Eastman rescues the ideality of the jeremiad by offering a critique of the United States from a position that is simultaneously of and outside of the mainstream. Eastman's invocation of this prophetic trope is in keeping with his reclamation of other Christian values in *Deep Woods*, which he reinscribes as authentically Indian.

By juxtaposing the submerged indictment of US culture in *Deep Woods* with Eastman's citizenship writing, one not only can challenge the critics who view Eastman as an assimilationist but also can recognize the productive element of Eastman's ambivalence. Between 1916 and 1919, Eastman devoted himself to promoting American Indian citizenship and contributed to debates about the relative value of citizenship bills circulating during this time.[146] One of Eastman's most eloquent justifications for Indian citizenship appears in "The Indian's Plea for Freedom." The speech's rhetorical power derives in part from Eastman's enumeration of American Indians' many contributions to US cultural, civic, and military life—including serving in and contributing financially to the First World War, paying taxes even when the benefits of citizenship were denied, and, Eastman claims, providing a model for "practically all the basic principles of the original articles of confederation of the Thirteen States," which "were borrowed, either unconsciously or knowingly, from the league of the Six Nations and the Sioux Confederacy."[147]

The rhetorical power of Eastman's "plea" also rests on his alignment of American Indians with the Greeks: "'We, too, demand, our freedom!' cry those modern Greeks, the Native American Indians."[148] Eastman's invocation of a group considered synonymous with civilization is part of the strategy by which he challenges the hierarchy of civilized life that social Darwinists promulgated and that lawmakers used to deny citizenship to Indians.[149] Here, as in much of his work, Eastman objects to an ideology that views Indians as less than civilized. Furthermore, he couples his insistence on full citizenship with the argument that American Indians shaped the nature of the "civilization" in which they are demanding legal inclusion. In Eastman's view, the Indian does not need to give up his native identity to assimilate; rather, he needs to assimilate mainstream US culture to a native point of view.

In his 1915 book *The Indian To-Day*, published a year before *Deep Woods*, Eastman promotes racial intermarriage as a productive solution to the problem in which the identity of the acculturated American Indian gets submerged beneath the "white" one. Eastman shifts away from using inclusive metaphors as he did in *Deep Woods*, where he depicted his identity in terms of a palimpsest, with his Sioux qualities overlaid by those of civilization. Instead, he describes the identity of Indians like himself with a substitutive metaphor, in which he imagines his identity as a building, made of completely new materials, which has replaced an outdated one: "Here is a system ['civilization,'] which has gradually taken its present complicated form during two thousand years. A primitive race has put it on ready made, to a large extent, within two generations. In order to accomplish such a feat, they had to fight physical demoralization, psychological confusion, and spiritual apathy. In other words, the old building had to be pulled down, foundations and all, and replaced by the new. But you have had to use the same timber!"[150] When Eastman explains how a "primitive race" has "put [civilization] on ready made," he employs the metaphor of culture as clothing that US educators often used to describe their goals for the boarding school system. As I illustrate earlier, these educators either celebrated or failed to recognize the violence with which boarding schools forcibly replaced Indian children's tribal clothing with American clothing.

Eastman abandons his own clothing metaphor of "put[ting] on culture 'ready made" and instead adopts a metaphor that depicts this transformation much more violently by calling attention to its impact on the body. This figurative shift evidences Eastman's recognition that clothing, as something that can be put on and taken off, does not effect a permanent transformation of one's identity. Instead, as he explains, the Indian's identity was "pulled down, foundations and all, and replaced by the new." This metaphor more accurately evokes how US educational institutions transformed the bodies beneath the clothing. Despite the pain and dismay with which Eastman describes this process, he also expresses pride in the Indian sources of American civilization when he emphasizes that the new building "used the same timber." This passage depicts the simultaneity of Eastman's American and American Indian identities and thus differs significantly from the ambivalence haunting his portrayal of identity in *Deep Woods*.

As he continues to advocate Indian citizenship in *The Indian To-Day*, Eastman ceases to depict the pain involved in the transformation of the Indian's identity. Instead, he emphasizes the possibilities offered by that transformation. As the book develops, it becomes a manifesto for intermarriage, which, Eastman suggests, is the source for the positive "American" qualities of "unequalled logic," "wonderful aggressiveness," and "dauntless public service" (124). In proposing intermarriage, Eastman reinscribes the historical trend whereby the assimilation of American Indians into mainstream US culture was represented as a path to their disappearance. Eastman himself was descended from a white man, Captain Seth Eastman (his maternal grandfather), and fathered six mixed-blood children with Elaine Goodale Eastman, so it makes sense that he promoted intermarriage as a means of saving the Indian's "physique" and "philosophy"—even if it was too late to "save his color" (147).

Eastman's embrace of racial intermarriage here is not bereft of the awareness of the violence that necessitated it. Eastman laments "the young [Indian] men [who] themselves have entirely abandoned their old purpose to keep aloof from the racial melting-pot" (presumably including himself), which resulted in their loss of "color" (147). Yet he ultimately adjusts to this inevitability, expressing a deep satisfaction that these young men "now intermarry extensively with Americans and are rearing a healthy and promising class of children. The tendency of the mixed-bloods is toward increased fertility and beauty as well as good mentality. This cultivation and infusion of new blood has relieved and revived the depressed spirit of the first American to a noticeable degree, and his health problem will be successfully met if those who are entrusted with it will do their duty" (147). Eastman bolsters his claim by providing an extensive list of the mixed-bloods who have influenced the development of US culture and history and by extolling their virtues and accomplishments. He introduces this list not merely to suggest that American successes have resulted from the presence of Indian blood but to argue that one cannot and should not distinguish the Indian from the white man in narrating US history. As he will later claim in "The Indian's Plea for Freedom," even though the first white men who came to the United States viewed the natives as "godless and heathen, they unconsciously, and in spite of themselves, absorbed enough of the Indian culture to modify their own."[151] According to *The Indian To-Day*, Indians not only have provided "the foundations of our national welfare" (178) but also are an essential ingredient for the country's future "well-being" (147). Both literally and symbolically, Eastman suggests, the United States is unimaginable without a joined history of native and white Americans.

The Indian To-Day concludes with Eastman's warning to the white man that the Indian's assimilation does not mean his disappearance.[152] Eastman insists that the Indian will live on "not only in the splendor of his past, the poetry of his legends and his art, not only in the interfusion of his blood with yours, and his faithful adherence to the new ideals of American citizenship, but in the living thought of the nation" (178). This passage is striking in the way it metonymically aligns the materiality of intermarriage (blood) with Indian cultural formations (history, poetry) and a "new," nativized version of American citizenship. By aligning the items in this list, Eastman envisions a future United States that is indelibly native in both its demographic makeup and its epistemology. Eastman concludes *The Indian To-Day* by locating his utopian vision in the mixed-race body, offering a radical counterpoint to the conclusion of *Deep Woods*, where Eastman admits to the inevitability of assimilation that results from another's "might." Thus *The Indian To-Day* invokes marriage to challenge "inevitability discourse," which, as Joel Pfister explains, assumed "that white American conquest was inexorable" and that the "digestive capacity of American society" would enable the "extinction of the 'Indian' as anything but a usable American individual."[153]

If we consider Eastman's increasing skepticism about "civilization" in the years leading up to the publication of *Deep Woods*, it seems difficult to read the autobiography as a lukewarm or even an ambivalent validation of mainstream US culture. *The Indian To-Day* points to the inadequacy of an assimilation policy that did not guarantee legal equality as its counterpart.[154] It is no surprise that after publishing *Deep Woods* in 1916 Eastman promoted full citizenship as a potential solution to the untenable ambivalence illustrated by the autobiography's structure. The constant shifting of *Deep Woods*, and the fact that the text never presents a definitive portrait of Eastman's identity, have led critics to disagree as to whether Eastman definitively embraced or rejected mainstream US culture. But if we revisit *Deep Woods* in the context of Eastman's other work, it becomes clear that in his acculturation he never abandoned the values of his own people. Recognizing that American Indians could not return to the traditional life that reservations had already disrupted, Eastman concluded that the only plausible objective was to convince the United States to confer value on the many under-recognized contributions that

American Indians had made to US society—contributions that Eastman spent much of his life both acknowledging and promoting.

This chapter emphasizes the challenges Eastman faced as he articulated his ambivalence in a variety of genres. The formal structure of *Deep Woods*, which submerges his critique beneath a surface of consent, attests to these challenges. Other individuals involved with citizenship education—female professionals, for example—also experienced limitations on the freedom to document their experience honestly and accurately. As a result, these women voiced their views insidiously, while still remaining within the boundaries of dominant narrative forms. Marianna Burgess is one example of this trend; as Jacqueline Fear-Segal argues, Burgess was a lesbian who created "an invisible male alter ego" (the MOTBS) that allowed her to "claim the power and control identified with masculinity."[155] As I argue in chapter 2 of this book, Frances Benjamin Johnston was another single, professional woman whose citizenship education photographs reveal the limitations that her professional aspirations may have imposed on her creative freedom. Though Johnston never publicly vocalized her opinions about the assimilationist education programs she photographed, her self-portraits suggest just how aware she was of the pressure to conform to gender norms. Because Johnston's self-portraits comment ironically on how her public persona was limited by gendered ideology, we might by extension conclude that her awareness extended to race and class ideologies. As chapter 2 illustrates, if we contrast the self-reflexive quality of Johnston's self-portraits with the tone of distanced formality marking some of her boarding school photos, we can see that the latter group might—like the self-portraits—have served as screens for Johnston's real views about assimilationist education: views she would have needed to suppress in the service of her professional aspirations.

2 / The Scenes of Seeing: Frances Benjamin Johnston and Visualizations of the "Indian" in Black, White, and Native Educational Contexts

Chapter 1 argues that Charles Eastman's educational autobiography, *From the Deep Woods to Civilization*, reveals his ambivalent embrace of the civic republican ideology he internalized at assimilationist boarding schools. It also demonstrates how in his procitizenship essays and curricular writing Eastman overcomes his ambivalence and attempts to infuse mainstream US culture with Sioux values. Eastman's formal choices reflect both his overdetermined identity and his awareness of the demands of genre and audience. Like Eastman's writing, Frances Benjamin Johnston's educational photographs—the subject of this chapter—reveal her multiple loyalties, as well as her awareness that framing and audience are central to the presentation of identity.

As a professional photographer, Frances Benjamin Johnston documented American Indian boarding schools, African American citizenship education programs, and the Washington, D.C., public schools. Johnston's educational photos are marked by highly formalized structures and distanced tones, which seem to mask any opinions she may have had about the institutions she documented. Though Johnston never offered public commentary about these institutions, we can gain a measure of insight into her photos by looking at a handful of her autobiographical self-portraits. Through these self-portraits, Johnston comments on the need for people with unconventional identities like hers—she was a single, professional woman—to manage the frameworks through which their identities are mediated and judged. In these photos, Johnston either playfully represents or challenges established options for

women's identities. In one photo, she figures herself as a wealthy conservative lady. In another, she projects a masculine persona, wearing pants and
holding onto a bicycle wheel.[1] In a third photo, Johnston adopts a modest
demeanor that she undermines by holding a cigarette and beer and pro-
vocatively revealing her petticoats (see figure 1). Yet another photo shows
Johnston with the artistic avant-garde group "the Push," of which she was
the organizing figure; this photo reminds viewers that Johnston rejected
marriage and motherhood to pursue a professional and artistic career. As
a group, these self-portraits emphasize Johnston's awareness that clothing,
demeanor, and stance play a role in upholding a normative feminine identity; they also point to her discomfort with that identity.

Looking at Johnston's self-portraits, one may wonder, who is the
"real" Frances Benjamin Johnston? Is she hiding behind, or between,
these varying representations? As a series, these autobiographical narratives portray Johnston's rejection of a normative, gendered identity and
as such fit within the tradition of the antibildungsroman. In other words,
these photos represent Johnston's resistance to being incorporated into
a society that limits the range of acceptable paths for women's development.[2] The radical quality of the photos derives from their mocking
representation of the pressure for women to be proper, pure, delicate,
and dependent.

If we were to examine Johnston's portraits of boarding school students
as narratives of education, we would have to characterize them as realist bildungsromane because they portray an intractable social order that
demands total conformity from the individuals assimilating to it.[3] In this
respect Johnston's boarding school photos represent the civic republican
ideology that informed assimilationist educational programs; however,
we should be careful not to align this ideology unequivocally with Johnston's documentary eye. Reading Johnston's educational photos through
the lens of her radical self-portraiture reminds us that Johnston was sensitive to the visual and behavioral conventions that affect the presentation of identity.

Johnston's photographs present American Indian, African American, and white students in temporal and visual registers that evoke the
social Darwinist ideology of her time. In particular, these photos feature
the symbolic "Indian" as a shifting signifier that offers insight into the
racialized hierarchy of difference within which new citizens had to articulate their identities at the turn of the twentieth century. This chapter
compares Johnston's representations of the "Indian" with Estelle Reel's
Course of Study for the Indian Schools of the United States, the government

FIGURE 1 *Frances Benjamin Johnston, Full-Length Portrait, Seated in Front of Fireplace, Facing Left, Holding Cigarette in One Hand and a Beer Stein in the Other, in Her Washington, D.C. Studio, 1896.* (Courtesy Library of Congress, Prints and Photographs Division, reproduction # LC-USZ62–64301.)

curriculum for American Indian boarding schools that Reel produced in 1901, while she was employed as the superintendent of Indian schools.[4] Juxtaposing Johnston's photos alongside Reel's curriculum reveals how not just one, but multiple, forms of evolutionary theory circulated in scientific and popular culture and influenced educational practice. The photos and curriculum also echo the "Indian craze" through which individuals profited from marketing frozen and detribalized manifestations of native cultures. Finally, these texts evoke (in Johnston's case) or employ (in Reel's) the representation of an overdetermined "Indian" through which racially diverse students were to internalize their status in a stratified public sphere.[5]

Johnston and Reel were not unlike other progressive female reformers of their time; many such women benefited from race and class privilege to further their careers and as a result supported educational institutions that undermined the democratic promise of US citizenship. Though Johnston's photos may be complicit with the dominant educational ideology in some respects, they also preserve a space that resists interpretation. By foregrounding this space, the photos ask us to consider what forms of student agency and individuality might have challenged the operation of social Darwinism in educational institutions. In an attempt to occupy these unreadable spaces in Johnston's photos, this chapter also examines archival writing by American Indian students. What results is an auditory narrative that counterbalances the stultifying impact of visual imagery (embodied by visualizations of the "Indian") through which Johnston materializes the discourse of assimilation. Whereas many critics emphasize Johnston's totalizing lens, I juxtapose ambivalent spaces in Johnston's photos with equally ambivalent letters and essays produced by American Indian boarding school students. While the scopic vocabularies of Johnston's photographs and Reel's curricula do not signify active resistance, writing by American Indians students does challenge the dominant culture's structures of representation, in particular as these students critically reimagine the "Indian." The archives also speak to the perhaps unintended contradiction of American Indian boarding schools, which failed to prepare students (as promised) for equal participation in US civil and civic life but gave them a language through which they were able to critique this failure.

In Nature's Time: Frances Benjamin Johnston and Evolutionary Race Theory

Hampton Institute, the boarding school that Johnston is most famous for photographing, was unique in that both American Indian and African American students enrolled there. Johnston showcased her photos of Hampton at the Paris Exposition Universelle of 1900, as part of a larger collection of photos representing progressive education. This exhibition featured photos that Johnston took between 1899 and 1902 as she made a visual record of students at Washington, D.C., public schools,

the Hampton Institute, the Carlisle Indian Industrial School, the Tuskegee Institute, and the "little Tuskegees" of Snow Hill and Mount Meigs.
Johnston's photos of African American and American Indian students
at the Hampton Normal and Agricultural Institute won a Grand Prix
award at the Paris Exposition.[6] The Hampton photos, which Johnston
took in the winter of 1899–1900, appeared as part of the exposition's
award-winning *Exhibit of American Negroes*, organized and curated by
Thomas Calloway and W. E. B. Du Bois.[7]

The simultaneous participation of Du Bois and Booker T. Washington
in this exhibit—Du Bois as compiler of the Georgia section and Washington as the author of a monograph on Negro education—emblematizes the internal contradictions of the exhibit, of Johnston's educational
photography, and of the philosophies and practices of the schools she
documented. Du Bois envisioned the Negro exhibit at the Paris Expo
as a showcase for African Americans' self-representations of their history, social conditions, education, and literature in the spirit of "reform
and uplift."[8] At the same time, however, the exhibit appeared as part of
an international fair through which the United States and other countries competed to promote superior national self-images.[9] To realize
this latter goal, the Negro exhibit, under the direction of Thomas Calloway, celebrated the progressive educational ideology of "learning by
doing" that informed the curricula at Hampton and Tuskegee.[10] As it
was implemented at these schools, hands-on learning was influenced by
the conservative objectives of Samuel Chapman Armstrong (Hampton's
founder), Booker T. Washington (Tuskegee's founder), and Thomas Calloway (vice principal at Tuskegee), who thought that African Americans
should become "better laborers, establish their economic independence,
and thereby earn the respect of whites."[11]

Hampton also mobilized progressive educational practices to educate
its American Indian students, for instance to enhance its English-only
policy. Some Hampton teachers drew on Francis Parker's model of the
"talking class" as they asked students to create sentences about their
lives by discussing objects and pictures. Others implemented Pestalozzi's
methods of "observation and direct participation" rather than relying on
an older method of teaching through "definitions and abstract rules."[12]
Ironically, Hampton teachers used student-centered methods to deprive
native students of their individuality, insofar as that individuality rested
in their tribal identities.

Hampton teachers drew on more traditional teaching methods, such
as recitation, when instilling the school's more overtly racist views. For

example, Hampton required its native students to memorize and repeat the racial paradigm through which William Swinton divided the human race into "five large classes," with "the Americans or reds" at the bottom.[13] Hampton rewarded students who could reproduce this paradigm correctly with high marks. Other students were asked to recite poems such as "The Indians of To-Day," which Hampton teacher Elaine Goodale (later Charles Eastman's wife) wrote in honor of the institution's 1886 anniversary exercises:

> My friends, I shake your hands! I'm ready
> To do the work I once despised,
> I've thrown away my bow and arrow,
> I've taken up the plough and harrow,
> I'm willing to be civilized![14]

Any American Indian student asked to memorize or recite this poem would, at least temporarily, have to inhabit its speaker's point of view, which validates the evolutionary hierarchy that infused many elements of the Hampton curriculum (and the boarding school movement more generally).

American Indian boarding school students did not always internalize assimilationist ideology.[15] Joel Pfister's discussion of Carlisle suggests that American Indian boarding schools denied students their *tribal* identities by convincing them to think of themselves as Indians and then proceeded to "individualize" them.[16] But Ruth Spack's discussion of English education at these schools suggests that many students continued to use tribal languages and identify with tribal cultures. As one example among many, Spack cites *The Middle Five* (1900), in which the Omaha Indian Francis La Flesche compares his classmates' "broken English" with the sophistication and fluency that native boys display as they recite stories in their own language.[17] Spack also highlights the dual-directional assimilation of Hampton's native students, for instance through their translingualism—the practice of translating native expressions into English ones.[18] Given this evidence of resistance to an English-only policy, it makes sense that Hampton educators adopted the student-centered techniques central to progressive educational practice to realize their linguistic objectives.[19]

The fact that Hampton teachers used progressive educational practices to realize a conservative agenda exemplifies the ideological flexibility of these practices. This flexibility also marks Johnston's educational photos, as well as their reception by critics. Johnston's biographer, Bettina

Berch, faults Laura Wexler and James Guimond for basing their critique of Johnston on the unrepresentative selection of Johnston's Hampton photographs collected in the Museum of Modern Art's 1966 publication *The Hampton Album*.[20] Berch argues that the museum's 1966 exhibit and eponymous book, with its post facto captions, represent Hampton falsely as an institute whose mission was to train African American and American Indian students for second-class citizenship.[21] Berch's commentary suggests that Hampton, Tuskegee, and Carlisle shared more characteristics with progressive educational institutions for white children than critics want to admit.[22] Berch correctly argues that schools for nonwhite children in fact offered the same types of education (ranging from the study of poetry to instruction in the hand drill) that mainstream schools offered to white children. Referencing a wider range of Johnston's photographs than those represented by the museum's publication, Berch emphasizes Johnston's status as a documentarian rather than an ideological apologist for assimilationist education.

Besides Wexler and Guimond, Shawn Smith and Judith Fryer Davidov have identified features of Johnston's Hampton photos that evidence her complicit acceptance of progressive educational practices that reproduced racial and economic inequality. Wexler identifies Johnston as a middle-class reformer whose positionality is complicit with a "white patriarchal stance."[23] Smith argues that Johnston's photographs of Hampton feature students who do not look at the camera, thus depriving them of a "'challenging' gaze" and "subtly [reproducing] a legacy of racial hierarchy in the turn-of-the-century South."[24] Davidov opines that the Hampton photos demonstrate an "absolute denial of subjectivity" to the students.[25] While these critics attribute varying levels of agency or resistance to Johnston's photographic subjects, they all work from the assumption that Johnston's photographs validate the use of progressive educational ideology to deny agency to African Americans and American Indians on the basis of their race.[26]

While misguided in some respects, Bettina Berch correctly faults Johnston's critics for attributing her complicity with dominant race and class ideologies to a handful of highly staged Hampton photos.[27] In fact, Johnston also took photos that were not staged and that do *not* abide by these critics' generalizations. The extensive collection of Johnston's work at the Library of Congress contains informal photos of white students gazing away from the camera, engaged by teachers or their work, as well as photos of nonwhite subjects that make different kinds of visual claims than those serving as objects of recent critical discussion.

Berch is correct that, when viewed comparatively, Johnston's visual representations of white, black, and native children point to parallel practices in educational institutions across the color line. Moreover, some of Johnston's photos portray nonwhite subjects in postures suggesting private contemplation and individual agency. The photographic structure, framing, and perspective in this broader range of photos suggest that Johnston is neither the neutral outsider that Berch claims she is nor the uncritical and unconscious spokesperson for a racially demeaning ideological program, as Wexler and others have argued.[28] Rather, Johnston variously aestheticizes and identifies with her subjects to tell a series of contradictory stories that mirror similar contradictions in progressive educational ideology and practice.

Johnston's photos of students engaged in hands-on learning testify to the presence of progressive educational practices in institutions promoting a narrow interpretation of civic republican ideology. Whereas John Dewey explicitly aligned progressive practices with the cultivation of a liberal democratic ideal, some institutions disregarded this objective. Dewey hoped that by validating individual learning styles and perspectives educational institutions could help reproduce a more democratic society, one marked by a communal and cooperative spirit rather than a private and competitive one.[29] Dewey thought that schools could model this form of democracy by promoting intellectual freedom in the service of the "public interest."[30] He also opposed the adoption of vocational and manual labor training that would result in economic inequality, arguing that this approach would undermine his democratic vision: "To split the system, and give to others, less fortunately situated, an education conceived mainly as specific trade preparation, is to treat the schools as an agency for transferring the older division of labor and leisure . . . into a society nominally democratic."[31] Though he did not comment directly on boarding schools such as Hampton, Dewey's statement suggests that he would have objected to programs that used progressive educational practices to bolster a racialized economic hierarchy.

We can gain insight into the social Darwinist elements of institutions such as Hampton by examining Johnston's portraits of detribalized "Indians" and tribal objects. Johnston's photograph *Louis Firetail (Sioux, Crow Creek) Wearing Tribal Clothing, in American History Class, Hampton Institute, Hampton, Va.* (see figure 2) has been the object of much critical discussion that emphasizes Johnston's role in drawing out the observer's masterful and objectifying gaze on a tribal Indian who seems to occupy an irretrievable past.[32] As Bettina Berch notes in her discussion

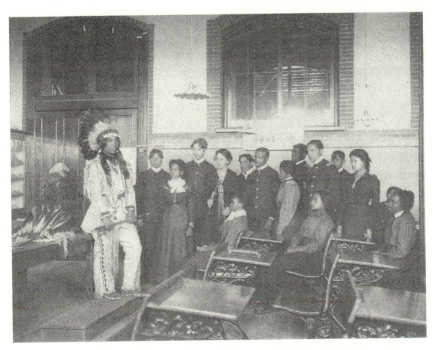

FIGURE 2 *Louis Firetail (Sioux, Crow Creek) Wearing Tribal Clothing, in American History Class, Hampton Institute, Hampton, Va.,* 1899. (Courtesy Library of Congress, Prints and Photographs Division, reproduction #LC-USZ62–38149.)

of this photograph, however, critics mistakenly have cited it as being representative of Johnston's educational photography, while neglecting other photos through which Johnston validates American Indian culture and celebrates Hampton's commitment to progressive education. Berch writes, "Against the MOMA-selected image of a class studying the nearly extinct Native American . . . one can juxtapose an image MOMA rejected . . . with its radiant Native American baby bound in the traditional cradle-board. For every manual-labor or field-hand scene, there is another with a cluster of elegantly uniformed African American men learning horticulture or browsing tomes of poetry. For every African American woman dressed in servile chambermaid clothes, there is another in a work smock learning to use a hand drill."[33] While Berch overlooks the social and economic inequality that American Indian and African Americans faced after completing their education, she nonetheless correctly emphasizes how educational institutions attended by white and nonwhite students often taught manual labor and academic subjects alongside each other.

In his analysis of Johnston's Carlisle photos, the sociologist Eric Margolis also draws attention to the practices of embodied self-regulation that linked school curricula across the color line. Margolis demonstrates how schools commonly organized activities such as sports and band practice to inculcate "Foucault's disciplines" of Time, Exercise, Rank, and Examination.[34] Nonetheless, as Margolis explains, progressive educational institutions for whites adopted "elements of discipline associated with modernity," whereas schools for natives (and, I would add, blacks) excluded their students from "the bargain of modernity [, which] is to exchange submission to an organization for increased knowledge and skill leading to upward mobility for the individual and stability for the social order."[35] In other words, despite some similar educational methodologies, evident through a comparative study of Johnston's school photos, students entered the civil and civic spheres of US life with unequal fields of possibility.

Though Johnston's photos highlight the progressive practices shared by institutions across the color line, her critics still conclude that she fails to individualize her nonwhite subjects and is thus complicit with their racialization. Margolis notes that Johnston's Carlisle photos emphasize students' group (versus individual) identities.[36] James Guimond calls attention to the way the Hampton photos deny student subjects the ability to gaze back at the camera's objectifying eye.[37] Guimond also argues that Johnston's Hampton photos validate assimilationist ideology by asking for the white viewer's "benevolent approval" of a utopian form of schooling, in which students are not "crowded, inattentive, bored, or distracted by anything."[38] Likewise, in her brief comparison of Johnston's Hampton and Washington, D.C., photos, Laura Wexler suggests that Johnston represents Hampton students in poses that indicate progress has already happened while portraying the D.C. students in movement, thus symbolizing their intellectual and economic mobility.[39]

Despite their compelling readings, these critics focus on Johnston's highly formal photos at the expense of others in which Johnston aligns white and nonwhite students. For example, figure 3, *Whittier School Students on a Field Trip Studying Plants, Hampton, Virginia*, appears in *The Hampton Album* but has not been the object of critical discussion. This photo, which Johnston shot at Whittier, Hampton's primary school, and titled *A Seed Lesson*, represents African American students in poses that suggest selfhood and individuality (see figure 3).[40] *A Seed*

FIGURE 3 *Whittier School Students on a Field Trip Studying Plants, Hampton, Virginia,* 1899. (Courtesy Library of Congress, Prints and Photographs Division, reproduction #LC-USZ62–38147.)

Lesson emphasizes students in the process of learning, thus illustrating the student-centered progressivism that was present in schools across the color line.[41] The photo shows three children in movement as they pursue individual forms of exploration: a boy in back looking at his collected weeds, a girl handing something to a teacher on the right, and a boy in front who is digging for plants. In this respect, the photo violates Guimond's generalization that students in Johnston's Hampton photos are never distracted. In fact, the level of student engagement in this photo evokes John Dewey's theory that in order to develop individuality, students must combine independent learning styles with experience working as part of a group.[42]

Edith Westcott captures the essence of Dewey's educational philosophy in the *New Education Illustrated* (1900), the journal that she and Johnston co-produced and that features selected photos from Johnston's D.C. collection. In the first issue of this short-lived quarterly journal, Westcott begins the chapter titled "Primary Education" by encouraging the reader to enjoy visions of (white) students engaged in learning: "Experience getting! What pictures are recalled by these words! A Herdie full of first grade children, en route to the Zoo. A field full of happy six-year-olds, waist-deep in daisies. A school room where the teacher is the center of an eager, inquisitive group, each intent upon the experiment which shall reveal the secret of some familiar phenomenon of nature."[43] Examining *A Seed Lesson* in the context of Westcott's text, we can see how it embodies the philosophy of progressive education emerging at the turn of the twentieth century. Johnston pictures the Whittier students in moments of real engagement; we can see them learning through experience in the very mode embraced by progressive educational reformers such as Dewey and Parker. These students, immersed in self-paced and self-directed forms of learning within the group setting, echo Dewey's belief that the individual pursuit of knowledge could not be realized "except under the stimulus of associating with others."[44]

Despite *A Seed Lesson*'s progressive elements, viewing it alongside a similarly themed photo of white D.C. children—titled *A Primary School in the Field* (see figure 4) and published in Westcott and Johnston's the *New Education Illustrated*—reminds us that unequal contexts often undermined progressive practices. In *A Primary School*, Johnston portrays a group of white primary-school students in a bright, vibrant, and dreamy atmosphere that is enhanced by the sunlight reflecting off the students' white clothing. Even given differences in lighting and vegetation that we can attribute to seasonal differences—Johnston shot *A Seed Lesson* in the winter and *A Primary School* in the spring—a comparative study of the photos suggests that white children could access more promising conditions of possibility. Most of the children in *A Primary School* wear frilly white clothing characteristic of the middle classes, as opposed to the heavy, dark uniforms worn by the Whittier students. Many wear jaunty hats. Most, if not literally "waist-deep in daisies," are either picking or contemplating their flowers.

The text that accompanies *A Primary School*, written by Edith Westcott, intensifies the photo's romantic promise. In the image, the teacher seems to be collecting her own flowers, while most of the students gaze in multiple directions, emphasizing their individuality. Facing this page, Westcott's text reads,

> The possibilities of such a trip, as is suggested by the opposite picture, are beyond enumeration. Appreciation of beauty, breathed in with every breath of invigorating summer air and sunshine; ethical

FIGURE 4 *A Primary School in the Field,* in *The New Education Illustrated, No. 1, Primary* (Richmond, VA: B. F. Johnson 1900). (Courtesy Library of Congress, Prints and Photographs Division, Frances Benjamin Johnston Collection, lot 2749.)

culture, from courteous association under new conditions, with little formal control; physical culture of the very best sort. . . . The child makes a beginning of learning many things; how plants grow—what neighbors this plant has, what familiar characteristics determine others of the same group or family, how the brook, in the lower part of the field, swollen with summer rains, has washed away the bank, carrying a muddy deposit for the formation of a miniature delta at its mouth; what birds are singing, what insects feeding, the inter-dependence of all myriad life of plant and bee and bird and stream.[45]

These comments recall the freedom of mind and body that Dewey saw as the precondition for his ideal of "investigation and experimentation."[46] The curly-haired girl toward the back of the photo, struck by a ray of sunlight, occupies the emotional center of the photo and seems to exemplify visually Westcott's idealized and romantic depiction of the educational process. In the spirit of Westcott's description, the photo invites us to align ourselves with this girl as she looks at her daisies and perhaps contemplates the "field . . . swollen with summer rains," the singing birds, the feeding insects, and the interdependence of all life. Nature here serves as a backdrop through which Johnston and Westcott imagine that students will acquire artistic appreciation, physical culture, scientific learning, and ethical behavior. As observers, we can also bask imaginatively in the ray of sunlight and recognize the possibilities offered by hands-on learning.

Though *A Seed Lesson* also pictures a few students in moments of contemplation and discovery, their natural surroundings are stark. The photo does not invite spectators to lose themselves in the fanciful, imaginative contemplation of nature, as they might do when looking at *A Primary School*. Knowledge of the Hampton curriculum further dampens whatever elements of a liberating atmosphere *A Seed Lesson* does possess; the Hampton students are studying seeds because they are being trained as agricultural laborers (or their teachers) in a rapidly industrializing society that has made the self-sufficient farmer an anachronistic ideal. Not all Hampton students were being shuttled into agricultural careers; some became craftsmen, industrial workers, or teachers who promoted these objectives. However, as Peter Schmidt explains, "Most of the skills taught at Hampton . . . could properly be called pre-industrial, such as farming, blacksmithing, and shoe-making, plus classes in how to wait tables and wash dishes for the men and, for the women, sewing, clothes repair, gardening, and cooking."[47] Moreover, though many African American graduates of Hampton became teachers, most native graduates fared much worse, becoming "subsistence farmers on the reservations or wives of such."[48]

Though Hampton students might have received some academic training, Hampton's founder, Samuel Chapman Armstrong, "rejected the idea of literate culture as either a civilizing force or appropriate preparation for morally responsible citizenship" and emphasized a curriculum that would "prepare the black masses for efficient service in racially prescribed occupational niches."[49] Not only was Hampton's "primary aim [as a normal institute] to work the prospective teachers long and hard so that they would embody, accept, and preach an ethic of hard toil or the 'dignity of labor,'" but Armstrong also "identified Hampton with the conservative wing of southern reconstructionists who supported new forms of external control over blacks, including disenfranchisement, segregation, and civil inequality."[50] Armstrong embraced manual and vocational training as a result of his belief that African Americans needed to proceed through a series of evolutionary stages toward civilization.[51] His views recall Herbert Spencer's embrace of a class-stratified society in which those already on the lower rungs of the social order would remain there because such populations were "immoral, irrational, and aggressive" and would pass on these traits to subsequent generations.[52] While there were differences in their positions, both Armstrong and Spencer assumed and even advocated the maintenance of rigid status distinctions based on biological difference.[53]

While John Dewey disapproved of an educational system that adopted vocational training in order to perpetuate "the feudal dogma of social predestination," other progressive educators were more invested in evolutionary ideology.[54] Progressivism in turn-of-the-century educational institutions, writes Peter Schmidt, was "a discourse of social engineering helping different groups progress at different rates determined by their inner destiny."[55] In this sense, both racial identity and character were not "inalienable" but "had continuously to be performed and claimed."[56] Whites, he explains, "were assumed to be superior, but they could only be properly trained to their role by a modern racial state governed in their interest."[57] In other words, evolutionary theory posited that both white and nonwhite children went through phases of primitiveness; whereas nonwhite children might not emerge from that phase, white children needed to be ushered through it by the educational apparatus. Drawing on Gail Bederman's work, Clifford Putney explains that this apparent contradiction functioned in a complementary way with the "developmental theories put forward by Progressive Era educators such as G. Stanley Hall. . . . Nonwhites in Hall's opinion might languish forever in a state of permanent primitiveness. But primitiveness for white boys was supposedly just a phase. . . . If white boys gained the requisite amount of strength and hardihood in their primitive phase, then they could go on to master the intricacies of civilization without fear of nervous collapse."[58] Hall's views informed the primitivist camps for white boys that I discuss in chapter 1 of this book. Given the contradictory nature of this ideology, one can understand why similar progressive educational practices could exist in schools designed for different races. Not only were these practices linked to varying objectives, but educators assumed that the progress of subaltern students would be inhibited by students' internal limitations—and barring that, by other policies that catered to their ostensible inferiority.

Returning to a comparison of *A Seed Lesson* and *A Primary School*, we can gain further insight into the overdetermination of progressive educational practices. Despite the social Darwinist trend in citizen-ship education, *A Seed Lesson* shares more similarities with *A Primary School* than differences, particularly in its representation of students as individuals with private inner selves. Johnston's educational photos are usually seen as complicit with a school system that denies subaltern subjects the emotional expression and legal protection that should be accorded to the interiorized individual. Eva Cherniavsky argues that access to rights in a liberal democracy depends on a concept of the interiorized individual that has been restricted to the white subject: "The industrial wage-worker and the (raced) laborer in combined systems of (neo)colonial production are wrongly conceived as mir-ror images of each other . . . inasmuch as race vitiates or suspends the proprietary structure of embodiment on which the social relations of industrial capital, including the civic apparatus of liberal democracy, come to rest."[59] Johnston's photos of white children evoke the inte-riority that Cherniavsky describes, symbolizing their access to legal protection of self and equality of opportunity promised by the liberal state. Yet Johnston's photos of nonwhite subjects similarly evoke their interiority. Though the nonwhite students might not have experienced full legal equality, *A Seed Lesson* and similar photos belie the logical corollary to Cherniavsky's claim: that colonial educational practices could prevent an individual from experiencing interiority. Johnston's photos that represent nonwhite students in contemplative states chal-lenge the argument that Johnston denied her American Indian and African American subjects interiority because of their race.[60]

At the same time, however, *A Seed Lesson* evokes the agricultural conditions that dominated African Americans' horizon of possibility in the South, recalling turn-of-the-century evolutionary views that figured civilization as a product of a racially conditioned distance from or mas-tery over nature. In this context, Johnston's representations of white and black students in contrasting relations to nature—pleasurable and use-ful, respectively—evoke the evolutionary science of Lewis Henry Mor-gan, which influenced schools such as Hampton, Tuskegee, and Carlisle. As this book's introduction notes, Morgan was an anthropologist who argued that progress along a savagery-barbarism-civilization continuum paralleled the shift from a hunting-gathering lifestyle to an agricultural one; Morgan imagined that progress culminated with "civilization [that] commenced . . . with the use of a phonetic alphabet and the production of literary records."[61] While Morgan admitted that ethnic and racial groups might (and would eventually) move through all three of these stages, he also argued that Aryans and Semitic peoples had progressed furthest along the savagery-civilization continuum.

In his discussion of Morgan in "The Turn-of-the-Century Concept of Race," George Stocking explains how evolutionary theory from this period aligned cultural development with racial and geographical particularities. Stocking writes,

> Social evolution was a process by which a multiplicity of human groups developed along lines that moved in general toward the social and cultural forms of western Europe. Along the way different groups had diverged, regressed, stood still, and even died out as they coped with various environmental situations within the limits of their peculiar racial capacities, which in fact their different environmental histories had created. The progress of the "lower races" had been retarded or even stopped, but the general level had always advanced as the cultural innovations of the "superior" or "progressive" [sic] races were diffused through much of the world. Leadership, as Lewis Henry Morgan argued, had often changed hands, but "from the middle period of barbarism . . . the Aryan and Semitic families seem fairly to represent the central threads of this progress, which in the period of civilization has been gradually assumed by the Aryan family alone."[62]

Morgan identifies most American Indian tribes as savage (hunting-gathering) societies, and African Americans as barbaric (agricultural) societies. Popular views such as Morgan's categorized both groups as being closer to nature, in an evolutionary sense, than were whites. However, Morgan also ascribed to the racist science whereby a dash of Indian "blood" would "improve and toughen" the Anglo-Saxon race; in turn, his theory supported Hampton's view that Indians could be "candidates for amalgamation with the white race," whereas law and custom prohibited African Americans—regardless of their evolutionary progress—from racial and social mixing with whites.[63]

Reproducing this distinction, educators imagined "progress" for natives and blacks differently, a difference emblematized by the tribal symbolism in Johnston's photos.[64] Morgan's time line helps make sense of the otherwise counterintuitive proliferation of "Indian" symbols that took on different valences in white, native, and African American educational institutions. For white students, the "Indian" could exist as a positive reminder of the stage through which they had recently passed; for natives, it could function as a derogatory symbol of the inferior status that they should hope to escape; and for blacks, it could serve as a bleak reminder of their unbridgeable distance from whiteness. Johnston's photographs, and the educational ideology they evoked, mimicked this contradictory quality of evolutionary theory: on the one hand, educators believed that American Indians were capable of progress and therefore encouraged them to replace hunting with farming—to manage nature rather than coexisting symbiotically with it. On the other hand, they portrayed natives as locked in a timeless, irretrievable past. This contradiction echoes the uncanny coexistence during this period of Lamarckianism—the principle that acquired traits could be inherited—and polygenism—the idea that different races derived from and remained on separate and unequal paths of descent.[65] In other words, evolutionists (and educators) ascribed to a diachronic, or Lamarckian, principle that American Indians could experience progress over time, but this was stained by the synchronic, or polygenic, theory that progress was biologically impossible.

Traces of the diachronic and synchronic strains of evolutionary theory mark two photographs by Johnston (figures 5 and 6, respectively). The first photo, titled *At the Museum—Fourth Grade*, appeared in number 3 (*Geography*) of the *New Education Illustrated* (see figure 5). This photo pictures a group of white, D.C. fourth graders looking at a museum exhibit of an American Indian man (tribe unknown) who is wearing a suit and a flowery hat. He is busy at work behind a glass enclosure, with students and teacher staring intently at him. This photo reifies the "Indian" as an object—a museum display—freezing him in time even as he engages in activity.[66] The "Indian" in this photo shows signs of "progress" by wearing a suit and by writing on a piece of paper. His enclosure within the museum display case, however, undermines this progress and symbolically captures the severely circumscribed freedom that education would offer him. By looking at the museum Indian, the D.C. students learn who they are by comparing themselves with a living (or apparently living) but nonthreatening remnant of an exoticized past.

In describing this photo on the facing page of the journal, Edith Westcott invokes the ideas of Lewis Henry Morgan. Her description, titled "The Study of Race Characteristics," defines geography as a "study of the Earth in relation to man" and encourages teachers to "train the child to form the habit of looking to physiographic conditions as determining the phase of development attained by different peoples." Explaining that the American Indian is the ideal object for geographical study, Westcott writes, "Our museums abound in Indian curios. . . . Scarcely a school

FIGURE 5 *At the Museum—Fourth Grade*, in *The New Education Illustrated*, *No. 3, Geography* (Richmond, VA: B. F. Johnson, 1901). (Courtesy Library of Congress, Prints and Photographs Division, Frances Benjamin Johnston Collection, lot 2749.)

can be found in which there is not some boy who is the proud owner of an arrow head or a pipe stone, and even such small beginnings may be made the basis for the study of the Indian. Insist on studying *things*, however limited your resources." Westcott's words disturbingly suggest that the Indian is himself a "curio" and that the act of looking at the museum exhibit is akin to experiencing ownership of him: yet what the onlooker will own is not "an arrow head or a pipe stone" but rather the knowledge that he or she occupies a more developed position along the trajectory of progress than does the "Indian."

The second, unpublished photo is archived with Johnston's comparative series, which she organized into two groups: "Children of Students Educated at Hampton" and "Children of Uneducated Parents."[67] This photo, titled *The Dawn of Civilization* (see figure 6), romantically captures an educated American Indian man in a moment of contemplation as he is about to either begin or complete his farming. Looking off into the distance, this

FIGURE 6 *The Dawn of Civilization*, n.d. (Courtesy Library of Congress, Prints and Photographs Division, Frances Benjamin Johnston Collection, lot 11051, box 2 of 2.)

man shares with the children of *A Primary School* the time and the ability to wonder at nature and relax in it. The positive valence of this photo intensifies when we compare it with Johnston's *Hampton Institute, Hampton, Va.—Before Entering School—Seven Indian Children of Uneducated Parents* (see figure 7), where the children stand uncomfortably in a field with tensed shoulders, severe expressions, and ragged, traditional clothing.

As a photo about the American Indian's progress, *The Dawn of Civilization* captures the strand of evolutionary theory that saw natives as capable of adopting the lifestyle, if not the identity, of white Americans. Like the rhetoric and policies of boarding school educators, this photo portrays the American Indian managing the land as part of his movement forward along a continuum of progress. Yet there is a telling difference between this photo and *A Primary School*. Because the former is about farming and the second is about picking daisies, a comparative view suggests that white people should (or could) adopt a playful, rather than useful, relation to the land—a consequence of their having reached beyond Morgan's "barbaric" stage of development.

FIGURE 7 *Hampton Institute, Hampton, Va.—Before Entering School—Seven Indian Children of Uneducated Parents*, 1899. (Courtesy Library of Congress, Prints and Photographs Division, reproduction #LC-USZ62-78702.)

While educators of American Indians pictured their students' progress as resulting from a newly productive relationship with the land, a similar agricultural curriculum directed at African Americans developed within a different context, with a corresponding tenor. Because many African American students who attended Hampton were former slaves, there was an irony to representing their agricultural training as a symbol of progress.[68] Likewise, some students at Tuskegee—the institute that the former Hampton student Booker T. Washington modeled after Hampton—were former slaves. Paradoxically, Washington saw agricultural labor as a move *backward* for the African American on his journey *forward* toward civilization. Invoking nature in his 1904 description of Tuskegee's curriculum, *Working with the Hands*, Washington explains that in "the course in advanced American History . . . little attention is given to the periods of discovery and colonization, except to show the student how the American people, as is true of all great nations, began as cultivators of the soil."[69] In suggesting that African Americans had to begin anew as "cultivators of the soil" before they could become a part of the great nation of America, Washington willfully disregarded the reality that the "great nation" of America was produced by African Americans' cultivation of US lands. This comment also exposes Washington's alignment with Hampton's founder, Samuel Chapman Armstrong, who embraced social Darwinism and thought that African Americans were best qualified to work in the fields because they occupied the lower rungs of an evolutionary ladder.

Educators such as Armstrong and Washington were not asking their black students to find the best qualities in themselves through an imaginative identification with nature, as does Edith Westcott in her depiction of white students in *A Primary School.* Rather, African Americans were to identify with nature as a substitute for entering the legal and imaginative world of the white liberal subject.[70] Viewing Johnston's photos in terms of the evolutionary ideologies that informed assimilationist programs, one might say that *A Seed Lesson* imagines nature as the end point of development for African American students, *The Dawn of Civilization* marks the beginning of the American Indian's progress-journey, and *At the Museum* represents the naturalized Indian as the foil against which white students were to envision their own identities.[71]

The Overdetermined Indian

Earlier in this chapter, I cited Bettina Berch's invocation of the "traditional cradle-board" baby as a symbol of Hampton's embrace of a rich American Indian cultural heritage (see figure 8). Berch's caption for this photo reinforces her position: "This photograph speaks to the vibrancy of traditional customs, not to their extinction."[72] Yet Johnston wrote on the back of this photo, "Children of uneducated parents," suggesting that, for her, it represented not an idealized culture but a degraded state of civilization in need of improvement.

This smiling baby, with its colorful and decorative blankets, undeniably contrasts with Johnston's other photos of sad or bitter "uneducated" children (figure 7). Johnston's inclusion of the cradle-board baby with the photos of "uneducated" students captures a development in American Indian boarding schools after 1905, when Francis Leupp became commissioner of Indian affairs and made "a concerted effort to increase the curricular focus on native culture."[73] In contrast to boarding school policy until that time, which sought to eradicate all traces of Indian culture in students, Leupp initiated policies that, he wrote, would avoid the mistake, "in the process of absorbing [the Indian], of washing out of them whatever is distinctly Indian."[74] In contrast with the policy prohibiting all aspects of native culture from boarding schools, after 1905 policy makers decided that educators should attempt to preserve certain

FIGURE 8 *Baby in Cradle-Board, Hampton*, 1899
or 1900. (Courtesy Library of Congress, Prints
and Photographs Division, reproduction #LC-
USZ62–121911.)

aspects of native culture. This shift perhaps explains the quaint tenor
of the image of the cradle-board baby. Even though the baby represents
the ostensibly "uncivilized" native, its visual appeal recalls the practice
whereby boarding schools began to romanticize visual representations
of the Indian, make "Indian" crafts for sale, and display these crafts in
the classroom.

The boarding school's embrace of the "Indian" is evidenced, for
example, in Estelle Reel's 1901 *Course of Study for the Indian Schools of
the United States, Industrial and Literary* (also known as the Uniform
Course of Study, or UCS). Between 1898 and 1910, Estelle Reel served
as the superintendent of Indian schools, supervising the training of

teachers, inspecting and reporting on the schools, and writing the UCS "to homogenize content and pedagogy across all federal schools."[75] Reel's curricular recommendations served as a template for the day-to-day curricula of both reservation and nonreservation boarding schools.[76] In her analysis of the UCS alongside letters, newspaper articles, and other archival sources, Tsianina Lomawaima demonstrates that Reel adhered to racist evolutionary theories in her reworking of mainstream educational trends.[77] As Lomawaima argues, even while Reel invokes educational theorists who advocated at least some practical education for most citizens, she clearly distinguishes between white "public high school graduates," whose training should "prepare them to pass the entrance exam to any college, or technical school, or school of law or medicine," and Indian students, whom she felt were "'too dull' to excel intellectually."[78] As Reel told a newspaper reporter in 1900, "The Indian child is of lower physical organization than the white child of corresponding age. . . . The very structure of his bones and muscles will not permit so wide a variety of manual movements as are customary among Caucasian children, and his very instincts and modes of thought are adjusted to this imperfect manual development."[79] Reel's comments here echo a shift away from evolutionary theories, which held that American Indians could achieve cultural whiteness. Her comments instead echo the eugenic perspective that emerged around the turn of the century, which conveyed increasing skepticism about whether Indians could assimilate fully. This "gradualist" belief that Indians could slowly, but never completely, be civilized mirrored "an emerging body of social thought that held that inherited race characteristics, not environment, were the source of primitive man's backwardness."[80]

Reel made an exception to her low expectations of American Indian children when it suited her economic aims. This tendency infuses Reel's *Course*, which she divided into sections that describe the ideal methods for teaching agriculture, sewing, baking, laundry, carpentry, blacksmithing, and other tasks. In the basketry section, Reel proposes educating workers with only elementary skills in non-native trades, *except* when a more sophisticated knowledge of tribal crafts might benefit the demands of a capitalist market economy. In other words, Reel promotes the wholesale eradication of American Indian cultures yet encourages instruction in commodifiable tribal crafts. As she writes, "In every school where the children are descendants of a basket-making tribe and where suitable materials are obtainable, a good teacher of basketry should be employed, and all the children must learn the art, since very many skilled workers are necessary to supply the demands of the times for these baskets. . . . Thousands are imported yearly."[81] Despite her posturing here, however, Reel's basketry curriculum lacked authentic tribal influence; in fact, Reel adapted techniques from the manual training movement, hobbyists, and books directed at mainstream elementary schools.[82]

The presence of basketry in Estelle Reel's curriculum speaks to the schools' attempts to produce an alienated, fragmented, and generic "Indian" identity. Reel's exhortation that "children must be led to see how important it is for them to learn the arts of making baskets as they were woven by their parents" partakes of a false cultural relativism,[83] as these "consumer articles no longer appear as the products of an organic process within a community."[84] In her exploration of the basketry curriculum, Elizabeth Hutchinson explains that the "relocation of traditional practices to Indian schools" isolated the younger and older generations from each other, "broke the learning down into lessons," and removed the making of baskets from the "seasonal cycles of gathering and preparing materials and producing the final work; the schools focused only on this last step, providing students with materials ready for assembly."[85] Reel's curriculum proposed that the school replace the parent in the service of capitalism and asked the students to produce and market "authentically Indian" products that were really only generically "Indian." Students were to be told "that the more 'Indian' the baskets are, the more valuable they are and the better price they will bring."[86] In other words, they were asked to see themselves as engaging in so-called "Indian" practices as they simultaneously underwent a systematic process of disidentification with everything "Indian" in order to adopt the ostensibly superior ways of the white man. The school thus functioned as a marketplace that manipulated the notion of authenticity to commodify both the actions and the identities of American Indian students. Being "Indian," in Reel's terms, meant engaging in reified cultural practices isolated from forms of meaning imparted by historical and communal use-value. In Reel's terms, "Indianness" would be represented only by decontextualized commodities to be made and sold in the service of cultivating US citizenship. Citizenship emerges here as the offspring of educational practices geared toward reinforcing a simultaneously consumerist and stratified economic sphere.

A return to Johnston's photo of Louis Firetail (figure 2) usefully demonstrates that the American Indian boarding school was not the only place in which the figure of the "Indian" was used to help establish students' identities. Both critical discussions of this photo and the work of Robert Frances Engs and Donal Lindsey exemplify how Hampton adopted reified representations of the Indian to model native culture for its African American students.[87] The photo of Louis Firetail captures the contradictory racial ideologies that African Americans and American Indians faced. This photographic scene suggests that the (black and native) students in the class have something to learn from this Indian warrior because of the noble history he represents; the photo thus echoes Armstrong's belief that American Indians were racially superior to African Americans. Engs argues that racial anxiety about miscegenation, which itself contributed to the increasing expansion of Jim Crow laws, prompted educators to deny the degree of "civilization" obtained by African Americans.

On the other hand, because Armstrong believed that African Americans were more assimilated than Indians, he used African Americans, at least in the school's early years, as models for American Indian behavior: "Armstrong began by giving each Indian student a black roommate, by making Indian boys walk while Indian girls rode in wagons, and by holding up the behavior of blacks as an example for Indians to emulate."[88] Hampton kept records of its graduates, which corroborate Armstrong's assumption. These records suggest that African American graduates experienced more success at assimilating than did American Indian graduates.[89] However, this outcome may itself have resulted from Hampton policies that denied American Indians the same opportunities as African Americans.

The static representation of the noble Indian in figure 2 is only one of several photos by Johnston that echo the logic, also adopted by Estelle Reel, whereby actual people were replaced with artificial emblems of their culture. In Johnston's D.C. photo *Indian Curios in the Schoolroom—Fourth Grade* (see figure 9), for example, the students gather around a table filled with "native" artifacts—model canoes, moccasins, arrows, and the like.[90] Westcott's accompanying text explains that looking at these objects not only will help students understand and love the poem *Hiawatha* but also will serve as models through which they can make their own "canoes, bows and arrows or tiny wigwams." In contrast with the Boy Scouts' curriculum through which Eastman asked white students to embody native practices, this photo asks them to identify with an imagined "Indian" culture (both literary and material) in a schoolroom that has been transformed into a miniature museum.[91]

As Johnston's photos of black, white, and native educational contexts suggest, the overdetermined symbol of the "Indian" mimicked the contradictory but coexisting forms of evolutionary theory at the turn of the

FIGURE 9 *Indian Curios in the Schoolroom—Fourth Grade*, in *The New Education Illustrated, No. 3, Geography* (Richmond, VA: B. F. Johnson, 1901). (Courtesy Library of Congress, Prints and Photographs Division, Frances Benjamin Johnston Collection, lot 2749.)

twentieth century. For native students, the "Indian" represented the production of a detribalized identity that was employed to sell crafts and support schools that paradoxically would teach native students to abandon their tribal identities in favor of Americanization. At Hampton, the "Indian" functioned in a confused manner, on the one hand reinforcing African Americans' practical knowledge that in many ways they were more assimilated than Indians, and on the other hand reminding them that the dominant culture considered even the unassimilated Indian to be racially superior to the black man—a condition that makes sense of laws that prohibited African Americans from intermixing as natives could. Finally, white students bolstered their own identities as representatives of "civilization" through imaginatively distancing themselves from "Indian" objects and people that had been transformed visually into simultaneous embodiments of progress and immobility.

Student Testimony and the Ambivalence of Consent

How successful were American Indian boarding schools in cultivating the detribalized "Indian" identity that this chapter outlines? And how successful were the schools in preparing students to achieve success in the competitive American marketplace? Letters sent to Carlisle's superintendent Moses Friedman and supervisor of Indian employment Charles Dagenett offer insight into Indian students' views of both their education and their activities after leaving boarding schools. In evoking the particularity of individual students, these letters provide an alternative to the abstract "Indian" identity emblematized by Johnston and Reel's imagery.

A 1909 letter from former Carlisle student and Nez Perce Indian Stephen Reuben illustrates the degree to which Reuben internalized Carlisle's production of "Indian" identity even as the letter expresses a tribal specificity that challenges the school's practices.[92] The letter contains a confession of remorse for wrongdoing and desire for praise:

> I had punishment once while I was [at] Carlisle School. It was every Saturday report was each individual student answered like this, Did you speak Indian during the past week? I said, yes. . . . I said truth because I spoke that time just a word to one of my friend Nez Perce, and in the evening the meeting was at Chapel [and] Capt. R. H. Pratt called us out who spoke Indian and used tobacco. I was officer, he called on me first then the rest of the boys and said to me, Stephen, you take charge these boys, take them down to lower farm there four miles below and soon as you would get down there and come right back to me to report. . . . So I took charge [of] about 30 of them boys. I said right face! forward march! And we went down to lower farm and some boys hided and some of them stole apples while down lower farm, but Capt. telephoned if we were down already. It was answered by the man who took charge the farm, here they are Capt., [he] said by phone, send them back right away, so we went back home. This was only one trouble I had and finished while I was at Carlisle School and I don't want to get punished again so I have to tell the truth and to do what right and I am thankful to Carlisle and I am friendly ask you to sent me Indian Helper and Red Man paper I will pay for it.[93]

Reuben's letter offers insight into the ongoing impact that education at Carlisle had on the psychic landscapes of its former students. The letter is confessional in nature: while Captain Pratt (no longer even at Carlisle) knew about Reuben's first infraction, speaking Nez Perce, he did not know about the second, that Reuben allowed the boys under his charge to hide, steal apples, and stay at the lower farm for longer than they were supposed to have stayed. The intensity of Reuben's guilt is impressive, considering that he left Carlisle in 1893, sixteen years before he wrote this letter. It is also noteworthy that he ceases to punctuate his thoughts toward the letter's end, evoking an intensified sincerity (one often associated with spoken language) and a heightened emotional investment in exchanging this confession for any future punishment.[94] Finally, in the very breath of the plea for leniency, Reuben asks for copies of the school's two newspapers. The letter, along with later correspondence from Reuben, suggests that Carlisle transformed his life in significant ways: he longs for the newspapers through which Carlisle created a pan-Indian community; he has become an evangelistic Christian; and he makes a living as a successful fruit farmer. Yet in recounting his experience Reuben replies to the question of whether he spoke "Indian" with a reply that he spoke a word of "Nez Perce." Reuben's knowledge—that it makes no sense to call a language "Indian" when no such language exists—testifies to the school's failure to eradicate his tribal identity, at least insofar as his identity rests in language.[95] This example also corroborates Ruth Spack's argument, cited earlier in this chapter, that tribalism persisted at boarding schools in spite of immersive assimilationist practices.

Priscilla La Mote (Menominee), a former Hampton student, more directly criticizes the boarding school's emphasis on eradicating tribal languages and communities. In a 1910 letter, she complains to Charles Dagenett about her dashed hopes of becoming a teacher:

> When I left Hampton I intended to return in the fall, but conditions have changed my plans. . . . Before leaving school I desired to take the civil service examination for teachers. The school authorities disfavored the idea as they wished me to return in the fall. . . . The agent here wished me to teach in this government school. The principal said that Indian teachers were forbidden to teach members of their own tribe. . . . The Tomah Indian School superintendent asked me if I'd accept the position of assistant laundress if it was offered to me. . . . It seems queer though when I've been to school so long and labored so diligently at my school work that I [can't] get a better place than that of an assistant.[96]

La Mote's letter testifies to the centrality of the detribalized "Indian" to boarding school policy and to at least one instance in which a school

policy organized around producing and maintaining tribal disidentification kept a student from achieving success.

Stephen Reuben's request for the *Indian Helper* symbolizes the relative success of boarding school ideology (as this newspaper was a vehicle
through which the school disseminated its ideology). However, Reuben
also requests the *Indian Craftsman*, another paper produced at Carlisle,
but one that exemplifies the students' agency in interpreting their experience and in "talking back" to assimilationist ideology.[97] The *Indian
Craftsman* was a monthly paper published at Carlisle in twenty issues
between February 1909 and January 1910. Some of the student writing
included in this paper comes in the form of depoliticized "Indian" myths
and stories, as well as autobiographical texts through which students laud
the boarding school experience and narrate their educational trajectory
as a journey of progress from savagery to civilization. Occasionally, however, the paper includes student testimonies that invoke and then inter-
rupt this narrative, evidencing how some students responded critically
to inaccurate, detribalized representations of themselves.[98]

In a short essay titled "The American Indian," published in the *Craftsman*'s December 1909 issue, Sara Hoxie (Nomelacki) begins by praising
the school's agenda: "Thirty years ago Carlisle was established for the
benefit of the Indian race. What did this mean? It meant patience and
perseverance. We, as students are thankful to all those who have taken
interest in us and our work, and who have done much for our advancement and promotion to a happier, nobler and more civilized life."[99]
While this essay's frame glorifies the racial hierarchy influencing school
policies, Hoxie later reveals her ambivalence about it. In the middle of
the essay, for example, Hoxie explains that popular conceptions about
American Indian culture have been mistaken:

> We ourselves are inclined to look upon our ancestors as warriors,
> but when defined as a warrior he has been misconceived. He knows
> nothing of standing armies or military tactics. . . . It is true he had
> the bow and arrow and the tomahawk, which were used only for
> slaying wild animals either for food or other comforts of life. His
> experience with wild animals has made him an excellent marks-
> man and a skillful Nimrod. He became such a perfect mimic of
> wild animals that he deceived both people and animals. His won-
> derful observation aided him in hunting and also in time of war.
> We read of many wars, but these occurred after the white men had
> immigrated and taken possession of various lands.[100]

With these lines, Hoxie demonstrates her confidence in the sophistication of her culture. She also blames its warlike characteristics on historical events set in motion by white settlers—thus contesting the narrative of progress central to the period's dominant educational ideology. Hoxie further challenges this progress narrative by disrupting the concept of an "authentic" tribal culture that American Indians were to leave behind; rather, she reminds us that natives have undergone continual transformation since their first contact with whites. Yet Hoxie most subtly and convincingly challenges boarding school ideology as she praises the hunter's skill in mimicry and his ability to deceive both animals and people. Is Hoxie pointing to her own skill at mimicry and deception, perhaps for the sake of getting her essay approved for publication? If so, we can imagine Hoxie's text as occupying one of the unreadable spaces in Johnston's photos, which otherwise would tell us stories of representation but not of transformation and resistance.[101]

The letters and essay discussed above suggest, in the words of Gerald Vizenor, that even if American Indians often simulated "survivance" in the realm of the symbolic, they did not allow their self-articulations to define them irrevocably as "the other of manifest manners, the absence of the real tribes, the inventions in the literature of dominance."[102] Like Charles Eastman, these students were warriors who counteracted "manifest manners" with "simulations of survivance . . . heard and read stories that mediate and undermine the literature of dominance."[103] In *Manifest Manners*, Vizenor clarifies that simulation is not assimilation and suggests that even as colonial language mediates self-expression its users can alienate the dominant ideology expressed in that language. This chapter concludes with the voices of Stephen Reuben, Sara Hoxie, and others to suggest that the official historical narratives reproduced by educational ideology, curricula, and photography cannot fully register the subtle ways in which students experienced agency. They found themselves in total institutions but nevertheless exercised some self-control over how they viewed and expressed themselves.[104]

Whereas students such as Reuben and Hoxie express their agency from within the confines of assimilationist ideology, other citizenship educators from this period challenged assimilationist ideology more overtly. Chapter 3 compares the approaches of three figures—Booker T. Washington, W. E. B. Du Bois, and Jane Addams—who not only educated new citizens but also philosophized about this practice. Chapter 3 prefaces its analysis of educational autobiographies by Du Bois and Addams with a short discussion of Booker T. Washington, whose Tuskegee Institute represents the dominant, assimilationist approach to citizenship education. Rather than focusing on Du Bois's fraught attempts to realize his minoritarian pedagogy in mainstream institutions, chapter 3 examines his autobiography *as* a curriculum. Likewise, the chapter interprets Addams's educational autobiography as a curriculum and argues that we can categorize both Du Bois's and Addams's educational autobiographies as dissensual bildungsromane.

3 / Curricular Cosmopolitans: W. E. B. Du Bois and Jane Addams

As chapter 2 demonstrates, Frances Benjamin Johnston's symbolization of the "Indian" at Hampton—as well as at other institutions—evokes the teleological structure of social Darwinist ideology. Hampton is also famous for being the school that Booker T. Washington attended and used as a model for Tuskegee, the Normal Institute he opened in 1881. Like Johnston, Washington portrays citizenship education with temporal metaphors that reveal the influence of evolutionary theory on his pedagogy. In *Up from Slavery* (1901) and *Working with the Hands* (1904), Washington reveals his commitment to embodied education for African Americans, with the goal of improving the quality of their status in civil society. This chapter briefly examines these texts before contrasting them with the cosmopolitan pedagogies of W. E. B. Du Bois and Jane Addams.

Du Bois, who famously opposed the "Tuskegee Machine" through which Washington exerted control over African American education, consistently articulated an educational philosophy that rejected the restrictive embodiment of African American citizens.[1] Like Washington, Du Bois invoked a temporal schema to relay his theory of citizenship education. However, he did so to suggest that African Americans should imaginatively revisit the experience of slavery in order to address its ongoing impact on African American identity. Whereas Washington's invocation of slavery reinscribed its living influence on both his own and his students' identities, Du Bois pursued a dialectical engagement with slavery, modeling an ideal African American citizen who overcame the limitations of embodied citizenship.

In Du Bois's unpublished 1895 "Diary of My Steerage Trip across the Atlantic," which he also revisits in *Autobiography of W. E. B. Du Bois: A Soliloquy on Viewing My Life from the Last Decade of Its First Century* (1968), Du Bois ruminates simultaneously on the history of the transatlantic slave trade and the European immigrant's journey to the United States, symbolically aligning the two as he articulates a theory of cosmopolitan citizenship. Envisioning a global framework for his own intellectual journey, Du Bois offers an alternative to the civic republican model of citizenship, refusing to represent his development as a process of negotiation with and consent to nationalist principles.

Through the cosmopolitan figure of the Rover, Du Bois also imagines an educational journey for the African American citizen that resists curricular implementation. In part, this choice exemplifies Du Bois's unfruitful attempts to realize his radical pedagogy within an institutional framework. In 1910, Du Bois resigned from his professorship at Atlanta University to become director of publicity and research at the NAACP, where he also edited the *Crisis*. In 1920, Du Bois began publishing the *Brownies' Book*, a children's monthly that had a run of only two years but during that time served as a platform from which Du Bois could circulate his radical pedagogy to African American youth. Through the *Brownies' Book*, Du Bois—alongside the magazine's literary editor, Jessie Fauset, and its business manager, Augustus Granville Dill—encouraged African American children to align themselves with black and brown people around the world and to emulate the successful men and women whose stories appeared in the magazine.

Jane Addams both knew and occasionally cooperated with Du Bois to develop alternatives to assimilationist education. As Mary Jo Deegan has demonstrated, Addams not only worked with Du Bois in founding the NAACP but also influenced his 1899 sociological study, *The Philadelphia Negro*, by recommending former Hull-House worker Isabel Eaton as its coauthor.[2] Addams also influenced Du Bois through her publication of *Hull-House Maps and Papers*, which, Deegan argues, served as a model for *The Philadelphia Negro*.[3] Deegan calls further attention to "nearly twenty documented professional contacts" between Du Bois and Addams during the period 1898 to 1935 in her quest to establish evidence of their close relationship, one that many critics have overlooked.[4]

Like Du Bois, Addams infuses her 1910 autobiography, *Twenty Years at Hull-House*, with a global sensibility that challenges civic republicanism. Both Addams and Du Bois wrote about and actively pursued alternatives to the assimilationist ideology and practice that dominated citizenship education at the turn of the twentieth century.[5] As Ross Posnock has demonstrated, both of these authors embraced a pragmatist pluralism through which they opposed "nativist and progressivist pressure to Americanize the immigrant via a thorough soaking in the melting pot."[6] They not only challenged the civic republican model of the nation as a "melting pot"; they also shared John Dewey's view that "the proper object of patriotic loyalty was not the American nation-state, but the ideal of democratic social reciprocity, for which the nation-state was a vehicle."[7] This resistance to normative nationalism is particularly evident in their educational autobiographies because these texts foreground the unstable boundary between their private and professional lives and emphasize the interconnectedness of individual and community interests.

In their educational autobiographies, Addams and Du Bois echo the conventions of the dissensual bildungsroman by refusing to compartmentalize their identities and infusing their challenge to normative nationalism with an international sensibility. As Franco Moretti argues, the dominant (idealist) form of the bildungsroman helped to reify nationalist ideology by situating the climax of the protagonist's development in the "private sphere" that he occupied after his "withdrawal from political life."[8] By contrast, the dissensual bildungsroman, as Joseph Slaughter explains, challenges the idea of a "singular national public" by emphasizing the "presence of competing publics within the domain of the nation-state."[9] Addams and Du Bois highlight the importance of these "competing publics" by intertwining narratives about the development of their private identities with evidence of their efforts to transform the public sphere. In other words, in contrast to the Rousseauian tradition, which requires citizens to sacrifice personal interests for the sake of the community, Addams and Du Bois acknowledge the multiplicity of private needs and interests that one inevitably encounters in the public sphere. Both authors also avoid reproducing the conventional journey of private growth central to the idealist bildungsroman: Addams does this by including narratives in *Twenty Years* about fellow settlement workers (including herself) whose development occurs in a communal, rather than private, setting; Du Bois attributes moments of intellectual discovery to the transatlantic journey he shares with a motley group of European immigrants.

By producing narratives of education characterized by freedom of movement and thought—and by defining citizenship in terms of this process—Addams and Du Bois evidence their alignment with pragmatist philosophy. While both authors sometimes rely on evolutionary language, they ultimately reject the deterministic and hierarchical frameworks central to social Darwinist thought. Addams, influenced by her close association with John Dewey and other Chicago philosophers, consistently demonstrates her willingness to allow events in the world to reshape her sense of self, goals, and educational methods.[10] In *Democracy and Social Ethics* (1902), Addams declares that it is a moral imperative for individuals to seek contact with a diverse range of people and to shed preconceived ideas about difference. Later, in *Twenty Years*, Addams demonstrates how she pursued this objective through her settlement work.

Du Bois, who was mentored by William James at Harvard, conveys his pragmatist philosophy through the figure of the Rover. Du Bois invents the Rover as a character type who, doubling as an avatar of himself, observes and gains insight from a diverse range of individuals traveling steerage class. The Rover follows an open-ended journey during which he seeks, but does not necessarily find, answers to his questions. The Rover thus embodies William James's imperative that the pragmatist not only follow new cognitive and practical paths but also focus on the value of the journey rather than its end point.[11]

Multiple parallels align the autobiographical writing and educational practice of Addams and Du Bois. Both authors thematize eye-opening encounters with a diverse, international citizenry as they narrate their journeys of intellectual and political development. Likewise, both promote cultural particularity in their curricular efforts—Addams by creating space for intercultural and intergenerational exchange in her Chicago settlement house, and Du Bois by using the *Brownies' Book* to encourage African American children (and their parents) to align themselves with heroic and successful figures of African descent.

The Transatlantic Voyage and the Memory of Slavery

From Reconstruction through the early twentieth century, conservative institutions such as Hampton, Tuskegee, and the smaller normal schools modeled on them dominated African American education in the South.[12] Most of these institutions trained African Americans for success in the civil sphere of work instead of offering them political education geared toward civic membership.[13] In part, this resulted from the efforts of southern white industrialists, who offered funding and political support for schools that would train a docile labor force and "instill in black and white children an acceptance of the southern racial hierarchy."[14]

At the same time, Reconstruction educators who sought to provide civic instruction under a federal mandate were hampered by conflicting institutional demands. The Freedmen's Bureau, which until its demise in 1870 provided funding for the education of former slaves, was beset by internal structural problems. Freedmen's Bureau schools were operated by missionary aid societies such as the American Freedmen's Union Commission (AFUC) and the American Missionary Association (AMA), which held varied and often incompatible mandates.[15] Teachers from the more radical AFUC who attempted to teach from the *Handbook for American Citizens* (which included the Declaration of Independence, a recently amended Constitution, and the Emancipation Proclamation) suffered violent reprisals from southern whites.[16] Conversely, the more influential AMA advocated a less civic-oriented training; its mostly northern, white, and female teachers stressed policies geared toward training a docile labor force. The Freedmen's Bureau itself commissioned textbooks that encouraged black students not only to be honest, industrious, and economical but also to adopt a conciliatory attitude toward their former masters. Freedmen's Bureau educators often went to great lengths to assure white southerners that education would be used to produce "efficient, dependable and contented laborers."[17] Even the abolitionist Lydia Maria Child toned down her radical sensibility in her widely circulated textbook *The Freedmen's Book*, in which she counseled, "If [southern whites] use violent language to you, never use impudent language to them. If they cheat you, scorn to cheat them in return."[18] In short, despite the fact that the Freedmen's Bureau funded industrial, normal, and higher education, on the whole it maintained a "conservative educational philosophy" that allowed it to garner "the support of Southern whites."[19]

By 1870, when the federal government curtailed funding for the Freedmen's Bureau, southern schools began to focus almost exclusively on industrial education for African Americans.[20] Rather than depend on unreliable state monies, many schools turned to northern philanthropists who funded industrial and manual training at secondary and college-level institutions instead of supporting basic literacy training for young black children. Even though many colleges for whites also promoted industrial education during this period, in 1900, northern philanthropists working with the Southern Education Board sought to bring elementary and secondary "white education in line with the best practices of the North"; conversely, the Board used its "tremendous influence to channel black education into 'industrial' lines, fitting black people for a secure—and subordinate—place in the South."[21]

It is true, as Adam Fairclough writes, that there were black educators in the post-Reconstruction South who not only opposed the legal disenfranchisement of black students but also opened private schools that offered "higher education, secondary education, and decent elementary education" to African Americans.[22] There were even savvy diplomats like Simon Green Atkins—who, as president of the Slater Industrial School, pretended, for fund-raising purposes, to emphasize industrial education, while actually focusing on academic instruction.[23] Though Fairclough emphasizes the importance of southern private schools run by African American educators, he also admits, "Private schools founded and taught by black teachers probably enrolled fewer than 5 percent of black children."[24] Fairclough further notes that these schools had a range of influence limited by religious disputes, meager resources, and competition from the more popular industrial model of education.[25]

In his 1911 Atlanta University study *The Common School and the Negro American*, Du Bois details the abysmal state of education for African Americans in the post-Reconstruction South. At the time of his study, not a single public college existed for southern African Americans.[26] As *The Common School* illustrates, the public schools that did exist were housed in below-standard buildings, with undertrained and underpaid black teachers, while African American tax dollars were used disproportionately to improve schools for white children. Moreover, many privately funded institutions were teaching "the Negro [to] be of greater service to others."[27] Service was such a dominant principle, Du Bois explains, that he felt alone in his call to train African Americans in the liberal arts.[28]

Early on, Du Bois had advocated some industrial training for African Americans and actually had sought out (and ultimately decided against) becoming a teacher at Tuskegee.[29] By the first decade of the twentieth century, however, Du Bois was speaking out vociferously against Washington's program.[30] In a 1906 talk titled "The Hampton Idea," Du Bois denounced Washington's curriculum as "educational heresy."[31] He instead advocated a model of higher education that would not merely teach African Americans to earn a living but also provide them with "training designed above all to make them men of power, of thought, of trained and cultivated taste; men who know whither civilization is tending and what it means."[32] Du Bois valued intellectual development and political rights over manual and trade labor. Though early on he promoted the elitist concept of a Talented Tenth within the African American community, in *Dusk of Dawn* he admits to the class stratification it implied and reminds us that he advocated an "aristocracy of talent [that] was to lie in its knowledge and character and not in its wealth."[33]

One irony marking Washington's educational policy is that at Tuskegee he enjoyed wealth, status, and freedom from having to labor, yet he promoted manual labor as an objective for his students.[34] Perhaps Washington championed manual labor because he attributed his own success to Hampton's work-oriented curriculum. Nonetheless, in two educational autobiographies—*Up from Slavery* and *Working with the Hands*—Washington exposes the incompatibility of his life narrative with the one he projects onto his students. These texts demonstrate that Washington, limited perhaps by his position as a well-respected educator, remains blind to the racist conditions of southern life that his students inevitably would confront. This obfuscation of the ongoing repercussions of slavery informs Washington's restrictive and embodied model of citizenship education for African Americans in the post-Reconstruction South.

In *Up from Slavery*, Washington describes his transatlantic voyage to symbolize his alignment with the American status quo, rather than using his distance from the United States to reflect critically on it. Describing his subsequent visit to Europe, Washington applauds the existence of a class-stratified society, revealing his identification with a white, upper-class subject position. Washington boasts of his freedom from financial care and right to leisure, recalling how his visit to the English countryside was paid for by friends of Tuskegee. Washington is impressed, he explains, "with the deference that the servants show to their 'masters' and 'mistresses'— terms which I suppose would not be tolerated in America. The English servant expects, as a rule, to be nothing but a servant, and so he perfects himself in the art to a degree that no class of servants has yet reached. In our country the servant expects to become, in a few years, a 'master' himself. Which system is preferable? I will not venture an answer."[35] Even though Washington's use of the terms *masters* and *mistresses* does not invoke the history of slavery overtly, US racial politics appears as a subtext to his statement. Washington pretends not to "venture an answer" to his rhetorical question, but the very circumstance of his being served in this scenario, coupled with his pleased and complimentary tone in describing such service, implies that he aligns himself with the "master" and feels no compunction about advocating a society of masters and servants. Even as Washington plays the master, however, he dares to voice disdain for the servant who would want to be master as well. This seems particularly ironic, given that *Up from Slavery* is a narrative about Washington's economic mobility.

If race does not appear overtly in the above passage, it does inform Washington's subsequent story about being waited on, this time aboard the ship that returns him to the United States. Carl Pedersen has argued that the memory of slavery is "not confined to the hold of the slave ship [but] invades the consciousness of all who enter the Atlantic zone."[36] Exemplifying the truth of Pedersen's statement, Washington writes,

> On this steamer was a fine library that had been presented to the ship by the citizens of St. Louis, Mo. In this library I found *A Life of Frederick Douglass*, which I began reading. I became especially interested in Mr. Douglass's description of the way he was treated on shipboard during his first or second visit to England. In this description he told how he was not permitted to enter the cabin, but had to confine himself to the deck of the ship. A few minutes after I had finished reading this description, I was waited on by a committee of ladies and gentlemen with the request that I deliver an address at a concert which was to be given the following evening. And yet there are people who are bold enough to say that race feeling in America is not growing less intense![37]

Though Washington invokes slavery in this scene, he represents it as a distant historical fact, not one that continues to qualify the realization of African American citizenship. By repudiating any connection between himself and Douglass, Washington implies that the history of slavery does not consciously affect his sense of self. As he articulates a class-conscious identity, Washington paradoxically reveals his preoccupation with race (invoking Douglass) while simultaneously proving his reluctance to acknowledge its impact on the lives of African Americans. Washington admits to his relish at being "waited on" by his (presumably white) admirers, using terms that recall his earlier stay in the English countryside and evidencing his glad intention to join the established economic order as a privileged member. He seems content to leave his fellow black men "on deck" with Douglass.

Because passengers on a transatlantic voyage are temporarily freed from the literal and symbolic limitations of the nation, African American authors often have invoked ships metaphorically to imagine an alternate set of social relationships and a fresh vantage point from which they might, at least temporarily, loosen themselves from the binds of history. The transatlantic voyage also has served as an educational experience, an opportunity to reframe the communities to which one belongs, and, in so doing, to gain transformative insight into them.[38] Washington does use the ship as a symbol of his independence from the binds of history. However, he also mistakenly aligns himself with the broader African

American population.[39] Washington concludes this passage by asserting that "race feeling in America is . . . growing less intense." Yet he is able to do so only by interpreting US life from aboard ship, where conventional race relations are suspended. As a result, Washington reproduces the ideological blindness that also characterizes his educational practice.

Comparing *Up from Slavery* and *Working with the Hands* offers further insight into Washington's dissociation from his students. In *Hands*, Washington's first-person narrative about Tuskegee's curriculum, Washington explains that Tuskegee students who arrived late or unpresentable at meals, despite working ten-hour days, would go without food: "It requires care and thought to make a hasty toilet after a ten-hour day on the farm or in the shops, and be ready for supper on the stroke of the bell. And a student late to meals goes without that meal unless he has a good excuse. But out of such a system arises a pride in personal appearance, and a spirit of self-respect that goes far toward making useful men and women."[40] Washington's rigidity in this matter is surprising, given that just three years earlier, in *Up from Slavery*, he admits how difficult it was for him, as a Hampton student, to prioritize both his appearance and his studies: "Shoes had to be polished, there must be no buttons off the clothing, and no grease-spots. [Yet] to wear one suit of clothes continually, while at work and in the schoolroom, and at the same time keep it clean, was rather a hard problem for me to solve."[41] Washington explains that he overcame his challenge with help from sympathetic teachers who procured secondhand clothing for him. Yet in describing the Tuskegee curriculum Washington reveals an inability or unwillingness to recognize that the demands he imposes on his students are the same ones that overwhelmed him at Hampton, and that he overcame only with the kind of sympathetic help he seems unwilling to offer.

Hands also figures Washington's development from a man who does manual labor to a man who aestheticizes manual labor, precisely because he neither has to nor is willing to do it. As the principal of Tuskegee, Washington did not depend on his own physical labor to survive. Yet in describing the Tuskegee curriculum Washington reveals that he identifies with his students on the basis of a misguided fantasy of shared circumstances. Describing his gardening activities, for example, the forty-four-year-old Washington claims to have a "great deal of [his] present strength and capacity for hard work"; yet he subsequently confesses that "the amount of time [he] can spend in the open air . . . is perhaps not more than an hour a day."[42] In contrast to Washington's hour of gardening, Tuskegee students worked ten-hour days, between two and six days a week, depending on how much tuition they could pay. Those who could not pay up front (as was Washington's case when he attended Hampton) had to work continuously for their tuition; the heavy workload meant that they had to spend years acquiring the basics of an elementary education. As the previous passage illustrates, Washington structures his students' development as a repetition of the conditions he encountered at Hampton, even though *Up from Slavery* emphasizes his difficult struggle to free himself from a life of physical labor.[43] If we read *Hands* as a sequel to *Up from Slavery*, we can see how Washington overcomes his former identity as a laborer—one he neither chose nor continued to pursue—by projecting this identity onto his students.

In *Hands*, Washington promotes an anachronistic philosophy that "work with the hands" is a "pathway to freedom."[44] Washington idealized the possibility that the majority of his students would become independent farmers who could "raise [their] food supplies . . . rather than to go in debt for them at the store."[45] Yet this agricultural ideal, and the freedom Washington hoped it would produce, was difficult to achieve for the majority of poor, southern African Americans at the turn of the twentieth century.[46] In 1900, "a quarter of all Southern black farmers owned the land they worked"; moreover, black workers in places such as the Mississippi Delta made relatively good money.[47] Nonetheless, most African American agricultural laborers, sharecroppers, and tenant farmers eked out a subsistence living in the post-Reconstruction South.[48]

In promoting farming for African Americans, Washington reveals his social Darwinist sensibility. In *Up from Slavery*, for example, Washington reproduces an ideology that assigned African Americans an inferior position on an evolutionary time line. Washington dreams, he tells us, of returning the urbanized black man back to a rural paradise of a timeless (but racialized) past; he hopes that "by some power of magic [he] might remove the great bulk of these [city] people into the country districts and plant them upon the soil, upon the solid and never deceptive foundation of Mother Nature, where all nations and races that have ever succeeded have gotten their start,—a start that at first may be slow and toilsome, but one that nevertheless is real."[49] This passage embodies Lewis Morgan's view, popularized in his 1877 book, *Ancient Society*, that cultures advance to higher levels of civilization by occupying successive positions on an evolutionary time line. As I discuss earlier in this book, Morgan's time line situates the development of culture along a savagery-barbarism-civilization continuum and argues that cultural sophistication resulted from increasing "control over the production of food."[50]

Morgan's developmental time line influenced Tuskegee's curriculum, which itself was complicit with the legacy of slavery that reverberated in both popular thought and postbellum agricultural conditions. Unlike Washington, however, Du Bois confronted the ongoing repercussions of slavery as he promoted intellectual freedom and embodied mobility for African American citizens.

The Citizen in Steerage Class: W. E. B. Du Bois and the African American Cosmopolitan

In keeping with the zeitgeist of the period, Du Bois's writing also reproduces elements of evolutionary ideology. For instance, in his 1895 "Diary" Du Bois creates a racialized hierarchy of immigrant citizens and suggests that the autochthonous American is a more promising candidate for citizenship than the immigrant. Nonetheless, the "Diary" does important work in exposing the intersections of race- and class-based discrimination. It also suggests that in order to cultivate an ideal cosmopolitan citizenship, African Americans must first address the residue of slavery in US life. As a result of this confrontation, the African American citizen can avoid reproducing an embodied identity and instead can take advantage of the promise of modernity. Though Paul Gilroy claims that Du Bois was skeptical of modernization as early as his years at Fisk (1885–88), the "Diary" embraces a cosmopolitan outlook that seems compatible with modernization.[51] Invoking a poetics of economic failure, first in the transatlantic "Diary" and later in the *Autobiography* (1968), Du Bois emphasizes the importance of broad-ranging intellectual inquiry for the African American citizen.

In his 1895 "Diary," Du Bois recalls the history of slavery as he reflects on the motley passengers traveling steerage with him to the United States. In this text, Du Bois assigns symbolic meaning to the physical space of the ship. He structures the "Diary" like a palimpsest, with a surface layer that evokes the European immigrant's elective immigration and an obscured layer that recalls the African's forced migration to the Americas. The "Diary" also suggests that the ideal cosmopolitan citizen will pay attention to these submerged historical layers without being limited by them. Casting himself as a Rover—an African American traveler who exists both with and apart from the masses—Du Bois articulates an anti-imperialist educational theory that emphasizes images, meditations, and narratives about black bodies that are not confined to the sphere of physical labor. Whereas Booker T. Washington's transatlantic narrative idealizes economic success and a class-stratified society, Du Bois's narrative foregrounds the insights he gains from moments of financial instability, suggesting that financial troubles might provide the opportunity to examine the conditions that normalize economic inequality.[52] In so doing, Du Bois promotes intellectual inquiry as the basis for African American citizenship.

At the same time, Du Bois's figure of the Rover captures his ambivalence about racial identification. While Du Bois often emphasized the centrality of race to his identity, he sometimes resisted racial identification in favor of a cosmopolitan outlook.[53] Depicting his return voyage to the United States in the *Autobiography*, Du Bois argues that the US citizen must directly confront the politics of race, because a refusal to acknowledge it allows for the reproduction of class inequality. Yet on his transatlantic voyages both to and from Europe Du Bois portrays himself as a world traveler who exchanges the limitations of a racial identity for the benefits of cosmopolitan citizenship. These seemingly contradictory points of view exemplify Ross Posnock's characterization of Du Bois as an "antirace race man" who "insisted on a dialectic between (unraced) universal and (raced) particular."[54]

In his 1968 *Autobiography*, Du Bois explains that on his sea voyage to Germany he discovered that a literal absence from the United States provided him with a fresh perspective on the problem of his racial identity and a vantage point from which to critique US racial politics. Including himself in a tradition of European thought, Du Bois writes,

> I crossed the ocean in a trance. Always I seemed to be saying, "It is not real; I must be dreaming!" I can live it again—the little, Dutch ship—the blue waters—the smell of new-mown hay—Holland and the Rhine. I saw Wartzburg and Berlin; I made the Hartzreise and climbed the Brocken; I saw the Hansa towns and the cities and dorfs of South Germany; I saw the Alps at Berne, the Cathedral at Milan, Florence, Rome, Venice, Vienna, and Pest; I looked on the boundaries of Russia; and I sat in Paris and London. On mountain and valley, in home and school, I met men and women as I had never met them before. Slowly they became, not white folks, but folks. The unity beneath all life clutched me. I was not less fanatically a Negro, but "Negro" meant a greater, broader sense of humanity and world-fellowship. I felt myself standing, not against the world, but simply against American narrowness and color prejudice, with the greater, finer world at my back.[55]

In this passage, Du Bois articulates a conflict between competing aspects of his identity. On the one hand, he employs metonymy to align the ship's voyage with the experience of studying and traveling in Europe. The em-dash evokes a coexistence between "the little, Dutch ship," "the blue waters," "the smell of new-mown hay," and in turn a long series of European localities and the historical and artistic knowledge that they represent—and that Du Bois came to acquire. As Paul Gilroy rightly argues in *The Black Atlantic*—and as this passage illustrates—Du Bois used his erudition, his "complete familiarity with the cultural legacy of western civilization," to demand "access to it as a right for the race as a whole."[56] Du Bois's academic training allows him to embrace the "humanity and fellowship" that informs the "unity beneath all life." In listing his visits to the cities, towns, cathedrals, mountains, and valleys of Europe, he includes the black man in this concept of "world-fellowship" and identifies with Europeans who become "not white folks, but folks." At the same time, however, Du Bois depicts himself as a "Negro," one group in the category of "folks" that he has just defined as having transcended race. This passage describes the paradoxical category of a race-less citizenry in which the black man is nonetheless an active presence.

This concept acquires depth in Du Bois's description of his return voyage to the United States. Du Bois invokes both race and slavery as he ruminates on the shifting composition of a US citizenry and revises the concept of universal fellowship to include those who share an economic bond. Paul Gilroy suggests that in the Du Boisian imagination the Atlantic symbolizes freedom from the memory of forced dislocation represented by slavery.[57] It rather seems that Du Bois—whose historical interest in the slave trade dates to his doctoral dissertation, "The Suppression of the African Slave Trade"—evokes the psychological residue of slavery in the ship's deck and hold, spaces he regularly moves between as he travels steerage class back to the United States. In other words, Du Bois dramatizes the US citizen's need to face the memory of slavery as one step in the process of becoming educated. In so doing, he activates historical memory as a form of resistance to the citizen's restrictive embodiment in the civil sphere. Moreover, by reflecting on his own identity in a public space (the ship's deck) and in international waters, Du Bois offers an alternative to the parameters of private and nationalist identity modeled by the idealist bildungsroman.

Traveling in the hold of the ship allows Du Bois to observe the dominant class of people who seek US citizenship, an opportunity that influences his cosmopolitan theory of national identity. Though he travels in the hold voluntarily, his experience recalls the forced displacement of slaves and their sea journeys to the United States since the seventeenth century. In his *Autobiography*, Du Bois explains that he ran short of money because he "stayed in Europe as long as the last penny allowed."[58] While he admits that he could have borrowed money from a friend to buy a first-class ticket home, Du Bois confesses that his "New England frugality" would not allow it.[59] Whether or not this explanation is sincere, Du Bois's "Diary" demonstrates the relish with which he took advantage of the opportunity to reflect on the spatial, historical, and symbolic aspects of the ship.

Du Bois's description of the ship's hold recalls the physical strife shared by all who have traveled steerage on their journeys to the United States. According to Maria Diedrich, Henry Louis Gates, and Carl Pedersen, the Middle Passage often has been theorized in terms of the dichotomy between the "tight packing" of the hold and the "marginally expanded space on the deck," where captives often would engage in forms of dance that served as originary moments of African American cultural unity.[60] In describing his daily routine aboard ship, Du Bois explains that he moves back and forth between the hold (where he sleeps and takes his meals) and a small portion of the deck, where passengers from the hold are able to take air. In a longer, unpublished description of the journey (titled "Sea-Sickness") than that which appears in *Autobiography*, Du Bois calls attention to the squalor that transatlantic passengers confront when traveling steerage:

> I'm not myself of the seasick getting kind but I must confess that the next morning as I felt the ship rising and fading away under my feet and rolling from side to side with something more than ordinary enthusiasm—I felt a certain settled melancholy which compelled me to confine my first breakfast to an orange and rush in rather undignified haste from its dark dungeons [to the] wet and dirty deck. . . . In spite of the efforts of the crew it was well nigh impossible to keep the deck clean. Everywhere lay unsightly messes . . . one can hardly realize how sick it is possible to get. Some of the pale drawn faces looked quite deathlike. . . . Such a sort of universal sickness however is a strange opportunity to view human character. These 350 human beings so accidentally thrown together learned to know each other best amid pain and suffering and the little friendships made there, the little deeds good and bad sank deeper with their souls than usual. It is perhaps this circumstance that gives a sea voyage its most peculiar flavor—its beginning of physical ailing.[61]

Even though the passengers in Du Bois's description are "accidentally thrown together," they forge a bond based on physical suffering that recalls some of the conditions that characterized the Middle Passage: the crowding in the "dark dungeons" of the hold, offset by moments of cultural solidarity on deck. Du Bois's experience of "settled melancholy" seems to arise from his attention to the residue of history. However, this narrative also suggests that paying attention to history can help us transcend the limitations of the historical present.

The 1895 and 1968 accounts of this voyage differ in significant ways. While both accounts present steerage as a society stratified by social difference, the earlier account echoes the evolutionary ideology dominant during this period. At the same time, however, the earlier account aligns Du Bois with his fellow passengers to suggest that their shared economic circumstances expose the artificiality of distinctions based on class status. In the 1968 *Autobiography*, Du Bois writes: "We have here of course all grades of society but a majority of what must be called lower. Yet I think that the better classes here, the better and more orderly elements though scarcely greater in numbers, have been distinctly more influential. The experience has proven in a degree what I have always thought, that the number of 'estates' becomes unlimited in a sense. One can scarcely bring any sort of a crowd of people together without finding a large number of distinct classes. . . . It is the same old strife of finer souls against brutality."[62] By concluding that this scene embodies the struggle of "finer souls against brutality," Du Bois suggests that it is in the nature of group consciousness to develop hierarchies of influence. Nonetheless, the hierarchy in this passage is informed only by differences in individual character, while the unpublished, 1895 version of this passage includes sketches of shipboard "types" that recall nineteenth-century evolutionary ideology.

In the 1895 account, Du Bois filters his portraits of fellow passengers through ethnic stereotypes, categorizing them as "The Evangelist," "The Rover," "The Jew," "The Negro," and "The Russian Pole." In particular, his descriptions of European immigrants undermine their contributions to the United States, a common response to the tense competition for jobs between immigrants and African Americans during this period. Du Bois describes the Russian Poles as "dirty and lousy and happy . . . [and] lazy," and the Jews as "dirty," "rough," and "sly." He contrasts these denigrating portraits with an image of the informed, curious, and internationally minded black man who represents the ideal citizen.[63] While Du Bois says he does not want to "join in any prejudice against [the Jew]," he admits that he feels compelled to, because in the Jew, "there seems to fail so far as I've seen that strong middle class which in every nation holds the brunt of culture." Whether encountering aristocratic or working-class Jews, Du Bois finds them sly. The Polish Jews in particular, he writes, are "as dirty and rough as the Poles themselves yet here again replacing the Polish innocence and greenishness with a sort of overbearing slyness." Du Bois ultimately concludes, "The Jew's national development is over widely different obstacles than that of my nation." While this last comment is somewhat vague, it supports this passage's implication that, unlike the Jew, the black man is born with his good qualities. The black man, Du Bois writes, has a "goodheartedness" and "straightforwardness"—a claim implying that any character defects have resulted from historical contingencies.[64]

Whereas Du Bois articulates these ethnic and racial stereotypes from a distant perch, he metaphorically descends from that perch to align himself with the Rover. He develops the figure of the Rover by contrasting him with the narrowly religious figure of the Evangelist. Unlike the Rover, who acquires knowledge as a result of his engaged movement through society, the Evangelist is a spectator who gleans his knowledge about the world from a disengaged and panoptical position. (Perhaps it is no coincidence that when Du Bois invokes ethnic stereotypes he does so as a distanced spectator.) As a result of his disengagement, the Evangelist is a closed-minded moralist, "one of those young and earnest and yet half-educated bigots" who silences his opponents and engages in "religious advertising which is so often defended as courage of one's opinions."[65]

On the contrary, the Rover, like Du Bois, is multilingual (he speaks seven languages), educated, well traveled, and full of insights into the racial and historical character of the places he has visited (Du Bois lists these places and the insights there acquired, just as earlier he offered up a list of his own). While Du Bois never specifically identifies the Rover as a black man, this figure nonetheless captures Du Bois's contradictory relationship to race by simultaneously evoking and transcending it—recalling Posnock's characterization of Du Bois as an "antirace race man."[66] This ambivalence about race informs Du Bois's increasing conviction that the African American needed to embrace a transnational perspective to avoid permanent minority status in the United States.

While the Rover's cosmopolitan perspective avoids both individualism and nationalism, this figure nonetheless differs from the modern, European cosmopolitan whose name, Du Bois explains, "savours of young nobility, riches and ennui."[67] Though the Rover is a curious and learned international traveler, his journey is not modeled on the "Grand Tour" that followed on the completion of one's formal education. In this respect, the Rover does not recall the cosmopolitan sensibility that is usually identified with "an apolitical leisure class."[68] The Rover is rather a "world-wanderer" who rejects the cult of the individual and takes pleasure and knowledge from group consciousness. Moreover, he represents an approach to cosmopolitanism that derives not from European high culture but from the working- and underclass experiences of those colonized by Europeans. In this respect, the Rover prefigures the black diasporan subject that increasingly preoccupied Du Bois.

By aligning the Rover with himself, Du Bois creates a figure marked by the elitist sensibility that Du Bois sometimes adopted. As Du Bois reminds us in the "Diary," though he travels steerage class, he only partially joins the masses. He spends much of his time sitting quietly on deck, analyzing the crowd as a kind of specimen. Nonetheless, the Rover's freedom of thought and movement prevent him from occupying a static identity, and in this respect he represents the promise of Du Bois's educational philosophy. By choosing to travel steerage class in the first place, Du Bois rejects a life lived, and narrated, from an isolated and individualized point of view. In contrast with the private intellectual discovery that characterizes his voyage out, on this return voyage Du Bois emphasizes his acquisition of cross-cultural insights. Moreover, he ultimately suggests that the cosmopolitan intellectual can offer a counterpoint to the social ranking that exists even in steerage. Concluding his discussion of the Rover, Du Bois claims, "I have here keenly realized how wide the world and that the wanderer's restlessness knows no bounds of rank or condition."[69] Even though Du Bois himself sometimes reproduces hierarchical modes of thought, the Rover embodies his pragmatist sensibility by refusing to identify himself with any particular perspective or belief—thus keeping open the possibility of future development.

Cultivating the African American Cosmopolitan: Du Bois and the *Brownies' Book*

Whereas the Rover's identity seems to know no bounds, as an educator Du Bois had to work within a national context if he wanted to exert influence on African American citizenship. As he reveals in *The Souls of Black Folk*, Du Bois was also aware that childhood was a formative moment in the development of one's racial identity and could influence whether that identity would become liberating or restrictive.[70] The *Brownies' Book* represents Du Bois's pedagogical effort to realize the vision of cosmopolitan citizenship that he articulated in his "Diary" and elsewhere. The *Brownies' Book* developed organically out of the annual "children's issue" of the *Crisis*, published every October between 1912 and 1919.[71] Though critics agree that Jessie Fauset was the dominant voice of the *Brownies' Book*, this magazine reflects Du Bois's desire for African Americans to cultivate citizenship by simultaneously ruminating on the history of slavery (and its ongoing repercussions for US life) and identifying imaginatively with black and brown transnational heroes.[72]

In part, Du Bois created the *Brownies' Book* as a response to the predominantly negative images of African Americans in both the popular media and school textbooks. Even before the first issue appeared, Du Bois detailed his motivations for producing the magazine in the *Crisis*; he writes, "Most of the books he [the African American child] reads are by white authors, and his heroes and heroines are white."[73] Because the "Negro" is usually presented as "a caricature or a clown," Du Bois explains, "he unconsciously gets the impression that the Negro has little chance to be good, great, heroic or beautiful." Other critics have called attention to the *Brownies' Book*'s challenge to dominant African American stereotypes.[74] What they have not said, however, is that the magazine dramatizes Du Bois's belief that confronting the history of slavery was an essential step in achieving cosmopolitan citizenship.

Like the transatlantic diary—which juxtaposes its revisionary portrait of the African American intellectual with a symbolic evocation of the Middle Passage—the *Brownies' Book* parallels its biographies of black cosmopolitans with two kinds of stories about African Americans: those who excelled despite limitations imposed by slavery, and those who continued to confront the ongoing repercussions of slavery in the post-Reconstruction South. The magazine not only featured stories about well-known figures such as Phillis Wheatley and Frederick Douglass but also exposed readers to biographies of little-known African American heroes such as Katy Ferguson, as well as stories of everyday black heroes such as Betsy Blakesley.[75] Moreover, the magazine featured biographies of child protagonists to inspire agency in its young readers.

The *Brownies' Book* also included fictional stories whose child protagonists might serve as role models for the magazine's young readers. For instance, "Why Bennie Was Fired" tells the story of a young African American girl named Bennie who gets fired from her job because she arrives late a few days in a row. Though Bennie is usually an exemplary employee who cleans the home of Mrs. Blair every morning before school, Mrs. Blair fires her without even asking why she has been late. One wonders if perhaps the employer has been quick to harbor low expectations of Bennie because of her race, attributing her tardiness to laziness despite evidence to the contrary. The reader knows that Bennie was late to work because she was preparing for an "oratorical contest for all the colored pupils in all the grade schools of the city"—a contest that she ultimately wins.[76] Instead of lamenting her loss of income after being fired, Bennie feels glad that she has extra time to prepare for the contest. This response recalls the poetics of economic failure that Du Bois symbolized in his transatlantic diary, not only because Bennie is relieved after being fired, but also because she refuses to take back her job (when Mrs. Blair offers it). As Bennie explains, she would rather enjoy the "delightful vacation" that her teacher has given her for winning first prize than go back to work for Mrs. Blair.[77] Bennie opts for the chance to improve herself at the expense of a meal.

By juxtaposing accounts of slavery with stories such as "Why Bennie Was Fired," the *Brownies' Book* contextualized the difficult choice faced by many African Americans in the post-Reconstruction South: it tried to make them self-conscious about the choice between becoming exemplary workers in the service-oriented jobs that were available to them or pursuing academic studies that did not necessarily promise concrete material benefits. By choosing her studies over her job, Bennie embodies Du Bois's approach to US citizenship. Like others of its kind, this story offers the magazine's readers an opportunity to reflect on the difficulty of making career choices in an economic sphere stratified by both class and race.

In addition to its exemplary tales for young African Americans, the *Brownies' Book* printed letters to the editor in a section of the magazine called "The Jury," thereby encouraging African American children to share their own experiences of race and economics. On one occasion, the magazine featured a letter in which a Philadelphia boy, Franklin Lewis, surely echoed the experiences of many African American children. In the letter, Lewis expresses frustration about a white boy's response to his statement that he wants to become an architect. After the white boy tells Lewis, "Colored boys don't draw houses," Lewis's parents recommend that he raise this issue with the *Brownies' Book*.[78] Lewis writes, "My mother says you will explain all this to me in your magazine and will tell me where to learn how to draw a house, for that is what I certainly mean to do."[79] This letter reveals how the magazine encouraged its parent-readers to shift discussion of their (or their children's) private encounters with racism into a public forum. By providing this space for a public discussion of the child's experience of double consciousness, the *Brownies' Book* realized a central aspect of Du Bois's cosmopolitan sensibility—its challenge to the boundary between private and public, individual and community. It also addressed the quandaries of racial identity during childhood, arguably the most fruitful period for cultivating race-proud African American citizens.

The letters-to-the-editor section of the magazine also evidences its success in achieving the intertwined objectives of critiquing imperialism and promoting a cosmopolitan identity. As Michelle Phillips argues in discussing Du Bois's monthly column "As the Crow Flies," the anti-imperial politics Du Bois articulated in the magazine challenged the black-white axis of African American identity by encouraging "the inter-activity of African Americans with subalterns of other nations and circumstances."[80] A child reading the magazine could learn about the heroic activities of people such as Toussaint L'Ouverture, Denmark Vesey, and Mahatma Gandhi. They also could read essays about anti-imperialist leaders in the Philippines, or about the accomplishments of Chinese culture. Stories of this kind regularly appeared in the magazine to expand the horizons of African American children: not only to inform them but also to inspire them to see themselves as world citizens.[81] A letter from one reader attests to the magazine's success with both of these objectives. Explaining that he wanted to travel to Asia and Africa, a boy named Thomas wrote: "I think colored people are the most wonderful people in the world and when I'm a man, I'm going to write about them too, so that all people will know the terrible struggles we've had. I don't pay any attention any more to the discouraging things I see in the newspapers. Something just tells me that we are no worse than anybody else. My father says no race is perfect. I'd like to have a newspaper some day, a daily one—and then 'I'd tell the world.'"[82] As this letter illustrates, the magazine exposed its readers to stories about people of color outside of a US context. In this respect, the *Brownies' Book* provided an alternative to racist stereotypes that circulated in the popular media. Moreover, it inspired young African Americans to pursue careers involving intellectual rather than manual labor.

Other letters from African American children evidence the magazine's ongoing success in cultivating a politicized, international, and intellectual sensibility in its readers. In one letter, Max Simpson from Toronto, Ontario, testifies to the magazine's international distribution.[83] Simpson asks if the editor can "take time to suggest a small library" for him because he wants "to know a great deal about colored people. I think when I finish school I shall go to Africa, and work there in some way. If I decide to do this I ought to know a great deal about our people and all the places where they live, all over the world, don't you think so?"[84] In another letter, Pocahontas Foster from Orange, New Jersey, explains how the magazine taught her to like history because of its stories about "Paul Cuffee, Blanche K. Bruce, and Katy Ferguson, real colored people, whom I feel that I do know because they were brown people like me."[85] These two readers—one who imagines his future in Africa, and the other who has become interested in African American history—exemplify one small but significant aspect of Du Bois's cosmopolitan vision.

Darwinism and Dissent at the Hull-House Labor Museum

Like Du Bois, Jane Addams made pedagogical choices that reflect the successes and limitations of her cosmopolitical ideal.[86] In *Twenty Years at Hull-House*, Addams narrates her experiences as a cosmopolitan educator on Chicago's West Side, revealing her efforts to validate the practices and viewpoints of a US citizenry varying in age, gender, ethnicity, and race. At Hull-House, Addams helped create a democratic space that encouraged citizens to maintain "overlapping affiliations"—a term Jonathan Hansen uses to describe John Dewey's similar objective.[87] Cosmopolitan theorists Gavin Kendall, Ian Woodward, and Zlatko Skrbis argue that because the cosmopolitical ideal is "fragile, and susceptible to threat" it can "disappear at those moments when exchange [with the other] becomes difficult or derogated."[88] However, Addams and her coworkers realized their cosmopolitical ideal by facing and overcoming such difficult moments of intercultural exchange. *Twenty Years* illustrates how Addams practiced a cosmopolitan ethics by maintaining a philosophical openness in the face of intercultural encounters that threatened to destabilize her commitment to difference.

Despite the cosmopolitan educational ideal it portrays, *Twenty Years* also reveals the influence of social Darwinist ideology on Addams's pedagogy. Moreover, because Addams's cosmopolitan ideal was influenced by Kant's universalist idealism, she sometimes reproduced the ethnic and racial hierarchies imbricated with that tradition.[89] Even though the humanist tradition posited equality based on shared human traits, it also understood universality through a Eurocentric lens.[90] Though Addams at times betrays her immersion in the humanist tradition, she also challenges the universalist assumptions of Euro-American cultural discourse by identifying with the (raced and racialized) minorities whom she encounters and represents in her role as educator and observer.[91] Though both Addams and Du Bois ultimately represent themselves as separate from the populations they seek to educate, they both foreground moments that symbolize their willingness to identify across boundaries of class and ethnic identity. In *Hull-House*, these moments dramatize Addams's challenge to individualism, materialism, and ethnocentric nationalism, as well as her ethical embrace of and care for the other (which is also central to the Kantian cosmopolitical tradition).[92]

The social Darwinist strain of Addams's thought informs her description of the Columbian Guards, a group of Hull-House boys who both engaged in marching drills and did neighborhood cleanup. In the following passage, Addams alludes to immigrant dirt with a tone that varies from her more typical, nonjudgmental attitude toward cultural difference:

> As the cleaning of the filthy streets and alleys was the ostensible purpose of the Columbian guards, I suggested to the boys that we work out a [military] drill with sewer spades, which with their long narrow blades and shortened handles were not so unlike bayoneted guns in size, weight, and general appearance, but that much of the usual military drill could be readapted. . . . I myself was present at the gymnasium to explain that it was nobler to drill in imitation of removing disease-breeding filth than to drill in simulation of warfare. . . . I can only look at [the sewer spade] in the forlorn hope that it may foreshadow that piping time when the weapons of warfare shall be turned into the implements of civic salvation.[93]

Addams admits that the need to facilitate the "civic salvation" of these Greek boys (by creating the Columbian Guards) justified violating Hull-House's long resistance to the military drill. In describing the Guard, Addams expresses her anxiety about the "disease-breeding filth" she has found in the immigrant communities served by Hull-House.

When Addams raises the question of hygiene in other contexts, she offers an overdetermined explanation that reveals her unwillingness to say whether this "filth" is a product of poverty or the immigrant's innate inferiority. In an early public address, for example, Addams explains, "One of the most discouraging features about the present system of tenement houses is that many are owned by sordid and ignorant immigrants. The theory that wealth brings responsibility, that possession entails at length education and refinement, in these cases fails utterly" (285). By suggesting that economic advancement has failed to counteract the immigrant's dirty habits, Addams attributes poverty to ignorance; yet she also notes that wealth does not automatically result in education and refinement (69). According to her reasoning, immigrant habits die hard, which accounts for the persistence of the immigrant's "wretched conditions . . . until at least two generations of children have been born and reared in them" (69). Addams does not explain precisely why the immigrants' habits prove so resistant to change; however, her language implies that she attributes the sordid circumstances in which immigrants live to ethnic difference.[94] A similar attitude marks Addams's lecture "Educational Methods," where she attributes the dull academic performance of the southern Italian student to the experiences of his ancestors: "Whatever interest has come to the minds of his ancestors has come through the use of their hands in the open air; and open air and activity of body have been the inevitable accompaniments of all their experiences."[95] Here Addams expresses the period's commonplace, Lamarckian assumption that children inherit the proclivities of their ancestors. Her evocation of an ethnic hierarchy informed by biology also recalls Du Bois's classification of ethnic types on his transatlantic journey.

Addams's discussion of embodied activity also reveals the influence of evolutionary ideology on her thought. Like other educators of her time, Addams valued "rhythmic motion" for producing "abstinence and the curbing of impulse" (284). Addams accedes that habitual, embodied practices could lead to shifts in behavior, and elsewhere she links shifts in behavior to intergenerational change.[96] In this respect, Carl Degler correctly aligns Addams with other progressive social scientists of her day, who associated the practice of transforming character through physical activity (part of the curriculum at Hull-House) with the popular Lamarckian idea that acquired characteristics could be inherited and the race improved through the transformation of individuals' bodies.[97] In other words, Addams promoted repetitive movement that ostensibly would transform future generations and represent forward movement along a racialized time line.

Recapitulation theorists popularized the idea that physical activity could affect character. First articulated by Ernst Haeckel but applied to educational contexts by Herbert Spencer, G. Stanley Hall, and others, recapitulation theory held that in order to achieve higher stages of development children needed to be ushered through the different stages of human culture. As Herbert Spencer states, "If there be an order in which the human race has mastered its various kinds of knowledge, there will arise in every child an aptitude to acquire these kinds of knowledge in the same order. . . . Education is a repetition of civilization in little."[98] In Twenty Years, Addams describes how ritualistic physical activity will help children move through the successive evolutionary stages that their development naturally requires. Addams writes, "Children seek a ceremonial which shall express their sense of identification with man's primitive life and their familiar kinship with the remotest past."[99] The commonality between Addams's invocation of repetitive physical activity and recapitulation theory lies in her assumption that repeating primitive movements will enhance an individual's cultural progress.[100] Throughout her educational autobiography, Addams continues to express the idea that rhythmical physical activity will facilitate the citizen's development, ideally culminating in a future "when the weapons of warfare shall be turned into the implements of civic salvation" (285). In other words, through proper education, the child's primitivity, itself an echo of cultural backwardness, will give way to civic-mindedness—and world peace.[101] Addams's comments about the training of children's bodies, alongside her evocation of an ideal future through the metaphor of the military drill, points to the bind that many progressive educators found themselves in at the turn of the twentieth century. Like others, Addams was limited by an outdated set of tools (ideological, linguistic, practical) for articulating and enacting her radical educational ideas. This contradiction explains why *Twenty Years* relies on the evolutionary language that was also common to the assimilationist paradigm.

In spite of moments in which mainstream educational ideology appears as a linguistic sediment in her writing, Addams articulates a progressive vision of citizenship education that validates cultural difference rather than seeking its erasure.[102] With this vision, Addams resists the idea of reproducing a stratified public sphere informed by ethnic and racial hierarchies.[103] Addams articulates this resistance in her 1907 book of lectures, *Democracy and Social Ethics*, arguing that we "limit the scope of our ethics" if we "grow contemptuous of our fellows and consciously limit our intercourse to certain kinds of people whom we have previously decided to respect."[104] This statement recalls the philosophy of John Dewey; both Dewey and Addams believed that as individuals not only are we "morally obligated to choose our experiences," but also we should choose to interact with "persons whose history, customs, beliefs, and ways of life differ from our own."[105]

Twenty Years illustrates how settlement workers at Hull-House realized a pragmatist ethical stance. Addams recounts how she and her cohorts both reshaped their policies in response to community needs and admitted when they had misjudged the tastes of the immigrants with whom they worked. In discussing Hull-House's efforts to improve the healthfulness of the immigrant diet through a public kitchen, Addams confesses, "[Even though] our hopes ran high for some modification of the food in the neighborhood . . . we did not reckon . . . with the wide diversity in nationality and inherited tastes" (90). In the end, Addams consents to the reality that habit is a better motivator than judgment, exemplified by "the woman who frankly confessed, that the food was certainly nutritious, but that she didn't like to eat what was nutritious, that she liked to eat 'what she'd ruther'" (90). Alongside similar experiences, this encounter teaches Addams and her coworkers "not to hold preconceived ideas of what the neighborhood ought to have" (91). As Addams continues, however, she hints at a potentially condescending attitude toward the community: "[We had to] keep ourselves in readiness to modify and adapt our undertakings as we discovered those things which the neighborhood was ready to accept" (91). To some readers, this comment might suggest that Addams believes in the superiority of things the neighborhood might eventually be "ready to accept." However, a turn to Addams's earlier essay on the settlement worker evokes her overarching position that settlement workers and members of the local community could be—and often were—mutually instructive to each other.

"Charitable Effort," published in *Democracy and Social Ethics*, exemplifies Addams's commitment to pragmatist diversity by depicting how experience has transformed the assumptions held by both charity workers and their charges. In the essay, Addams describes the poor people who would give their last crust of bread to an ailing neighbor and who feel confused at the charity worker's hesitant and selective contributions. She writes, "The neighborhood mind is at once confronted not only by the difference of method, but by an absolute clashing of two ethical standards."[106] Addams characterizes these differences not in terms of the superiority or inferiority of the individuals involved but in terms of class status and life experience, which have shaped their viewpoints and lifestyles. Here Addams promotes mutual understanding between people by encouraging them to understand difference as a function of experience rather than biology. This commitment to cross-cultural communication constitutes one strand of Addams's cosmopolitan philosophy, which promotes an openness to transformation that can result from lived experience. In this respect, Addams echoes Du Bois's figuration of citizenship through the Rover.

When Addams describes her receptive audience of foreign-born immigrants at Hull-House, we also see the influence of Dewey's vision of a democratic realm whose members cultivate "overlapping affiliations."[107]

For example, Addams writes in *Twenty Years* about "Italian and Bohemian peasants . . . [who] tramp along with at least a suggestion of having once walked over plowed fields and breathed country air" (153). Given Addams's distaste for the crowded and dirty conditions of city life, it makes sense that she idealizes these countrified folk as though they themselves provide a breath of fresh air to the city dweller. Her portrait of these peasants calls attention to their distinctive style of movement and their ability to inhabit more than one identity at a time. As a metaphor for the urban denizen, Addams's vision contrasts with the "melting pot" popularized by Israel Zangwill's eponymous 1908 play.[108] The city that Addams describes is a diverse quilt of cultures that exist alongside each other, sometimes even within a single individual. The peasants whom Addams admires obviate the boundary between urban and rural; moving through the city in their "bright holiday clothes" and on their way to visits with cousins, they offer an imaginative release from the reality of an overcrowded and alienating urban environment. With her description of them, Addams portrays the city as a space forgiving enough to encompass the countryside without stifling it, thereby allowing expression of the living history embodied by the immigrant's habits of movement. By attributing cultural meaning to the ostensibly private self expressed in embodied movement, Addams also develops her challenge to the private/public binary. Nonetheless, this portrait functions less as a description of the neighborhood in the realist mode than as an imaginative vision, which perhaps relieves Addams of her preoccupation with "disease-breeding filth" and "sordid" conditions.

Here and elsewhere in *Twenty Years*, Addams qualifies her idealization of difference by expressing hope that immigrants such as these country folk will undergo some degree of Americanization. She explains that Hull-House workers merely seek to "preserve and keep whatever of value [the country folks'] past life contained and to bring them in contact with a better type of Americans" (153). Despite valuing the cultural contributions of immigrant citizens, Addams hopes they will continue to develop through association with a "superior" form of American culture. This same attitude informs Addams's narratives about the efforts of Hull-House workers to improve the relationships of immigrants and their American-born children. These chapters demonstrate how Hull-House validated immigrant culture by creating a space for its expression. However, they also recount the ghettoization of immigrant culture in the Hull-House Labor Museum, emblematizing the coexistence of cultural relativism and evolutionary ideology at the settlement house.

Describing a series of recreational evenings devoted to German immigrants, Addams recalls the newfound appreciation that the children of immigrants developed after being exposed to their parents' cultural heritage. She writes,

> I have seen sons and daughters stand in complete surprise as their mother's knitting needles softly beat a time to the song she was singing, or her worn face turned rosy under the hand-clapping as she made an old-fashioned courtesy [sic] at the end of a German poem. It was easy to fancy a growing touch of respect in her children's manner to her, and a rising enthusiasm for German literature and reminiscence on the part of all the family, an effort to bring together the old life and the new, a respect for the older cultivation, and not quite so much assurance that the new was the best. (154)

This passage reveals Addams's view that physical movement embodies culture. By metonymically aligning the soft beat of the knitting needles and the audience's hand-clapping with the mother's German poem and Old World curtsey, Addams evokes the distinctly foreign quality of the mother's character. We can identify the moment that this Old World character emerges, because the mother exchanges the worn expression of an immigrant laborer for the rosy face of a German peasant. This nostalgic description suggests that the immigrant mother prefers her older German traditions to the experience of American life (either that, or Addams prefers it). The passage also highlights the spontaneous element of parent-child encounters at Hull-House: a woman transforms the regulated activity of knitting into song, and her children "stand in complete surprise." The result, Addams concludes, is an unexpected improvement of intergenerational relationships. This scene, like others, illustrates how Hull-House creates a space in which a traditionally private experience (such as knitting) shifts into a communal experience that in turn precipitates the development of cosmopolitan citizenship.

As Addams depicts them, events at Hull-House vacillated between spontaneous exchanges such as the one described above and activities held in the formal setting of the Hull-House Labor Museum, an "educational enterprise" that, Addams hoped, would "build a bridge between European and American experiences in such wise as to give them both more meaning and a sense of relation" (155). Whereas museums traditionally exhibit a distant past, the Hull-House Labor Museum served as a site devoted to the living histories of its immigrant visitors. In recounting her inspiration for the museum, Addams reveals her goal of emphasizing the continuity between historical and contemporary practices. Addams recalls seeing an old Italian woman on the street, spinning thread to make socks for her goddaughter, and wonders, "Could we not interest the young people working in the neighborhood factories, in these older forms of industry, so that, through their own parents and grandparents, they would find a dramatic representation of the inherited resources of their daily occupation?" (156). Exposure to the past in this form, Addams explains, would allow American children to develop by teaching them to recognize how their present evolved from their past. She imagines that visits to the Hull-House Labor Museum would help children "make a beginning towards that education which Dr. Dewey defined as 'a continuing reconstruction of experience'" (156).

Addams organizes the museum so as to represent the teleological progress-narrative evoked earlier. Her discussion of the museum is worth citing at length because it offers insight into the twinned influences of evolutionary thought and cultural relativism on daily life at Hull-House. Addams explains,

> We found in the immediate neighborhood, at least four varieties of these most primitive methods of spinning and three distinct variations of the same spindle in connection with wheels. It was possible to put these seven into historic sequence and order and to connect the whole with the present method of factory spinning. The same thing was done for weaving, and on every Saturday evening a little exhibit was made of these various forms of labor in the textile industry. Within one room a Syrian woman, a Greek, an Italian, a Russian, and an Irishwoman enabled even the most casual observer to see that there is no break in orderly evolution if we look at history from an industrial standpoint; that industry develops similarly and peacefully year by year among the workers of each nation, heedless of differences in language, religion, and political experiences. (156–57)

In this passage, Addams uses the same developmental time line to evaluate the spinning activities of different nations. In so doing, she reveals the humanist underpinnings of her cultural relativism: these women engage in diverse, equally valid modes of spinning that nonetheless evidence a hierarchy of human development. Even though Addams accords equal value to the immigrant cultures she describes, she suggests that "factory spinning" is superior by stating that every culture naturally progresses to this end point. Addams invokes a "historic sequence" to suggest that contemporary industry naturally eclipses primitive forms of spinning. With its echo of recapitulation theory, this passage contrasts with Addams's earlier description of the spontaneous German cultural evenings in which the children of immigrants learn to doubt their feelings of superiority over their parents' generation.

The paradox of the Hull-House Labor Museum is that it asks real immigrant women to engage in quotidian activities in a museum context while at the same time reifying these practices as part of a distant past. Nonetheless, by inviting living women to serve as exhibits at the museum, Addams allows the space to become an unstable territory, which opens it up to a variety of uses. At least some of the time, immigrants transformed the Hull-House Labor Museum into a living cultural space, disregarding the reifying intent of the exhibits and instead using them to engage in cultural activities that they inflected with their own meaning.

The fact that Addams accepted the immigrants' repurposing of Hull-House is exemplified by her pride in recounting the means by which a group of Russian women spontaneously took over the museum one evening. The women arrived at Hull-House in anticipation of an event they mistakenly thought was taking place. They subsequently discovered the Labor Museum's weaving room and created their own event: "The thirty sodden, tired women were transformed. They knew how to use the spindles and were delighted to find the Russian spinning frame. . . . They turned up their dresses to show their home-spun petticoats; they tried the looms; they explained the difficulty of the old patterns; in short, from having been stupidly entertained, they themselves did the entertaining. Because of a direct appeal to former experiences, the immigrant visitors were able for the moment to instruct their American hostesses in an old and honored craft, as was indeed becoming to their age and experience" (160).[109] This anecdote is appealing on a number of fronts. First, it challenges the vision of mainstream citizenship education programs that sought to assimilate new nationals to dominant US cultural norms. As Addams herself notes, the museum transforms "immigrants into the position of teachers" (159) while the settlement workers become students of those they had hoped to educate. This spontaneous display of live culture undercuts the exhibit's teleology, belying the narrative that spinning and weaving have given way to "the present method of factory spinning" (157). Moreover, the museum space facilitates an unusual exchange not just between immigrants and settlement workers but also among immigrant women themselves. In other words, the museum allows its immigrant visitors to experience a virtual Old World setting, creating an international space that encourages European cultural practices to thrive within the borders of Chicago. In this example, Hull-House validates the internationalism that persists within national space. In so doing, it exemplifies an ideal manifestation of Addams's cosmopolitan sensibility.

The museum also functions to enhance the reader's sense of *Twenty Years* as a dissensual bildungsroman. Though Addams is a settlement worker who seeks to facilitate the adaptation of European immigrants to US life, in this scene she portrays herself as the student of European peasants whose living practices undermine the ostensible lesson of the museum's exhibit. Addams not only allows this experience to displace her authority but also thematizes the fact that this transformation occurs in the Hull-House Labor Museum. In this respect, the museum space enhances the dissensual nature of the text by preserving permeable borders between individuals with culturally specific practices (which in many cases are also international) and a nationalist public culture.

The reverie that overtakes Addams as a result of this museum experience nonetheless also reveals the humanist elements of her internationalism. Watching the European scene evokes a tapestry of memories for Addams, one that includes "shifting pictures of woman's labor with which travel makes one familiar; the Indian women grinding grain outside of their huts as they sing praises to the sun and rain; a file of white-clad Moorish women whom I had once seen waiting their turn at a well in Tangiers; south Italian women kneeling in a row along the stream and beating and beating their wet clothes against the smooth white stones; the milking, the gardening, the marketing in thousands of hamlets, which are such direct expressions of the solicitude and affection at the basis of all family life" (160). From one perspective, this passage points to Addams's desire to forge international solidarity by figuring domestic labor as an occupation that minimizes cultural and national difference. Nonetheless, the passage also exposes Addams's desire for the museum's female audience to experience kinship based on a common set of interests and practices. In articulating these commonalities, Addams reveals her gender and cultural biases. Aligning Indians, Moors, and Italians through the medium of the family and the woman's role in upholding it, Addams expresses her middle-class idealization of the female caretaker. At the same time, Addams imaginatively places Indians, Moors, and southern Italians in a distant past characterized by ancient religious practices (praise-songs), biblical images (the well), and glorified preindustrial labor (grinding grain and cleaning one's clothes at the river).

What can we make of Addams's vision of cosmopolitan kinship articulated through images of nonwhite, non-Protestant women engaging in domestic labor?[110] Maybe Addams seeks to mobilize peaceful visions of preindustrial activity and rural life to heal the rifts between immigrant mothers and their American-born daughters. After all, this vision echoes other moments in which Addams finds solace in pastoral fantasies, as when she portrays peasants traipsing through the city streets as though they were on country lanes. By this logic, if the invocation of historical practices can relieve the tensions of industrial Chicago for Addams, then perhaps immigrant parents might invoke Old World practices to minimize the stresses experienced by their American-born children.

Addams is thrilled to discover an example of intergenerational reciprocity as she witnesses the transformation of a mother-daughter relationship at Hull-House. She recalls that when the pair first started coming there on a weekly basis, they separated at the front door, the girl to take a cooking class and the mother to spin in the Labor Museum. At first, the girl always entered the house separately out of fear of being associated with her mother: "She did not wish to be too closely identified in the eyes of the rest of the cooking class with an Italian woman who wore a kerchief over her head, uncouth boots, and short petticoats." One evening, however, the girl saw her mother surrounded by a bunch of visitors from the School of Education (presumably from the University of Chicago) and "she concluded from their conversation that her mother was the 'best stick-spindle spinner in all of America'" (161). After ascertaining that this was true, the daughter underwent a miraculous change in attitude toward her mother: she began to learn about her mother's life and to respect her wisdom and experience. The two began to enter Hull-House through the same door.

This anecdote speaks to the interpersonal benefits of the cosmopolitan citizenship practiced at Hull-House. Other moments of *Twenty Years* evoke the more overtly political tenor of Addams's educational philosophy. Addams surmises that "internationalism engendered in the immigrant quarters of immigrant cities might be recognized as an effective instrument in the cause of peace" (201) and offers up examples of how bringing together diverse people has transformed individuals, community relations, and even the demographic makeup of her West Chicago neighborhood. Addams recounts a friendship that develops between a southern Italian Catholic and an Austrian Jew and uses it to exemplify "internationalism as sturdy and virile as it is unprecedented" (200). Though the two befriend each other out of exigency, their friendship soon belies their prejudiced expectations; as a result, both men go on to renounce other nationalistic and religious prejudices. As Addams explains, "He thus modifies his provincialism for if an old enemy working by his side has turned into a friend, almost anything may happen" (201). We can see in this example the development of ideas Addams would later articulate in *Newer Ideals of Peace* (1906), where she argues that cosmopolitan environments encourage universalist humanism, which in turn can produce peace.

In *Newer Ideals*, Addams envisions an ideal, cosmopolitan community that will provide an alternative to nationalism and the wars that it inspires.[111] Ideally, this community "of highly differentiated peoples" will by necessity develop "a deeper and more thorough-going unity" than that achieved by very similar people. Illustrating her humanist sensibility, Addams supposes that regular contact with cultural difference will lead people to recognize a more essential commonality: individuals will be "forced to found their community of interests upon the basic and essential likenesses of their common human nature." In this ideal cosmopolitan city, individuals will also abandon attachments based on nationalism and patriotism. Ultimately, Addams hopes, they will even give up war, understanding that "it will be as strange to wage war on the other side of the globe as it would be to wage it against one's neighbor."[112]

To the extent that she could, Addams sought to realize this cosmopolitan vision at Hull-House. In *Twenty Years*, she explains how her approach to citizenship education did not merely transform the immigrant population; it also benefited the settlement workers. Addams recounts the transformation of one settlement worker who belonged to Hull-House's Social Extension Committee. After an extraordinary evening with a group of southern Italian men, this woman confessed her change of heart about leaving the neighborhood: "I have been nagging my husband to move off M Street because they [the Italians] are moving in, but I am going to try staying awhile and see if I can make a real acquaintance with some of them" (232). As a result of one of the spontaneous, international exchanges made possible by Hull-House, this woman begins her transformation into a "citizen of the world"; she not only learns to understand and respect difference (among "all kinds of people with their varying experiences") but also expresses her desire to continue benefiting from this difference (232).

This chapter has argued that despite their occasional invocation of evolutionary ideology, both Addams and Du Bois articulated a cosmopolitan sensibility that rejected nationalistic xenophobia and envisioned the creation of world citizens. Du Bois sought to cultivate world citizenship for African Americans, while Addams sought to realize it for the mostly white, working-class immigrants whom she encountered at Hull-House. The cosmopolitan stance expressed by these two visionaries also prefigures the radical ethics of a twenty-first-century cosmopolitanism as articulated, for example, by Kendall, Woodward, and Skrbis in *The Sociology of Cosmopolitanism*. The ideal cosmopolitan subject, Kendall explains, "looks outward to see difference as an opportunity for connection rather than as a pretext for separation."[113] This form of cosmopolitanism "requires putting oneself in the place of the other" to achieve, in Bryan Turner's words, a "critical recognition ethics" through which the individual can practice "respect for difference, critical mutual evaluation, and finally care for the other."[114] Through their representation of potentially fragile intercultural encounters, Addams and Du Bois demonstrate how one might avoid the ethical threat that can arise "when exchange [with the other] becomes difficult or derogated."[115] They both illustrate how one can develop an ideal cosmopolitan ethics by maintaining philosophical openness in the face of cultural difference.

Though Du Bois does engage in cultural typologization and does flirt with a superior stance as he observes his shipboard types, he nonetheless immerses himself in the world of the displaced exile-in-transit and economic subaltern. Aligning himself with this population by traveling steerage, Du Bois mobilizes their shared economic position to challenge the nationalist assumptions of his time. As an "ironic, detached" cosmopolitan who nonetheless maintains a "fundamentally ethical concern for the other," Du Bois uses his voyage to question the narrow assumptions of a liberal ideology that is limited to the nation-state.[116] In this sense he evidences Hansen's claim that Du Bois (like Addams and John Dewey) saw that "the proper object of patriotic loyalty was not the American nation-state, but the ideal of democratic social reciprocity, for which the nation-state was [merely] a vehicle."[117]

While *Twenty Years* does not depict Addams's travels outside the United States, it articulates her realization of cosmopolitanism within the urban space of Chicago. Like Du Bois, Addams aligns herself with the European immigrants she depicts. Whereas Du Bois identifies with European immigrants by ruminating on a shared economic sensibility, Addams celebrates moments when she and her fellow educators have their expectations and plans reversed—when the immigrant visitors to Hull-House transform the teachers, lessons, and methodologies that threaten to reify them. Both Du Bois and Addams model, philosophize about, and practice a democratic reciprocity by imaginatively releasing their subjects from the burden of economic and cultural pressures.

Offering a contrast to these idealistic visions of cosmopolitan citizenship, chapter 4 examines citizenship education programs through which established German American Jews sought to assimilate a newer generation of eastern European Jews. However, it also juxtaposes an archival analysis of these programs with a comparison of Abraham Cahan's dissensual bildungsroman *The Rise of David Levinsky* and his Yiddish-language autobiography *The Education of Abraham Cahan*. Though Cahan does not directly articulate a cosmopolitan politics, he illustrates the difficulties of exchanging an Old World identity for a new, Americanized one. Cahan's novel acknowledges that the extranational elements of Levinsky's identity persist even after he has assimilated to mainstream US culture; it further questions the benefits of Cahan's desire to abandon this Old World. Cahan develops his cosmopolitan outlook in his nonfictional autobiography by challenging the idea that a singular, Old World Jewish culture even exists and by emphasizing its multiple and conflicting characteristics.

4 / Educating the *Ostjuden*: Abraham Cahan and Gestures of Resistance

As chapter 3 demonstrates, Booker T. Washington and W. E. B. Du Bois defined success differently: Washington viewed it as freedom from material cares, whereas Du Bois envisioned it in terms of intellectual freedom. While both educators projected these ideas of success onto their students, their pedagogies also reveal traces of elitism—of wealth in Washington's case, and of talent in Du Bois's. At the same time that Washington was promoting manual labor at Tuskegee, in the service of cultivating a working-class ideal of capitalist success, German Jewish educators were pursuing a similar agenda for their eastern European coreligionists in New York City. Their citizenship education programs provided English-language education, as well as manual and industrial training, for the eastern European Jewish immigrants—or *Ostjuden*—who were arriving to the United States in large numbers at the turn of the twentieth century.[1] German Jews adopted an assimilationist educational agenda through which they could encourage the *Ostjuden* to embrace capitalism without threatening the Germans Jews' status as owners of capital.

This chapter juxtaposes an archival analysis of these citizenship education programs with interpretation of poetic, novelistic, and autobiographical texts in which eastern European Jews dramatize problems with the German Jewish educational paradigm and the vision of success it promoted. Records of life at the Educational Alliance (EA) and Hebrew Orphan Asylum (HOA)—two institutions funded and run by German Jews—testify to the Germans' anxiety that their assimilated status would suffer from association with the Yiddish-speaking newcomers who isolated themselves into ghettos and either practiced Orthodox Judaism or engaged in leftist political activities.[2] Influenced simultaneously by social Darwinism and racialized shame, German Jews instituted English classes to promote a secular and capitalist sensibility; they also provided embodied activities to instill patriotism and transform what they perceived as the immigrant newcomers' weak, un-American physiques.[3] Ironically, these educators, who were disturbed by the repetitive movement, musicality, and communalism of both the Yiddish language and Orthodox Judaism, used rhythmical and communal movement to enhance their students' assimilation.[4]

The vision of success adopted by German Jewish educators infused US educational culture more generally, evident in books by authors as diverse as Booker T. Washington, Horatio Alger, and Mary Antin. As this book's introduction illustrates, Horatio Alger's *Ragged Dick* celebrates its protagonist's achievement of capitalist success despite the fact that Dick makes less money after becoming a clerk than he made as a bootblack. In the fashion of sentimental fiction, the novel attributes Dick's increased status to his honesty, hard work, and frugality, when his success results largely from good luck. By privileging Dick's moral qualities over his luck, the novel's narrator reifies the myth that other homeless bootblacks might easily have mimicked Dick's success by emulating his capitalist sensibility. Likewise, this myth of capitalist success was validated by the work of assimilated eastern European Jews such as Mary Antin.[5] Assimilationist autobiographies such as Antin's *The Promised Land* celebrated Americanization by featuring protagonists who gave up Yiddish, adopted secularism or Reform Judaism, and achieved financial success by becoming efficient laborers or owners of capital.[6] At the same time, leftist authors such as Abraham Cahan and Charles Reznikoff critiqued this narrative trajectory. This chapter examines such critiques by analyzing fictional, nonfictional, and poetic accounts of Americanization by Cahan and Reznikoff, both eastern European Jews—born in Russia and Brooklyn, respectively—whose portraits of Jewish immigrant life in New York City comment on the German Jewish educational paradigm.

Cahan's *The Rise of David Levinsky* (1917) and Reznikoff's "Early History of a Writer" (collected in his 1969 book, *By the Well of Living and Seeing*) not only dramatize problems with the capitalist success narrative reified by *Ragged Dick* but also express disappointment with the form of citizenship education institutionalized by German Jews.[7] As a mock-bildungsroman, *Levinsky* satirizes the myth of capitalist success by representing its protagonist's assimilation as an alienating experience and by evoking the persistence of Levinsky's indelible foreignness through his embodied gestures and accent. Reznikoff's poetry also registers disappointment with the American success narrative but does so through adopting an elegiac tone that emphasizes his speaker's loss of family, language, and culture. From Reznikoff's perspective, alienation inevitably accompanies the American-born Jew's successful assimilation.

Both Cahan and Reznikoff invoke the genre characteristics of the idealist bildungsroman, which, as Joseph Slaughter writes, narrates its protagonist's alignment with the nation-state as a story of "normative assimilation" that nonetheless requires a "frustrated incorporation."[8] Both authors call attention to the artificiality of a nationalist assimilation narrative that balances awkwardly atop actual experience.[9] While Reznikoff invokes the idealist bildungsroman with an elegiac tone, and Cahan does so through satire, both authors critique its central premise, highlighting the "frustrated incorporation" that is central to the experience of "normative assimilation."

By ironizing elements of the idealist bildungsroman, Reznikoff and Cahan also participate in the tradition of the dissensual bildungsroman. Reznikoff's speaker experiences a sense of loss as he adapts to mainstream US culture, but he accepts the goal of assimilation validated by the idealist bildungsroman. At the same time, however, Reznikoff challenges the myth of a "singular national public" by emphasizing the "presence of competing publics within the domain of the nation-state."[10] Likewise, Cahan represents these "competing publics" to belie the myth of belonging reproduced by the idealist bildungsroman. As this novel demonstrates, the idealist bildungsroman cannot represent the experiences of citizens whose integration is always-already undermined by the multiplicity of linguistic, cultural, and historical influences on their identity—influences they either cannot or will not abandon. In this respect, the novel prefigures Cahan's Yiddish-language autobiography, *Bleiter Fun Mein Leben*—translated as *The Education of Abraham Cahan* (1926)—which foregrounds the multiple identities that Cahan inhabited as a European Jew, identities he continued to embrace after immigrating to the United States.[11] Ultimately, all of these texts—Reznikoff's poem, and Cahan's fictional and nonfictional autobiographies—suggest that a liberal, rather than a civic republican, model of citizenship will most accurately represent the diversity of a US citizenry.

Language and the Body: The *Ostjuden*'s Difference

Established German Jews who had been living in the United States since the 1840s and 1850s worried that they would be identified with the much more visible eastern European Jews who were immigrating to New York City between 1880 and 1924.[12] The HOA and the EA were two institutions through which German Jewish educators sought to Americanize the new wave of Jewish immigrants; to realize this objective, they offered English classes, vocational education, military-style regimentation, and strict dress codes, alongside forms of discipline that included isolation and corporal punishment. The HOA, founded in 1822 by Sephardic and German Jews of the Hebrew Benevolent Society, grew to become one of the largest homes for destitute Jewish children and orphans, admitting over thirteen thousand children between 1860 and 1919.[13] Because the HOA effectively replaced parents in its function as an orphanage (whether the parents were dead or simply unable to care for their children), its archives offer useful insight into the values and practices that German American educators sought to instill in this impressionable population. Likewise, the archives of the EA house material evidence of the values and practices of German Jewish educators. The EA opened in 1891 and advertised itself as a "nonsectarian citizenship and character-building agency devoted to the making of new Americans."[14] Its primary role was to provide English classes to immigrants of all ages and stages of assimilation, for the purpose of streamlining their entrance into public schools.[15] The German Jews of the EA heavily emphasized English education in part because they felt anxious—however unfounded that anxiety might be—that the persistence of Yiddish among the *Ostjuden* would threaten their own assimilated status.

The linguistic diversity of US immigrants at the turn of the twentieth century figured prominently in popular media, the literary world, and educational circles as a real or imagined threat to a unified national identity.[16] Anti-Yiddish prejudice had intensified among German American Jews in the postbellum United States, paralleling the increase of anti-Yiddish feeling among German Jews after the unification of Germany in 1871.[17] In both Germany and the United States, popular theories located Jewish inferiority in the accents and gestures of Yiddish.[18] Though German American Jews in New York City were not subject to this particular theory—being fully assimilated English speakers—they were nonetheless influenced by the assumption that a Jew's assimilation is never complete. As Sander Gilman explains, even if the assimilated Jew did not call attention to his Jewishness, he still carried "the mark of difference which offends even after the Jew is integrated into the mainstream of American culture."[19] German American Jews suffered discrimination from Protestant elites, as well as from Sephardic Jews who traced their presence in

New York City to the seventeenth century.[20] In turn, the German Americans may have projected their experience of discrimination onto a newer generation of *Ostjuden*.[21]

In both Germany and the United States, linguistic anti-Semitism was imbricated with stereotypes about the inferiority of the Jewish body. Historians and theorists have offered competing explanations for why nineteenth-century Jews were associated with an inferior physiology: Did this association originate as a form of anti-Semitism, or did Jews cultivate physical weakness in order to avoid conscription in European armies and subsequently suffer from the naturalization of this adopted trait? In his *Memoirs*, EA director David Blaustein suggests that in "Europe . . . the necessity of military service created a philosophy of unfitness as a means of escape."[22] In the late nineteenth century, however, countries such as Germany and Austria relaxed their restrictions against Jewish military service; as Sander Gilman argues, the increased visibility of Jews in the army led to an intensification of anti-Jewish stereotypes.[23] Whatever its source, the belief that the Jew had "never exhibited . . . a high physical standard" pervaded popular thought in Europe and the United States at the turn of the twentieth century.[24] In Germany the Zionist leader Max Nordau went so far as to call for a "new Muscle Jew," explaining, "[The Jews] have killed our bodies in the stinking streets of the ghettoes and we must now rebuild them on the playing fields of Berlin and Vienna."[25]

German American educators were influenced by theories about the Jew's linguistic and bodily deformity, associating "a specific Jewish physiognomy" with "a specific manner of speaking."[26] In addition to seeing embodied inferiority and linguistic difference as interconnected phenomena, these educators believed that the *Ostjuden*'s physique was stunted from an overreliance on intellectual and religious pursuits: a belief they expressed through the framework of social Darwinism. Moreover, because the *Ostjuden* spoke Yiddish while engaging in leftist political activities or Orthodox religious rituals, German Jewish educators blamed this language for undermining civic republicanism and preventing the *Ostjuden* from embracing a capitalist sensibility. In their citizenship education programs, German Jews sought to combat the immigrant Jew's language, politics, and religion with English-language classes and instruction in manual and vocational labor.

Though German Jewish educators authentically believed their Americanization programs would improve the lives of the *Ostjuden*, they described this group with anti-Semitic language (a contradiction that recalls the boarding-school policies and English-only program promoted by ostensibly pro-Indian reformers, as I discuss earlier in this book).[27] In *The School and the Immigrant*, a manual published by the New York City Department of Education in 1915, Albert Shiels expresses anxiety about a Jewish "immigrant problem [that continued] to be segregated, speaking its own language, maintaining its own customs, crowding itself into congested sections, housing itself (or being housed) in dirty tenements and rookeries, [and] adopting its own schemes of private litigation and private vengeance."[28] Here, Shiels expresses his anxiety that segregation from the mainstream equals negative visibility and therefore poses a symbolic threat to the nation. Other German Jews, who were distressed by this tendency, revealed anti-Semitic sentiments as they depicted their fears of an unpleasantly emotional, "fervent Yiddish culture with leftist inclinations that would obstruct assimilation."[29] These Germans disdained the "miserable darkened Hebrews" who used "piggish jargon [Yiddish]" to express "dangerous principles."[30] Fearing the transmission of both political radicalism and Orthodox Judaism through the medium of Yiddish, EA educators banned the language from their curriculum until 1898 (at which point they incorporated it in an effort to increase their audience).[31] Likewise, American public school bureaucrats suffered the anxiety of influence about leftist political ideas emerging out of the Yiddish-speaking community; Abraham Cahan was famously fired from his job as an evening public school teacher because he was seen giving a socialist speech.[32]

German elites demonized political radicals by claiming that these "agitators and demagogues" used Yiddish to make "tools of innocent Jews" who were "ignorant of the principles which underlie [their] government."[33] Since Yiddish was also the language at *cheders* (Jewish elementary schools) where the children of Orthodox Jews were educated, its absence from the EA discouraged traditional Jews (along with political radicals) from attending its programs.[34] In excluding the language and accompanying traditions of Yiddish-speaking immigrants from their programs, both the EA and the HOA encouraged immigrants to cultivate assimilated Jewish personas that would fit neatly within an American mold.[35]

The prospect of assimilating Orthodox Jews presented a real challenge to German Jewish educators, in part because Orthodox identity emerged from a triangulation of study, song, and movement. According to William McNeill's sociological study of the role of rhythm and music in human history, tightly knit communities of Orthodox men historically have remained cohesive as a result of movement in unison alongside singing or chanting; these activities characterize their religious elation and social connection.[36] Prayer based in movement and song remained a feature of Jewish Orthodoxy in turn-of-the-century New York City, as Cahan illustrates when describing his visit to an Orthodox synagogue: "As I made my way through the market-place, a merry, bizarre hubbub of singing voices broke upon the stillness of the street. The voices came from a tumble-down frame house. . . . A Holy Ark and a reading-desk betokened the character of the place. The little synagogue was crowded with bewhiskered, pious, ragged old men, swaying and nodding, curling their sidelocks or stroking their beards, as they sang a joyous Sabbath melody. Their faces shone and their voices trembled with emotion."[37] Cahan conveys the sense that these worshippers could be meeting anywhere. In other words, the physical surroundings of their practice signify little when compared with the spiritual elation, the rapt attention and joy, with which these men approach their prayer. Through chanting, these worshippers suspend time and invoke the presence of a transhistorical community of believers. Cahan's depiction of a "tumble-down frame house" also points to the public nature of Jewish life on the Lower East Side, a visibility that troubled German Jewish educators. This insistence on a strict divide between public and private culture was characteristic of the assimilationist ideal upheld by German Jewish educators, just as an attempt to dissolve this divide was central to the cosmopolitanism of Addams and Du Bois. As this chapter later illustrates, Levinsky's need to hide his religious identity is characteristic of both assimilationism and its correlative, the idealist bildungsroman.

Rather than promoting strict secularism in the *Ostjuden*, German Jewish educators tried to replace Orthodox Judaism with Reform Judaism (their own invention), in part because it provided an alternative to the visible—and one might argue, exhibitionist—quality of Orthodox prayer. In place of the public and communal Orthodox tradition, German Jews offered a mode of prayer that was private, isolated, and curtailed. In an undated brochure titled *Scenes in the Daily Life of an Orphan Child*, the HOA describes the compartmentalization of prayer that results from the ritual of synagogue attendance: "To bring the children up in the faith of their fathers has ever been the foremost aim and object of the Asylum authorities. The children are taught the principles of their religion, and prayers are recited each morning and evening, grace is said before and after meals, and divine services are held on the Sabbath and on all holidays."[38] By isolating and minimizing religious practice, German Jewish educators sought to enhance the integration of Jews into mainstream US society. As Rabbi Kaufman Kohler states, "It will not do for us as teachers of humanity to remain Hebrews in garb and custom, in views and language."[39] Reform Jews referred to their synagogues as temples and held services in English; some of them even celebrated Christmas or bought Christmas trees. In the 1880s and 1890s, some uptown temples such as Emanu-El even attempted "to transfer the Jewish Sabbath from Saturday to Sunday."[40]

German Jews who became involved in public school administration used their positions to help reduce the isolation of Orthodox Jews from mainstream US life and were assisted in their efforts by new laws that mandated public school attendance.[41] The public schools cultivated a normative American identity by promoting Protestant values and emphasizing English-language education.[42] The public schools also taught "American" ethics and morals.[43] As education superintendent William Maxwell explained in his 1903 *Course of Study*, the public school was a "central agent in the transformation of immigrant aliens into the logic and lifeways of the dominant culture."[44] The "dominant culture" to which Maxwell referred was one that celebrated manual labor and promoted a working-class identity for the public school's immigrant students.

In his *Course of Study*, Maxwell recommended that in teaching geography, teachers should intertwine "American" values such as cleanliness and orderliness with capitalist ones such as a love of work. Maxwell wrote, "The ethical purpose of the teaching of geography are [*sic*] to lead to the moral lesson that all men must work and that each man should so work that his labor will benefit not only himself, but the whole community."[45] He encouraged teachers to use geography, alongside other ostensibly academic subjects, as a medium for inspiring students to engage in industrial and manual labor. The curriculum defined citizenship training as teaching students "to keep garbage and paper separate from ashes; to keep receptacles covered . . . to refrain from throwing anything from windows . . . [to keep] cleanliness of body, of clothing, of dwelling, of streets."[46] As this passage illustrates, Maxwell was like other citizenship educators in his preoccupation with the upkeep of the body and the benefits of labor.

With the creation of Ira Wile's 1913 curriculum, German Jews successfully increased industrial and vocational education in the public schools and removed the study of science and foreign languages.[47] German Jewish educators hoped that by emphasizing vocational training they might prevent the *Ostjuden* from ghettoizing themselves in the realm of commercial market activity. These educators feared that Jewish immigrants who made a living from buying and selling goods, rather than producing new ones, would intensify stereotypes that Jews were parasitic.[48] Some *Ostjuden* actually shared this concern; as Abraham Cahan explains, "Neither the enlightened immigrants nor the uneducated orthodox newcomers undertook peddling. They looked upon it as a shameful occupation. It was work, real work with one's hands, that they sought. Only such work was considered an honest way to make a living."[49] Ironically, however, many German Jewish educators who encouraged the *Ostjuden* to adopt trades so they would not be perceived as parasitic were themselves business magnates who had made their fortunes through ownership of banks, garment factories, and department stores. Whether or not they were aware of this contradiction, German Jews emphasized vocational education, perhaps as a function of their fear that innovative immigrants would challenge their economic dominance. This was already beginning to happen in the garment industry, which this chapter's later discussion of Cahan highlights.

Archival materials from German Jewish citizenship programs echo the dominant trend in US education, whereby educators adopted movement-based education to reproduce a class-stratified society.[50] Public and vocational schools attended by working-class whites accustomed students to the repetitive work they would encounter in the industrialized city and prepared them to enter a class-stratified civil sphere.[51] Likewise, public school education geared toward a range of immigrants used vocational training to impart working-class values. As Henry E. Jenkins—New York City's district superintendent in charge of evening schools—explains in his 1916 treatise "Development of the Social and Recreational Life of the Foreigner," once manual training replaced other forms of social interaction, the immigrant would learn to find joy in her work because it would feel like play.[52] Describing an evening school for immigrants, Jenkins writes, "The principal found that his vocational classes could be made, so to speak, social extension tentacles. Classes in dressmaking, millinery, embroidery, flower making, etc., have become much more than vocational. They possess a large socializing influence. To the tired laundress, the housemaid, to the drudge in her own household, the evening school comes as a haven of rest, a sanctuary in which to learn to do that work which, because of the joy in it, is most like play."[53] Jenkins's use of "tentacles" as a metaphor suggests that the worker needed some strong convincing that work was like play. Moreover, play itself was mobilized to bolster a capitalist sensibility. At the EA, for instance, educators sought to replace the "spontaneity, self-hood, and inner-directedness" embodied by the outdoor street games of eastern European Jews with games that were codified, formalized, and organized in the service of "establishing ruling class hegemony."[54]

Jenkins's discussion of Jewish education also reflects this desire to reproduce a class-stratified society through linguistic and physical education. Describing an evening elementary school serving an "entirely Jewish and male" population, Jenkins writes, "In miscellaneous classes where foreigners without a specific trade struggled with our vowels and consonants, the teacher emphasized the importance of choosing vocations correctly and endeavored to help in the choice. . . . [This] kindly sympathetic interest often makes the immigrant aware of the fact that somewhere among the trades there is a place for him."[55] The metonymical association between an education in "vowels and consonants" and an education in "choosing vocations" emphasizes the teacher's function as a producer of working-class consciousness. Concluding his essay, Jenkins stresses the "importance of physical fitness . . . in its relation to work and to the survival of the fittest."[56] With his reference to Herbert Spencer's famous phrase, Jenkins evidences the influence of evolutionary ideology on physical education programs that promoted class stratification. The presence of evolutionary ideas—and recapitulation theory in particular—in Jenkins's essay is not surprising, given that the nineteenth-century physical culture movement attributed the acquisition of moral superiority to movement-based activities.[57]

As James Salazar explains, at the turn of the twentieth century the United States experienced an "explosion of interest" in "the practices of physical exercise, organized sports, and athletic displays that collectively came to be known as 'physical culture,' at the center of which stood the revalorized image of the visibly muscular body."[58] Educators associated with this movement worried that Anglo-Americans were being emasculated, as a result of not only corporate life, the women's rights movement, and a decline in agricultural labor, but also the increasing diversity of the US population. These educators "laid stress on the importance of developing a muscular, 'preindustrial' body" and sought to improve their students' physiques through summer camps, organized sports, and the YMCA movement.[59] Men such as G. Stanley Hall, Theodore Roosevelt, and S. Weir Mitchell hoped that a superior muscular physique would emblematize the Anglo-Saxon's racial and moral superiority. This "revalorized" male body would be "hardened, expanded, and empowered to withstand not only the enervating demands of modernity, but also the 'race-diluting' effects of massive immigration and the challenges to traditional white male authority posed by the 'New Woman' and the 'New Negro.'"[60]

The *Ostjuden*, who were popularly viewed as nonwhite, were more likely to be seen as an impediment to the white subject's development than as candidates for physical training along these lines. Neither were they the intended audience of recapitulation theorists, who interpreted the physical culture movement in evolutionary terms. Proponents of recapitulation theory, such as G. Stanley Hall, imagined that, in the process of becoming more civilized, Anglo-Saxons would identify imaginatively with the ostensibly overembodied nonwhite subject. This identification would, Hall imagined, inspire white Americans to acquire a stronger physique, which in turn would enhance their civilized status.[61] Though immigrant Jews were seen as overly intellectual and physically deficient—and therefore in need of physical training—they were not to tread the same recapitulative pathway that Anglo-Americans would. Instead of reaching back to progress forward, in line with recapitulation theory, the eastern European Jew was supposed to reach forward in an attempt to play catch-up with those who embodied whiteness more successfully. Physical training would allow the Jew to achieve "just enough" in the way of civilized mannerisms and economic success.

At the turn of the twentieth century, almost nobody was immune to some influence from evolutionary theories that aligned physical superiority and racial progress. Even several decades into the twentieth century, German Jewish educators were attributing differences in the *Ostjuden*'s character and status to organic, rather than materialist, causes. In spite of this belief in the Jew's biological inferiority, many proponents of citizenship education subscribed to the neo-Lamarckian idea that physical and cultural characteristics could be transformed during the course of an individual's life and passed from one generation to the next. German Jewish educators who embraced this view hoped that new habits would, over time, replace the inferior qualities of the *Ostjuden*.[62]

Increasingly, however, German Jewish educators were influenced by the new science of genetics.[63] As genetics became more prominent, citizenship educators lamented that cultural traits would not disappear as a result of educational training.[64] The shift from evolutionary to genetic ideology was catalyzed by August Weismann's discovery that acquired characteristics could not be passed on to future generations unless genetic material had been altered.[65] Weismann's theory challenged the neo-Lamarckian assumption that education could result in racial improvement.[66] Carl Degler argues that neo-Lamarckianism gave way to

Francis Galton's eugenics movement and its emphasis on racial improvement through breeding.[67] However, as the archives illustrate, during the first two decades of the twentieth century, German Jewish educators were motivated by a combined influence of evolutionary and genetic theories.[68] In this respect, the archives illustrate the truth of Sarah Wilson's claim that "range, contradictoriness, and mutability" characterized evolutionary thought during this period.[69]

We can see the influence of genetic science on a 1902 report from the EA, which, in describing its summer camp for the "East Side boy," reveals the author's perception that physiology was the source of indelible psychological and cultural traits.[70] The report laments the Jew's overintellectual nature: "It is a discouraging fact, but nevertheless true, that the East Side boy despises manual labor of whatever sort. He has not learned Emerson's 'nobility of labor' nor Ruskin's 'duty and love for work.' Apart from intellectual exertion, all labor appears menial to him. The few duties at the camp—none of them irksome or onerous—were shirked and evaded with perplexing regularity."[71] The "discouraging" tone of this report points to the author's fear that the camp's physical activities would not improve the Jewish boy's innate character. The report further echoes this deterministic expectation by overlooking historical explanations for the *Ostjuden*'s antipathy toward the muscular ideal. Cary Goodman claims that in creating their educational policies the German Jewish barons of the EA ignored the "vociferous antagonism" that many eastern European Jews had "towards anything military."[72] This antagonism resulted in part from the forced conscription of Jews in eastern Europe, which had prevented them from practicing their religion. Exemplifying their disregard for historical explanations, the German Jews of the EA supported school and camp programs that relied heavily on a militaristic program of "patriotic songfests, sports meets . . . [and] military drills," as well as weekend camps that were conducted entirely "under National Guard rules and regulations."[73] This report's anxiety about the potential failure of physical activity to improve the *Ostjuden* was in keeping with the new science of genetics.

In contrast to this report's skepticism, other EA materials reveal the institution's adoption of repetitive, embodied training to instill mainstream US values in eastern European Jews. For example, an article from an EA newsletter expresses confidence that physical activity was improving the immigrant Jew's character, and in turn his fitness for citizenship. The headline, "Strong and Healthy Bodies and Ideals of Fair Play Make for Good Citizenship," suggests indirectly that cultural characteristics (like "ideals of fair play") naturally result from a well-cultivated physique.[74] The newsletter's photo collage includes images of Jewish children doing calisthenics in Busby Berkeley–style formations, evidencing the EA's desire to align students with each other through simultaneous movement. Other photos show the children playing basketball and lifting free weights. In one photo, a burly muscular weightlifter—the photo's central figure—is being observed by a group of less muscular but visibly impressed boys who wait their turn on the sidelines. The photo visualizes both identification and competition among the boys. The weightlifter smiles mildly as if he knows he is the center of attention. But the boy to his left waits with a challenging air, as though he believes he can do a better job. While the boys who flank the weightlifter pose in less challenging stances, all three spectators reveal their interest and eager anticipation to be at the center of the action. Somewhat eerily, a thin, lanky boy shadows the weightlifter in the right-hand corner of the frame, as if to say, "I am a shadow of this weightlifter's former self, the un-muscular Yiddish Jew whose body is to be transformed by muscular activity."

Adam Bellow, an EA historian, claims that it was mostly non-Jews who were responsible for attacks on the Jewish physique. The archives, however, demonstrate that German Jews also contributed to this trend. Bellow cites Anglo authors who represent Jewish stereotypes as immune to eradication: for example, sociologist Edward Alsworth Ross wrote in *The Old World in the New* that "on the physical side the Hebrews are the polar opposite of our pioneer breed. Not only are they undersized and weak-muscled, but they shun bodily activity and are exceedingly sensitive to pain."[75] Ross himself refers to an unnamed settlement worker who claimed, "You can't make boy scouts out of the Jews. There's not a troop of them in all New York."[76] Ross inflates the authority of this comment by highlighting its author's profession as a settlement worker; seemingly, he wants his readers to assume that this worker has tried, unsuccessfully, to "make Boy Scouts" out of the Jews. This statement reflects the belief, informed by genetic science, that moral and physical training would do nothing to contradict the Jew's innate inferiority.

In a promotional brochure, the directors of the EA similarly undermine the Jew's innate physical stamina but, in a social Darwinist vein, suggest that their programs can remedy this fault. The directors emphasize the importance of "physical training for our down-town brethren," which ostensibly would improve the immigrant Jew's physique and his future success as a manual laborer.[77] They also express confidence that their programs will counteract the Jew's physiological inferiority: "Our co-religionists are often charged with lack of physical courage and repugnance to physical work. Nothing will more effectually remove this than athletic training. Let a young man develop his body, and he will neither shrink from imaginary danger nor shirk manual work which falls to his lot."[78] This passage reinforces the popular assumption that immigrant Jews were cowardly and averse to hard work; it also proposes a solution that will limit the immigrant Jew's success to the civil sphere of work. In this respect, though the brochure testifies to the directors' belief that education will improve the Jew's abilities, it also justifies their cultivation of a working-class status for the *Ostjuden* by naturalizing the view that "manual work . . . falls to his lot."

At both the EA and the HOA, German Jews instituted regimented military drills, uniform dress codes, and physical fitness activities to realize their vision of a public sphere defined by civic republicanism and economic stratification. These two objectives are embodied in another photo from the EA newsletter discussed earlier. That photo pictures a group of children wearing military uniforms and carrying US flags, under a banner that reads, "The Educational Alliance Commando and Athletic Contest." This kind of military exercise enabled students to acquire bodily dispositions compatible with the objectives of the school and, by extension, the nation. Patriotic symbolism, alongside marching exercises that organized the students' time rhythmically, together trained the student's body to remember the ostensibly nationalistic lessons of organization, focus, and precision. As one might imagine, the cultivation of organized, focused, and precise bodies would also assist in the production of efficient industrial workers.

These materials—as well as this chapter's later analysis of *Levinsky*—evidence Pierre Bourdieu's insight that our "deep-rooted linguistic and muscular patterns of behavior" are subject to manipulation by symbolic power. As Bourdieu argues, habitual practices can objectify social institutions in our bodily *hexis*, a "political mythology realized, embodied, turned into a permanent disposition, a durable way of standing, speaking, walking, and thereby feeling and thinking." In analogous processes, the child learns "to think in (rather than with) the language" while her body "enacts," rather than memorizes or repeats, "the past."[79] Bourdieu's theory suggests that at any moment in one's life a linguistic or muscular pattern can appear suddenly and suspend time, in such a way that the past will appear as vivid and palpable as if it were present. This theory is important for understanding why assimilationist educators employed a methodology incompatible with their aims. An individual's seemingly complete identification with mainstream culture can come undone with the activation of certain phrases, patterns of thought, or habitual movements, which may represent lessons or beliefs the individual acquired under different material and ideological circumstances. As Bourdieu explains, certain uses of the body, even insignificant ones, "are predisposed to serve as 'memory joggers' charged with the [social and class] group's deepest values, its most fundamental 'beliefs.'"[80] Moreover, the culture's deepest values become embodied in children "without their consent or contract"; this results in a situation in which individuals become powerless to resist their function as "depositories of deferred thoughts [and states of mind] that can be triggered off at a distance in space and time."[81] Thus, even if an individual ostensibly has assimilated to US culture, his or her previously formed identity can emerge at any time to belie the appearance of assimilation.[82]

We can observe the process that Bourdieu describes in Maurice Bernstein's unpublished memoir about his childhood at the HOA, "All Still! Life among a Thousand Siblings." Bernstein illustrates how the definition of consent becomes murky when we apply it to orphans, who not only are powerless to refuse but also cannot usually understand the long-term implications of consent. In depicting the imbrication of physical training and patriotism in the institution's weekly military drill, Bernstein emphasizes the complex hierarchy of authority at the school. He explains how the upper-class, German Jewish trustees of the HOA—"rich people . . . [who] came in automobiles with chauffeurs and wore dark or black pin-striped suits and 'stove-pipe' hats"—enjoyed "watching the children play on the field or engaged in military drilling in their khaki uniforms, led by the Band."[83] According to Bernstein, the military drill

> was a major Sunday feature. . . . On those days, after breakfast we
> changed into our khaki drilling uniforms and then lined up in
> company formation on the big field. We obeyed commands given
> by the older boys who were designated as Sergeants, Lieuten-
> ants, and Captains. One of the oldest boys had the distinction of
> being the Major in charge of the whole battalion. Each company
> rehearsed for about an hour. Privates in the ranks carried wooden
> guns, remaindered from the Spanish-American War, with triggers
> that clicked but couldn't fire bullets. The Captains carried blunted
> swords with silver type hilts. The Major had a gold type hilt for his
> sword. Majors and Captains gave the orders and marched proudly.
> At Sunday drilling, after rehearsal time, the Major stood in the
> middle of the field with the troops up before him. At the top of his

voice, he gave orders. . . . The whole "army," well trained, obeyed instantly. Anyone who didn't could expect to be nudged, not always gently, by an officer's sword. Then after a while, came the trooping of the colors, the Pledge of Allegiance and, when the order was given, the Band played "The Stars and Stripes Forever," or another of Sousa's marches. The regiment then marched around the field several times, passing before the Trustees, their guests and all the girls. Officers were proud to be seen strutting, in command.[84]

Bernstein's description suggests that the military drill was geared toward training the orphaned children of eastern European Jews to be physically vigorous, obedient to authority, and patriotically American. This description elaborates the pleasure experienced both by the German spectators and by the children who took a turn being in charge of the other orphans. Allowing the children to discipline each other was one way the school could get students to internalize the value of obedience symbolized by the military drill. Moreover, the spectators' pleasure in observing this patriotic obedience highlights the importance for them of eradicating displays of Jewishness that might appear un-American.

Bernstein's description also recalls how America's imperialist sensibility was intertwined with its anxiety about the immigrant's threat to national unity. The passage cited above represents the military hierarchy being superseded only by the trustees who, standing in metaphorically for the children's parents, look on contentedly while the children parade their obedience. Bernstein's language—his description of being in charge as a "distinction" and of the "strutting" of the "proud" officers—suggests that children who were not in charge probably aspired to be so one day and adapted their behavior accordingly. The symbolic effect of having the students mimic the HOA's institutional authority—which was all the more powerful because it replaced parental authority—was intensified by the students' symbolic use of weapons from the Spanish-American War.[85] In this respect, American patriotism involved identifying with the nation as an imperial force. Authority thus resided in one's ability to command other children while also imagining oneself to be representing the national interest.[86] By metonymically conflating the authority represented by the educational institution, the army, and the nation, Bernstein emphasizes the cultural capital to be gained by adapting oneself to ideals of cleanliness, order, and obedience.[87] As the passage illustrates, one way to relieve anxiety about the immigrant's threat to cultural unity was to stage his transformation into a symbol of the imperialist nation.

Bernstein's depiction of growing up in an orphanage represents an extreme but not quite rare example of assimilationist citizenship education; like American Indian boarding schools, the HOA literally replaced the parental function, which had the effect of intensifying its curriculum. Even in less exaggerated circumstances, however, children of eastern European Jews became alienated from their family, language, and culture as a result of the German Jewish influence. In his autobiographical poem "Early History of a Writer," Charles Reznikoff speculates about this very topic. Though Reznikoff's poetic style is usually minimalist, when he describes the good-bye scene between himself and his grandfather—he is leaving for law school—Reznikoff's minimalism seems perfectly aligned with the point he is trying to make. This scene suggests that an excess of language would be useless to remedy the loss—itself linguistic—that characterizes Reznikoff's attempt to communicate with his grandfather. Reznikoff confesses that because he speaks no Hebrew and only "broken Yiddish" he does not fully understand his grandfather's blessing or the subtleties of their interaction. He bluntly explains, "I did not know what he was saying."[88] After blessing Charles, his grandfather begins crying, prompting Charles to speculate about why his grandfather might feel so sad:

> Perhaps my grandfather was in tears for other reasons:
> perhaps, because, in spite of all the learning I had acquired in high
>   school,
> I knew not a word of the sacred text of the Torah
> and I was going out into the world
> with none of the accumulated wisdom of my people to guide me,
> with no prayers with which to talk to the God of my people, a soul—
> for it is not easy to be a Jew or, perhaps, a man—
> doomed by his ignorance to stumble and blunder.[89]

Of course, Reznikoff does not know why his grandfather is really crying. However, his speculation evokes the irony in the loneliness he feels: the good-bye is not really a good-bye, since language has already distanced Reznikoff from his grandfather.

This passage's shifting punctuation further evokes how assimilation has resulted in Reznikoff's alienation from Jewish tradition. Whereas the stanza's initial lines comprise a flowing sentence, its final lines articulate a series of incomplete thoughts separated by em-dashes. The staccato rhythm created by these dashes mimics the difficulty of walking through the world without the language—and therefore the prayers and wisdom—of Judaism. The speaker suggests that the absence of religion deprives him of a soul, which in turn causes him to doubt whether he is even a Jew. He concludes with an onomatopoetic image of an assimilated American whose linguistic disconnection from tradition dooms him to "stumble and blunder" through the world. This imbalance is intensified by the disconnected syntax of the stanza's last three lines. As this scene illustrates, knowing only English causes Reznikoff to experience an alienation that is at once linguistic, physical, and philosophical.

In another section of this poem, Reznikoff depicts the public school's appeal for the children of immigrants. Stephan Fredman explains that Reznikoff "learned at his mother's insistence to speak only English at home" while he simultaneously underwent Americanization in the New York City public schools.[90] Though Fredman also argues that Reznikoff nursed a lifelong regret about his inadequate command of Jewish culture, this poem recalls Reznikoff's youthful confidence in the possibilities that his public schooling materialized. Reznikoff writes that his high school was situated on "blocks of quiet streets, / shaded by maples, / and the building itself, partly covered with ivy, / was a pleasant, if sober, red brick. / It had seemed to be, when I first saw the building, / that I should be happy there."[91] The image of the school's solid brick foundation is mirrored by the speaker's tale of the solid academic foundation he acquired there, reading and studying authors from Latimer to Donne, from Rosetti and Swinburne to the *Rubaiyat*, and from Ben Jonson to Beattie to Keats.[92] By contrast, as Reznikoff explains in an interview with Reinhold Schiffer, he was disturbed by the Hebrew *cheder*, with its basement location, "unpleasant" and "atrocious" atmosphere, and "terrific turmoil."[93] Despite its positive representation of the public school, this poem also reveals Reznikoff's alienation from both eastern European and German American Jews. The poem's speaker both critiques German Jews' assumptions about their Yiddish-speaking students and distances himself from these students. Departing from the first-person voice in which much of "Early History" is told, the speaker describes the tensions between these groups of Jews:

The school, which had never had more than a few Jews,
suddenly had many—half a class, sometimes, Jewish.
Besides, those who had come in the past
were generally sons of German or Hungarian Jews
who had been in the United States quite a while,

and even before that
had lived in a civilization somewhat like this country's.
The parents of those pupils often had money
and a home in the tree-shaded neighborhood of the school.
But the new boys were, for the most part, children of poor people
who had hardly had time to learn much of the speech and accent of
    the land;
boys with strange and difficult Polish or Russian names,
in ill-fitting clothes and often ill at ease,
who, because of this, were sometimes loud and brash.[94]

This portrait of these students as self-conscious and "ill at ease" suggests that the German Jew's distaste for his coreligionists must have affected their psyches. On the one hand, this passage adopts a distanced, sociological tone to highlight—in Reznikoff's characteristically "Objectivist" fashion—the linguistic and cultural differences at the school.[95] On the other hand, it evokes a Marxist perspective to suggest that the boys might have acted "loud and brash" because they—or their parents—did not have the time or resources to assimilate (a point further bolstered by the reference to "ill-fitting clothes").[96] Reznikoff's absence as a first-person subject in this passage emphasizes his alienation from both German educators and eastern European students. Like the students he describes, Reznikoff carries a strange Russian name; yet, as he explained earlier, he could not understand "the accumulated wisdom of [his] people."[97] Unlike these students, Reznikoff is fluent in "the speech and accent of the land"; at the same time, however, he does not share the educators' negative reactions to the *Ostjuden*.

As this discussion of Reznikoff has suggested, his autobiographical poetry evokes a sadness that is in keeping with the formal attributes of the idealist bildungsroman: the poem's speaker experiences loss in the process of adapting to mainstream US culture but nonetheless accepts the trajectory laid out for him by his parents, the school, and the culture at large. Though "Early History of a Writer" does not explicitly resist the German Jewish educational paradigm, it offers a muted critique of the demand that Jewish children alienate themselves from their language and culture. In thus exposing the exclusionary nature of the assimilative process, the poem participates in the tradition of the dissensual bildungsroman, as Joseph Slaughter has defined it and as the introduction of this book illustrates. By contrast, the next section of this chapter emphasizes Abraham Cahan's evocation of both unconscious and conscious resistance to assimilation, in the manner of the dissensual bildungsroman.

Assimilation and Critique in *Levinsky* and *The Education*

In an April 19, 1919, article for *Forverts* (*Jewish Daily Forward*), the Yiddish poet Abrom Liessen argued that assimilation, particularly through English education, weakened the immigrant child's commitment to family and community: "Why do they not feel their obligation to the poor? . . . Something has gone wrong in the American [public] school . . . that rends a terrible tear in the Jewish soul. . . . It touches and destroys the foundations of that which is the holiest and most beautiful in our long-suffering Jewish life: the Jewish family. In those schools our children have become estranged from us, and we are separated by an abyss of the soul."[98] Like Liessen, many Yiddish-speaking Jews critiqued the assimilation programs promoted by educational institutions such as the EA and HOA. These Jews not only developed a rich cultural life on US soil—through lectures and union activities, as well as Yiddish-language newspapers and literary texts—but also sent their children to camps and after-school programs that taught Yiddish. They did so with the hope of instilling both a radical political sensibility and a secular Jewish identity in their children, which ostensibly would serve as an antidote to the negative effects of assimilation. Through this Yiddish secular school movement, leftist activists sought to "bridge the deep and painful separation between children and their immigrant parents, which resulted from a language conflict between the students' English and their parents' Yiddish, as well as from the culture clash that developed when children began to feel more secure in their new homelands."[99]

The mass migration of eastern European Jewish radicals to New York City beginning in the 1880s resulted in the proliferation of socialist and Zionist newspapers in Yiddish. While anti-Semitism in eastern Europe had relegated Yiddish to the home, in the United States the language was a basis for cultural and political community among immigrants. Though Cahan claims he was bothered both by the "Yiddish of American-born children" and by "the Americanized Yiddish of the immigrants, studded with English expressions," he also applauds himself for starting a socialist paper "written in the simplest Yiddish so that even the most uneducated worker could understand it."[100] In fact, describing how Yiddish served new purposes in the United States, Cahan suggests that it took on a distinctly American quality.[101] Nonetheless, Cahan's Russian-speaking comrades ridiculed his attempts to revive Yiddish in a US context; when he proposed to make socialist speeches in Yiddish so he could reach a wider audience, Cahan recalls, "All who were standing around us laughed. Yiddish, they thought, was suitable for daily talk at home, in the *cheder*, or while bargaining with a Jewish merchant. But the idea that one could make a serious political speech in this homey language seemed comical to them."[102] Not only did Cahan make speeches in Yiddish, but he also defended the language and "showed how racy and powerful it could be and how it lent itself to the most subtle and delicate thoughts."[103]

Cahan also saw the potential for *Yiddishkeit* to reform the spiritual emptiness of US capitalist culture. When in 1897 Cahan became editor of the *Jewish Daily Forward* (*Forverts*), he transformed it into an organ that would unite the Jewish immigrant community.[104] The *Forward* was a Yiddish-language weekly whose function was to circulate a socialist sensibility among working-class Jews.[105] Alongside his journalism and speech making, Cahan wrote a Yiddish-language autobiography, *The Education of Abraham Cahan*, which validates the humanitarian, communitarian, and anticapitalist values that were central to Yiddish culture.[106] The *Education* also dramatizes the multiple allegiances, languages, and practices that informed Cahan's experience of US citizenship. It illustrates his ability to move fluidly between Yiddish, Russian, and English and shows how these languages represent different aspects of his identity. By dramatizing the simultaneous presence of these languages (and their respective cultures) in his life, Cahan rejects an assimilationist paradigm that defines successful Americanization in English-only terms. This simultaneity also recalls Jonathan Hansen's concept of "overlapping affinities," which not only characterizes the personas of Addams and Du Bois, as chapter 3 illustrates, but also informs the identities of Cahan and his fictional avatar Levinsky.

Juxtaposing *Levinsky* with *The Education* highlights *Levinsky*'s challenge to the myth of middle-class superiority and the assumption that successful immigrants would remain satisfied with subpar economic prospects. In the novel, David Levinsky goes from being an unemployed, Yiddish-speaking immigrant to a financially successful businessman as a result of his innovations within the garment industry. Nonetheless, the capitalist values that Levinsky acquires leave him spiritually bereft. Despite his financial success, Levinsky is plagued by a sense of loss, both for an older self that was centered in Orthodox religious practice and for a leftist political community that he cannot join because of his status as a capitalist. In this respect, the novel represents the Yiddish immigrant's uneasy adoption of nationalist structures of belonging. Not only is Levinsky haunted by a simultaneous distaste and desire for Yiddish culture, but also his assimilation to mainstream US life is undermined by the linguistic habits and gestures that persist as irreducible aspects of his Yiddish self. (This "Yiddish" identity developed from Levinsky's immersion in the culture and religion of Yiddish-speaking Jews; it is not, as the racist science of the day would suggest, a product of biology.) Thus, even though on the surface Levinsky embraces American capitalist attitudes and a secular nationalist identity, as the novel's first-person narrator Levinsky ultimately concludes that his assimilation has been unfruitful.

Levinsky is pained by the embodied persistence of his Yiddish identity, and Cahan employs this persistence to question the assimilationist model of citizenship. Even though the novel tracks Levinsky's transformation from a Russian yeshiva student to a successful American capitalist, its conclusion belies this development as Levinsky confesses that his inner self remains that of a Talmudic scholar: "I cannot escape from my old self. My past and my present do not comport well. David, the poor lad swinging over a Talmudic volume at the Preacher's Synagogue, seems to have more in common with my inner identity than David Levinsky, the well-known cloak manufacturer."[107] With this passage, placed at the very end of the novel, Levinsky finally admits that his adopted identity as an American businessman constitutes only a temporary and unstable layer of his self, whose buried characteristics reemerge with the invocation of certain words and gestures. Because Levinsky's earlier self materializes in his language and gestures—the twinned categories through which he exerts agency—Levinsky's assimilation becomes an impossible task.

The novel's location of identity in language and movement emerges as Levinsky recalls the repetitive and systematic features of his religious upbringing. As a youth in Antomir, Russia, Levinsky spent most of his time at the yeshiva. From "nine in the morning until bedtime every day, and an all-night vigil every Thursday," he stood "at a gaunt reading-desk, swaying to and fro over some huge volume, reading its ancient text and interpreting it in Yiddish" (43). Levinsky studied regularly with an older Talmudic scholar, Reb Sender, who, "as he read and interpreted the text . . . would wave his snuff-box, by way of punctuating and emphasizing his words, much as the conductor of an orchestra does his baton" (28). Levinsky explains that "one cannot read Talmud without gesticulating" (30), but he also admits that the habits he acquired during his Talmud study reappear even years after he has abandoned his religious practice: "[A] trace [of that experience] still persists in my intonation even when I talk cloaks and bank accounts in English" (28).

By the end of the novel, Levinsky is living as a wealthy, American-ized businessman who belongs to a "fashionable" German synagogue and has abandoned any pretense to religiosity (528). Moreover, Levin-sky has embraced a social Darwinist perspective; he writes, "I had no creed. I knew of no ideals. The only thing I believed in was the cold, drab theory of the struggle for existence and the survival of the fittest" (380). Despite this claim, Levinsky's old self haunts him; its reappear-ance not only undermines his public persona but also belies the linear narrative of progress through which he has portrayed his development. In this respect, the novel varies from the idealist bildungsroman. It inter-rupts a narrative that tracks Levinsky's increasingly seamless adaptation to US culture. In place of this narrative, the novel features moments in which Levinsky's gestures and linguistic habits testify to the living his-tory that has made an indelible mark on his consciousness. In a dream-like moment symbolized by the wavering flame of a candle, Levinsky describes how mental images of his childhood "took possession" of him: "[The images] turned my present life into a dream and my Russian past into a reality" (389). Levinsky's use of *possession* here emphasizes the involuntary nature of historical memory; his depiction of the memory as a dream calls attention to the warping of time that happens when the past inhabits our minds and bodies.

It is not only in such dreamlike moments that Levinsky's Old World self emerges; elsewhere he flatly attributes his economic success to his Russian Jewish sensibility. Levinsky explains that though the German Jews "were of a superior commercial civilization" (201), the "Yiddish-speaking immigrants from Russia or Austrian Galicia" were bound to be more successful because the "Russian competitor was a tailor or cloak-operator himself, and was, therefore, able to economize in ways that never occurred to the heads of the old houses" (337). In attributing his success to a Russian/Jewish habit of mind, Levinsky again reminds us of the instability, or perhaps artificiality, of his studiously acquired American identity. No matter how badly Levinsky desires to shed all evi-dence of his former self, it persists as a part of him because it developed before he was able to adopt an identity through "consent or contract."[108] Levinsky's gestures and linguistic tics are like living fossils of the past, which collapse space and time when invoked. These seemingly innocu-ous moments or slips of the tongue are like fault lines that destabilize the narrative of development that Levinsky desperately wants to follow.

Aware of this instability, Levinsky confesses his need to use the ges-tures associated with English. With this objective in mind, Levinsky attends a public evening class taught by a Jew of German descent whom he simultaneously dislikes and slavishly imitates: "I would hang on his lips, striving to memorize every English enunciation, but also his gestures, manners, and mannerisms, and accepting it all as part and parcel of the American way of speaking" (129). Levinsky stresses how important it is for him to abandon his habitual manner of moving, because, as he opines, "One can tell the nationality of a stranger by his gestures as readily as by his language. In a vague, general way I had become aware of this before, probably from contact with some American-born Jews whose gesticulations, when they spoke Yiddish, impressed me as utterly un-Yiddish" (129–30). This comparison calls attention to the artificiality that accompanies any individual's attempt to adopt a new set of cultural practices, not just those trying to become "Americans." This comment also testifies to the influence of Cahan's own experience on the novel, for his autobiography similarly thematizes the centrality of gesture to language. In *The Education*, Cahan explains that when he first arrived in the United States he could not understand the gestures of a trolley conductor: "Unfortunately his gestures seemed strange to me, for the gesture of an American has an 'accent' that makes it different from the same kind of gesture by a Jew in Vilna."[109]

For Levinsky, failure to adopt the gestures of English, as well as certain slang phrases, makes him feel physically defective. In the following passage, Levinsky reveals his perception that verbal inadequacy marks his body:

> If I heard a bit of business rhetoric that I thought effective I would jot it down and commit it to memory. In like manner I would write down every new piece of slang. . . . The Americans I met were so quick to discern and adopt these phrases it seemed as if they were born with a special slang sense which I, poor foreigner that I was, lacked. That I was not born in America was something like a physical defect that asserted itself in so many disagreeable ways—a physical defect which, alas! no surgeon in the world was capable of removing. (291)

Describing his language difficulties synesthetically, as visible markers, Levinsky recalls the means by which Yiddish (even as a residue in accent and gesture) served as a locus for the racialization of the Jew's body.[110]

A similar inability to disguise or repudiate markers of his former self characterizes Cahan's self-description in *The Education*. In this autobiography, the young Cahan seems to believe that the performative nature of identity will allow him to move easily between different public personas that he adopts while trying to escape the country. Cahan finds himself on the run from the Russian police because they have discovered his association with nihilist revolutionaries who assassinated Tsar Alexander II. To avoid detection, Cahan disguises himself as a yeshiva Jew: "I put an ordinary cheap hat on my head and twisted two strands of hair down the side of my face, making them look like the sidelocks of a pious Jew." Fearing discovery by the family with whom he is taking shelter, he writes, "I checked out the details of my identity. My trousers were properly tucked into my boots, my scarf was around my neck, I reached under my old hat and gave my sidelocks a few extra twists, for by this time I had cut my hair so as to have real sidelocks. I had pangs of remorse every time I contemplated myself in the mirror because I had come to look like a real yeshiva boy."[111]

Yet Cahan's attempt to mimic an Orthodox persona fails when a stranger recognizes the signs of a university education in his demeanor. An older man, who wants Cahan to watch over his son on the trip to America, lowers his voice and explains, "'I assume you're going to America. . . . So is my son.' Then he dropped his voice lower. 'He's a high school student. You are probably a university student yourself. I beg you, take care of my son on the way to America.'" Cahan confesses, "It came to me as an unpleasant shock that despite my hat and my sidelocks he guessed so easily that I was 'probably a university student.'"[112] Notwithstanding the visual exactitude of his disguise, Cahan does not come across as a yeshiva student, presumably because his gestural language, immune to disguise, has exposed his embodied identity.[113] Just as Cahan fails to disguise himself, the German Jewish educators who sought to transform the identities of the *Ostjuden* through embodied training must have encountered resistance in their students' already-formed habits of gesture and thought.[114]

Levinsky evokes the psychological complexity of the *Ostjuden's* desire to exchange visible signs of his foreignness for an assimilationist identity shaped by the German Jew. Levinsky is happy to have learned English in classes funded and taught by German Jews, but he also explains that he dislikes the German Jew's affect and prejudice. As a cloak manufacturer and salesman, Levinsky encounters elite German Jewish businessmen on the job. Levinsky's depiction of the German Jewish sensibility becomes increasingly negative as he becomes more successful financially, culminating in his representation of a self-hating Jew named Loeb.

One of the bitterest encounters between Levinsky and Loeb occurs when Levinsky is attempting to emulate the American habits of his

fellow train passengers, a scene that highlights Levinsky's internalization of embodied inferiority: "I would watch American smokers and
study their ways, as though there were a special American manner of
smoking and such a thing as smoking with a foreign accent. . . . There
seemed to be a special elegance in a smoker taking a newly lighted cigar
out of his mouth and throwing a glance at its glowing end to see if it was
smoking well. Accordingly, I never did so without being conscious of
my gestures and trying to make them as 'American' as possible" (326).
Here as earlier, Levinsky's use of synesthesia to describe gesture and
language—"smoking with a foreign accent"—points to the simultaneity
of these two registers in forming and maintaining identity. Loeb mocks
Levinsky's attempt to imitate "American" gestures and ridicules the
obviousness and inescapability of his "Talmudic gesticulations" (327).
Loeb is correct in assuming that his barb will affect Levinsky, who confesses to the reader, "My . . . gesticulations worried me like a physical
defect. It was so distressingly un-American. I struggled hard against it.
I had made efforts to speak with my hands in my pockets; I had devised
other means for keeping them from participating in my speech. All of
no avail" (327). In an article about this novel, Phillip Barrish suggests
that Levinsky depicts the materiality of his body (like his gestures in
this scene) as constructions from which he distances his assimilated and
Americanized self in order to attain cultural distinction.[115] However,
when Barrish suggests that Levinsky manipulates his lapses into an older
self to bolster his cultural capital, Barrish assumes that Levinsky can
control his embodied memories. On the contrary, it seems that Levinsky's embodied memories resist his attempts to repress or manipulate
them and that in this respect they undermine his efforts to embellish the
superiority of his American self.[116]

In the scene above, Levinsky is unable to resignify his embarrassing
gestures because Loeb witnesses and mocks him. Through his loud and
ruthless provocation, Loeb seems to be overcompensating for an internalized shame over the ethnic heritage he shares with Levinsky. Loeb
further repudiates this kinship by extending his attack on Levinsky,
telling a series of nasty jokes about Yiddish Jews who refuse to speak
in situations where they cannot also gesticulate.[117] After hearing these
jokes, Levinsky asks Loeb if he isn't himself Jewish, and Loeb responds,
"Of course I am . . . and a good one too. I am a member of a synagogue"
(328). Here Loeb points to the choice he has been able to make, as an
American-born Jew, about the forms through which he expresses his
Jewishness. Being Jewish is something he can "put on" when he goes to

synagogue and hide when he is in the world of business; it is a set of practices rather than an embodied extension of his self. (In this case, there is no need to rely on synesthesia to evoke the embodiment of accent.) Levinsky, on the other hand, is racialized on account of gestures that he cannot abandon even after serious effort. Levinsky, caught between his desire to emulate German Jews and his discomfort about this desire, "laughed with the others, but . . . felt like a cripple who is forced to make fun of his own deformity" (328). While this scene stereotypes Levinsky by figuring him in terms of an unpleasant physical appearance coded as Jewish, he nonetheless soothes himself with the comfort of knowing that his experience as a laborer and his Russian sensibility have enabled him to succeed as a businessman. In a moment of poetic justice later in the novel, Levinsky discovers that Loeb has lost his job because the cloak industry "was now in the hand of [Russian Jews] . . . some of whom were Talmudic scholars like [Levinsky]" (372).

Late in the novel, Levinsky testifies to his increasing Americanization by explaining that he has joined a Reform synagogue. As a result of his membership, Levinsky has come to associate socially with German Jews, and he expresses pride about his membership in their community:

> Most of the people at my hotel are German-American Jews. I know other Jews of this class. I contribute to their charity institutions. Though an atheist, I belong to one of their synagogues. . . . I am a member of that synagogue chiefly because it is a fashionable synagogue. I often convict myself of currying favor with the German Jews. But then German-American Jews curry favor with the Portuguese-American Jews, just as we all curry favor with Gentiles and as American Gentiles curry favor with the aristocracy of Europe. (528)

This passage's boastful tone reveals that Levinsky has come to embody some of the shallow motivations he critiqued earlier in the text, even though he simultaneously "convict[s]" himself for the practice. Moreover, he has lost contact with the people in his life who used to offer him real spiritual satisfaction; not coincidentally, these people were members of the two groups, Orthodox Jews and political radicals, that German Jews considered a threat to their assimilated status.

Levinsky's loss is captured by his two descriptions of the New York synagogue attended by Jews from his hometown of Antomir. When he first arrived in America, Levinsky went regularly to this synagogue: "This would bring my heart in touch with my old home, with dear old Reb Sender, with the grave of my poor mother. . . . At times I would feel the tears coming to my eyes for the sheer joy of hearing my own sing-song, my old Antomir singsong. . . . My former self was addressing me from across the sea in this strange, uninviting, big town where I was compelled to peddle shoe-black or oilcloth and to compete with a yelling idiot" (109). During these visits, music, movement, and prayer temporarily dissolve the time and space that distance Levinsky from his origins, while they also relieve him temporarily from his economic worries.

At the same time, this scene foreshadows the inevitability of Levinsky's secular transformation. Looking back on his early visit to the synagogue, Levinsky explains,

> The orthodox Jewish faith, as it is followed in the old Ghetto towns of Russia or Austria . . . is absolutely inflexible. If you are a Jew of the type to which I belonged when I came to New York and you attempt to bend your religion to the spirit of your new surroundings, it breaks. It falls to pieces. The very clothes I wore and the very food I ate had a fatal effect on my religious habits. A whole book could be written on the influence of a starched collar and a necktie on a man who was brought up as I was. (110)

In this passage, clothing not only symbolizes the transformation of the visible self but also participates in transforming the self. The "fatal" effect that clothes and food had on Levinsky's religious identity was to eradicate it. Nevertheless, the novel's conclusion reveals that Levinsky's adopted lifestyle, along with its accompanying belief system, is as changeable as the clothing he uses to symbolize it.

Levinsky's second description of Antomir's New York synagogue evokes the spiritual emptiness that has marked his Americanization. Levinsky, now an atheist who has shaved his beard, aligns his spiritual emptiness with the synagogue's new location, a former Presbyterian church that makes him uncomfortable: "The place reminded me of a reformed German synagogue rather than of the kind with which my idea of Judaism had always been identified. This seemed to accentuate the fact that the building had until recently been a Christian church. The glaring electric lights and the glittering decorations struck me as something unholy" (388). The clash between belief and architecture that Levinsky describes symbolizes the incompatibility between the inner self and the normative structures of belonging required by civic republicanism. Like the Protestant church, the assimilationist narrative fits awkwardly over the Jewish immigrant's embodied identity, which is marked by history.

As he continues to describe this second visit to the synagogue, Levinsky further reveals the artificial spirituality he has come to inhabit. At first he ruminates on how a candle flame in the temple invokes his Russian self, turning his "present life in to a dream and [his] Russian past into a reality." Yet he abruptly interrupts this reverie to exclaim, "Thank God, mother dear! I own a large factory. I am a rich man and I am going to be married to the daughter of a fine Jew, a man of substance and Talmud" (389). No longer a man who studies the Talmud himself, Levinsky still prides himself on associating with a religious man. It seems he has come to believe that the value of one's religion lies in its recognition by others rather than in the practices and values it inspires.

In the first of these parallel scenes at the synagogue, Levinsky invoked the candle flame to symbolize his religious and Russian identities; in the second scene, the flame comes to represent Levinsky's pride in his material wealth (389). Later in the novel, the image of the candle flame returns to figure Levinsky's irrational attraction to Anna Tevkin, a woman whom he loves in spite of her leftist politics. Levinsky repeatedly has described his contempt for the "socialism, anarchism, and trade unionism" of the intellectual Lower East Side as "something sinister, absurd, and uncouth" (410). Yet despite his ostensible dread for the socialist world of the Tevkin house—and Miss Tevkin herself—Levinsky confesses, "Moth-like, I was drawn to the flame with greater and greater force. I went to the Tevkins' with the feeling of one going to his doom" (469). When he described his second visit to the synagogue, Levinsky recalled how the nebulous candle flame momentarily froze his inevitable path toward spiritual emptiness. In the Tevkin scene, the flame symbolizes a similar aporia: it evokes the irresistible yet forbidden possibility of spiritual fulfillment, represented in this case by the idea of marrying Anna Tevkin. Levinsky harbors an almost tragic confidence that he ultimately will find fulfillment in the one world from which he has been barred because he has chosen to live and identify as a capitalist. Ultimately, however, the novel concludes that spiritual fulfillment is impossible because it relies on the unstable categories of memory and desire.

The Tevkin scene also echoes the second synagogue visit in that both scenes represent spiritual fulfillment and material success as mutually exclusive objectives. Levinsky describes going to the Tevkins' as going to his doom, probably because these visits recall the spiritual dissatisfaction that has accompanied his financial success. Levinsky depicts his attraction to Anna Tevkin as a metaphor for the irresistible yet ultimately unsatisfying attraction of his success. He draws a parallel between his obsession with Anna and his irresponsible financial speculations when he explains, "I was literally intoxicated by my new interests, and the fact that they were intimately associated with the atmosphere of Anna's home had much—perhaps everything—to do with it" (482). With this statement, Levinsky suggests that it is only in an intoxicated state that he can hope for Anna to requite his love; yet this intoxication results from and symbolizes Levinsky's risky, and therefore untenable, financial activities. Confessing that his "gambling mania was really the aberration of a love-maddened brain" (484), Levinsky expresses awareness that the at-homeness he hopes to find at the Tevkins' home is incompatible with the stable financial status he has acquired through hard work and is unwilling to give up. The metonymical linkage of Levinsky's "gambling mania" and "love-maddened brain" suggest that the Tevkin home can only ever represent an unsustainable deviation from the normative path Levinsky has chosen to follow.

Levinsky concludes that there is no relief for the unhappiness that he also shares with other wealthy men of his acquaintance. One of these men, Levinsky tells us, has come to the wistful conclusion that all the luxuries his money could buy would not equal "one spoon of [his] wife's cabbage soup" or "the bread cider [his] mother used to make" (484). In other words, cabbage soup and bread cider symbolize a set of homey experiences that are incompatible with the demands of assimilation. Like these men, Levinsky longs for the impossible; he thinks he sees it in Anna, but even their simplest conversations are held as "through a thick window-pane" (480); though the window is inviting, its opacity represents the unbridgeable distance between them. In this respect, Levinsky's pursuit of spiritual fulfillment through Anna makes perfect sense; he knows that spiritual satisfaction and marriage to Anna are equally impossible. Because he decides that Anna is the only wife he will accept, Levinsky's story cannot end—as a more conventional bildungsroman might—in marriage. Instead of marriage, Levinsky's tale ends with disappointment and silence. After being rejected by Anna and recovering his fortune—which had been threatened temporarily by his risky financial speculations—Levinsky confesses that his "sense of triumph" at being Americanized was accompanied by "a brooding sense of emptiness and insignificance" (526). As if to say that Levinsky's success is incompatible with community, the novel parallels the noise of this success—"the pandemonium of [his] six hundred sewing-machines"—with the "deadly silence of solitude" (526).

Abraham Cahan's autobiography, on the other hand, represents the memory of home, and of Yiddish, as an antidote to the homesickness and alienation Cahan sometimes experienced in America. In *The Education*, Cahan confesses that he can make himself feel at home by singing or writing in Yiddish. This is an effect of Cahan's cosmopolitan sensibility; unlike Levinsky, Cahan does not envision Americanization as the replacement of an older identity with a newer one. Cahan speaks and thinks in Yiddish and Russian—the languages of his childhood—and learns English (so well that he can teach it) after he immigrates to the United States. In *The Education*, Cahan explains that he realizes different aspects of his self through different languages. "Russian," he tells us, "was the language of my intellectual self." Yiddish, on the other hand, is the language of home: "Oh, how pleasant it was to write home! I wrote frequently and at great length. I wrote in Yiddish."[118] Yiddish seems to have a cathartic impact on Cahan. When homesick, he feels better only after writing a letter home in Yiddish. Not only does Cahan feel more at home in Yiddish, but by writing positively about America in Yiddish he is able to interpret his difficult experiences as fruitful ones.

Cahan depicts the happy coexistence of his Russian and Yiddish identities by confessing that when he felt sad he "would walk the streets humming one of the prayer melodies I had heard my father sing. Or suddenly, I was singing one of the [Russian] folk songs I had learned at the Vilna Teacher's Institute." Both sets of songs relieve his loneliness, but in different registers. As Cahan explains, "Russian folk songs are filled with the poetry of sad loneliness. They sing of the broad fields and the high heavens, and the mixture of sadness and grandeur had stuck deep roots in my heart. My father's songs lacked the poetry and folk quality of the village songs. But then, they had a quality far more precious. They were the songs I could still hear my father singing."[119] Cahan describes his experience of Russian songs as both embodied (they are rooted in his heart) and intellectual (his enjoyment of them derives from his rumination on their poetic qualities). In this latter sense, the pleasure Cahan takes in the Russian songs seems tied to the linear, discursive structure he uses to analyze their likable qualities. Conversely, he recalls his father's Yiddish songs as emotional memories. Like Levinsky listening to the Antomir sing-song, Cahan can hear his father singing, but in such a manner that it stops the flow of time for him. Cahan explains that he knows the songs are precious but cannot say why. In other words, Cahan cannot translate this experience into a temporal register that would allow him to offer a rational explanation for why the prayers soothe him. This pleasure is unspeakable because it comes from memories that are not primarily linguistic. Rather, Cahan remembers how the songs made his body feel.[120]

In this respect, *The Education* is like *Levinsky*: they both illustrate how embodied memories collapse time and provide an alternative to a concept of identity understood in teleological terms.

Voices from the Archives: A Conclusion

The Jewish educational archives house recollections from children who lived at the HOA, as well as letters from Jewish immigrants who attended classes at the EA's Baron de Hirsch Trade School. On the whole, these narratives offer positive accounts of assimilation, and—in the vein of Charles Eastman's *Deep Woods*—bury their authors' critiques of citizenship education beneath articulations of praise for these institutions and expressions of satisfied belonging to mainstream US culture. At the same time, these materials echo David Levinsky's awareness not only that assimilation is accompanied by embodied shame but also that mainstream US culture is marked by unavoidable class stratification.

In "All Still!," Maurice Bernstein explains that in the 1930s, when he was working toward a degree in social work, he attempted to conduct one hundred interviews with ex-inmates of the HOA. Even though he claims to have stopped after twelve and subsequently lost the manuscripts, the interviews remained vivid for him. Bernstein recalls, "Some of the alumni, when interviewed, would begin with praise of the institutional regime. . . . 'The Home made a man of me.' . . . 'The discipline was what I needed.' . . . However, when [I] probed more deeply, they would elaborate on the cruelty of Captains and Monitors, the beatings they had been given by those in charge, sometimes at the hands of the Colonel. Then, as the interview was ending, they would revert to the initial praise of the discipline."[121] Unlike the activities of marching and athletics that appear in accounts of citizenship education promoted by German Jews, Bernstein's discussion points to the embodiment of pain that accompanied assimilation. However, Bernstein uncovered these painful memories only when he "probed more deeply." The former HOA residents structure their memories with frames that allow them to screen out their more negative recollections; these frameworks, and the phrases the inmates use to describe their experiences, echo the institution's ideology.

This type of narrative structure informs Emanuel Weinstock's recollections of his 1917 residency at the HOA. Weinstock tells of the "silk hat, wealthy European Jews, with lots of conscience," who funded the HOA and insists that he does not "have any inclination to belittle or degrade or demean the efforts of all these people. It was all very noble." Weinstock continues, "And the bottom line on it is that I came out with a profession." Yet Weinstock goes on to confess that HOA authorities "would, excuse the expression, beat your God damned brains out if you didn't toe the mark."[122] Ironically, Weinstock expresses a solicitous concern to protect the very people who apparently belittled and seem to have abused him. This may signal Weinstock's denial of trauma, but it also suggests that he has identified so deeply with the ideal represented by his German Jewish benefactors that degrading them, even in memory, would be akin to degrading himself.

As he continues to recall life at the HOA, Weinstock confesses that even though the school helped him succeed, it punished inadequate performance quite severely. Weinstock praises the "athletics . . . orchestra, glee club and band" at the orphanage and the fact that attending the HOA enabled him to go to college.[123] But he also recollects the beatings students would get if they did not do their (inanely repetitive) chores properly: "We had all kinds of . . . bed fixing lessons . . . where they would turn over about 25 or 30 beds and you had to make them . . . again. And they came around, and if there was a wrinkle on top they'd spill all 30 of them . . . so they'd make you do a whole afternoon of that. You know. Until we got tired. And if you opened your mouth or if you talked back to anybody, you'd get your mouth smashed in."[124] Despite this evidence of how the HOA micromanaged children's bodies by alternating repetitive work activities with corporal punishment for disobedience, Weinstock stresses how grateful he is to the HOA. He explains that the institution made it possible for him to have a "remunerative profession"; he even offers excuses for its use of corporal punishment, justifying the abuse by stating, "Taking care of 1200 kids has to be a pretty big chore."[125]

As these passages demonstrate, Weinstock provides a narrative justification for the embodied pain that accompanied his citizenship education at the HOA. He also offers a violent symbol of the literal injunction to silence when he says that you would "get your mouth smashed in" if you "opened your mouth" or "talked back to anybody." This literal prohibition against complaint at the HOA seems to inform the narrative elisions and denials that mark Weinstock's recollections. Weinstock comments on this phenomenon when he explains to his interviewer, "Some of the things I spoke about are . . . very difficult to speak about, because no one can have total recall. I can only give you impressions."[126] Weinstock's partial impression of the difficult experiences he underwent leaves us to imagine how difficult life might really have been for him on a day-to-day basis at the HOA.

Like Weinstock, former vocational students at the Baron de Hirsch Trade School frame their complaints with expressions of appreciation.

In their letters, these students praise their vocational training in abstract terms that echo the American rhetoric of success but simultaneously reveal how inadequate their training actually was.[127] In one such letter, dated October 11, 1913, David Gordon addressed the school's superintendent, Ernest Yalden. In the letter, Gordon explains that though he was working as a plumber's helper, it was only "theoretically" that he was "turned out a good plumber (to a certain extent)"; in fact, Gordon writes, he lacked a "profound knowledge of the trade."[128] Nonetheless, Gordon concludes his letter by announcing, "The Baron de Hirsch Trade School is a great factor in helping to make out of almost unproductive people honest workingmen and good mechanics."[129] Though Gordon has offered evidence of the school's failure to provide him with the vocational training that would ensure his success, he asserts that the institution was successful at providing such training. Gordon's juxtaposition of the details of his own case with abstract praise for the institution recalls Charles Eastman's adoption of this very technique. It is difficult to say definitively why Gordon uses this narrative structure. Perhaps it evidences his internalization of the idea that "productiveness" was a desirable ideal that eastern European Jews did not embody naturally. Or it might simply represent Gordon's strategic invocation of the narrative demand to represent his experience through the lens of the dominant educational ideology.[130]

The next chapter examines the libertarian Modern School through which politically radical Jews in New York City provided an alternative to the dominant form of Jewish immigrant education that this chapter has represented. Though the Modern School was small, it represents a unique trend in the history of US citizenship education. Unlike the institutions previously discussed in this book, Modern School educators fully realized the child-centered ideal of progressive education envisioned by Pestalozzi and Froebel, interpreting it even more radically than John Dewey had done. As chapter 5 demonstrates, Modern School educators were unswayed by the social Darwinist or genetic ideologies that influenced the majority of citizenship educators at the turn of the twentieth century. Chapter 5 also argues that the autobiography of one Modern School educator, Emma Goldman, models an educational path that refuses to confine the individual's development to the overarching structure of the bildungsroman.

5 / Emma Goldman, the Modern School, and the Politics of Reproduction

Emma Goldman begins her autobiography, *Living My Life* (1931), not with the story of her childhood in Russia or her immigration to the United States but rather with the tale of her dramatic exodus from a traditional Jewish marriage at the age of twenty. Announcing that her "entire possessions consisted of five dollars and a small hand-bag," Goldman calls attention to the economic instability that results from leaving her husband.[1] Yet she also suggests that her life need not climax or dead-end in marriage. In fact, her life only really begins once she is able to leave the marriage. Not only does Goldman refuse to remarry throughout her life, but she also resists inner urges and outside pressures to have children.

In the autobiography, Goldman offers two competing explanations for why she never had children: physical inability (due to what she thinks is an inverted womb) and the incompatibility of motherhood with her political goals. Goldman confesses that she has refused an operation that would have enabled her to have children and be free from physical pain. The text's confused presentation of this issue raises the question of whether Goldman has refused the operation because she is attached to her physical pain or perhaps is dependent on the psychological pain that occupies her childhood memories and her ailing body. Though Goldman repeatedly aligns her pain with inescapable memories of childhood abuse, her refusal to have the operation ultimately reads as a feminist objection to being defined by her biology. As a feminist, Goldman also lobbied on behalf of the birth control movement, remained unwilling to marry a series of men whom she loved but discovered to be antifeminist, and, at one point in her life, simultaneously cohabited with two lovers because each fulfilled a different need for her. Together, these choices emblematize Goldman's queering of the traditional family.

As this chapter demonstrates, Goldman's queer politics of reproduction not only shapes the formal structure of her autobiography but also informed her educational activism. In Joseph Slaughter's terms, *Living My Life* is an antibildungsroman: by rejecting oppressive family structures, it displays Goldman's refusal to be incorporated into a "deformed and insular" society.[2] Not only does Goldman's autobiography object to a narrative of success defined by marriage and motherhood, but her political activism challenged the reproductive ideology that informed the education of new US citizens. In part, Goldman realized this latter goal by helping to envision, establish, and fund the Modern School of New York (later of Stelton, New Jersey), a libertarian educational experiment that spanned the years 1911 to 1953.[3] As this chapter's archival analysis illustrates, the Modern School queered reproductive education, replacing the traditional family-school dyad with a community that enacted leftist ideals about education and citizenship for working-class immigrants. Modern School educators instituted progressive educational practices untainted by social Darwinist ideas and in so doing rejected civic republican and assimilationist ideologies. Viewed in the context of the Modern School archives, *Living My Life* reads as a form of curriculum itself: an example of the educational path Goldman envisioned for new citizens, which did not limit individual development to the narrative confines imagined by the bildungsroman.

The Libertarian Ideal: Cultivating Freedom at the Modern School

Emma Goldman, along with Alexander Berkman and other associates of the Ferrer Center of New York, founded and funded the first and longest-lived of the US-based Modern Schools.[4] As Alice Wexler writes, "Goldman played a critical role in the early stages of the Ferrer Center and School. She publicized it on her 1910 lecture tour and recruited financial backers such as Alden Freeman and Gilbert Roe and teachers such as Robert Henri and Bayard Boyesen."[5] The school was initially influenced by, but did not exclusively adopt, the ideas of the Spanish anarchist and educator Francisco Ferrer.[6] From its original location at the Ferrer Center of New York City, the Modern School sought to provide a leftist alternative to public school education for the city's working-class immigrant children.[7] Once it moved to Stelton, it became a combined intentional community and school. Though teacher turnover was high, over time the school developed a libertarian philosophy of education that it publicized in the *Modern School* magazine (1912–22).[8]

The magazine, which was printed on the school's own press, featured essays, speeches, and symposia transcripts in which Modern School educators articulated a libertarian resistance to associating the school with a particular set of beliefs or practices. Nonetheless, their comments evoke a shared commitment to individual freedom and social change. In the "Symposium on Libertarian Education" held at the school, Leonard Abbot announced the school's antipathy to any particular ideology: "While its 'tone' is radical, while its background is Anarchism, Syndicalism, Free Thought, [libertarian education] does not teach any set of doctrines authoritatively or exclusively."[9] William Thurston Brown, an early principal at Stelton, also argued that libertarian education could not "be reduced to a formula"; rather, it was "preparation for a free life."[10]

In fact, most Modern School educators employed the term *freedom* when describing their views about libertarian education. This usually referred to the child's freedom to become his true self, in keeping with the philosophies of Pestalozzi and Froebel.[11] As William Shulman explains in his symposium comments, "Libertarian Education consists chiefly in aiding each [child] to realize his or her inner needs, dreams, and desires."[12] Modern School educators also saw their school as an alternative to mainstream education, which in their view transformed children into minions of the dominant culture. According to these educators, school should teach children to reconstruct, rather than reproduce, social structures and ideologies. As one Modern School educator, M. Epstein, bluntly stated, "On leaving the Modern school, the child should find the world unsatisfactory, repulsive, as indeed it is, and should be a rebel for the purpose of reconstructing society."[13]

In opposing state-funded schooling, Modern School educators replicated the views of Francisco Ferrer. William Thurston Brown quotes Ferrer's assertion that schools should cultivate "men who will continue unceasingly to develop; men who are capable of constantly destroying and renewing their surroundings . . . men always disposed for things that are better, eager for the triumph of new ideas."[14] Because "society fears such men," Ferrer adds, one could hardly "expect it to set up a system of education which will produce them."[15] Though public schools claimed to be "turning out an improved brand of citizens," Brown argues that in fact the schools "are not turning out citizens at all. They are turning out a mass of human beings who do not possess a single ideal superior to their parents."[16] Emma Goldman opposed any school—public, private, or parochial—that sought to "pound, knead and shape [the child's will] into a being utterly foreign to itself."[17] Goldman's use of "foreign" here seems to signify doubly: on the one hand, it critiques mainstream schools for alienating children from themselves; on the other hand, it seems to indict these schools for training foreign characteristics out of immigrant children.[18] Like her cohorts, Goldman thought the school should let "each pupil" be "free to his true self."[19]

Educators such as Emma Goldman, Joseph Cohen, Harry Kelly, and Carl Zigrosser, who funded and operated the Modern School, shared an objection to the public school as an institution that reproduced the status quo, particularly as it reflected a statist perspective. For example, Harry Kelly indicted the public school for being "a powerful instrument for the perpetuation of the present social order with all its injustice and inequality" and for seeking "to mold obedient citizens who would submit to the authority of the state and function as loyal workers within the capitalist system."[20] In a 1907 speech to the International Anarchist Congress, Emma Goldman identified the public school's complicity in reproducing inequality, stating that the "ordinary public school is a veritable barrack, where the human mind is drilled and manipulated into submission to various social and moral spooks, and thus fitted to continue our system of exploitation and expression."[21] By contrast, Mike Gold's recollection of his visit to Stelton contrasts starkly with Goldman's description of the public school:

> [The children] are in the barn, helping milk the cows, or currying old Fred, the horse, whom they love. They are working in the fields with Sherwood [Trask], each proud of his little garden, each planting seeds and marveling at the mystic chemistry of Nature, that turns loam into vivid flowers and clean, sweet vegetable food. They build little houses of their own, and write plays and act them, and they dance and sing, and draw, and edit and type for their magazine, and raise chickens, and sail rafts on the pond, and fly kites and wash dishes. They do as much useful work every day as the average man, and they learn more, and yet you would think it was all play. They do it with noise and barbaric exuberance, and it is like a constant hymn of joy sung in the worship of life.[22]

This glowing portrait of Stelton is particularly striking in that it appears in Gold's 1921 *Liberator* article, which claims that colonies such as Stelton (where Gold lived for a time) were failures. In this description, however,

Gold paints an image of children learning academic subjects (drama, science, and carpentry, among others) in a practical, self-directed manner. This mode of learning, which felt like play and was identical with living, realized the goals of the Modern School's founders and provided an alternative to the more mainstream mode of "learning by doing" that this book has described.

The Contested Discourse of "Learning by Doing"

John Dewey famously promoted "learning by doing" as an antidote to the conservative educational models that preceded him. In their 1915 book about progressive education, *Schools of To-morrow*, John Dewey and his daughter Evelyn explain, "'Learning by doing' is a slogan that might almost be offered as a general description of the way in which many teachers are trying to effect this adjustment [between the child and his environment]." Many progressive educators shared this goal of adjustment as they instituted hands-on education as an alternative to an outdated form of rote learning. Rote learning required children to be seated "in rows, far enough apart so they [could not] easily talk to each other.... [Teachers would provide facts] to the child, and have him repeat them often enough so that he [could] reasonably be expected to remember them, at least until after he '[was] promoted.'"[23] Even conservative programs that offered citizenship education to racial and ethnic minorities replaced rote learning with hands-on education. As this book has illustrated, the conservative adoption of "learning by doing" often prevented students from experiencing upward mobility as a result of their schooling.

In *Schools of To-morrow*, the Deweys laud a number of schools that offered hands-on education (from the Organic School at Fairhope, Alabama, to the Wirt schools of Gary, Indiana). According to the Deweys, these schools did *not* use manual training to prevent upward mobility. The Deweys emphatically reject the claim that the progressive schools they describe sought to "turn out good workers for the steel company" or to "save the factories the expense of training their own workers"; rather, these schools implemented manual training "for the educational value of the work [it] involved." The Deweys also reject the imputation that the controversial Wirt schools prevented economic mobility by taking "the unpromising immigrant child and [turning] him into a self-supporting immigrant, or ... [attempting] to meet the demand of an industrial class for a certain sort of training."[24] The Deweys instead argue that the progressive Wirt schools taught children to think critically about and therefore better adapt to their circumstances.[25]

Compared with such mainstream progressive schools, however, the Modern School appears radically unconventional in its interpretation of "learning by doing." Modern School educators rejected the goal of using education to adapt students to US society. Rather than helping students conform to urban, industrial life, the Modern School taught them to develop and maintain their individuality in a world set on minimizing it. Elizabeth and Alexis Ferm—two Modern School educators who successfully realized their vision of libertarian education at Stelton—exemplified this approach by preaching "a general aloofness from all occupational roles."[26] In this respect, the Ferms differed from John Dewey, who "closely linked the idea of democracy with vocational training."[27]

Other Modern School educators, such as Anna Koch-Riedel, also instituted a radical interpretation of "learning by doing" at Stelton. Koch-Riedel illustrates her child-centered approach by describing a typical basketry class in the *Modern School* magazine: "Without guidance or suggestion from any teacher—in this case the teacher knows but little more than the pupils—we try to work out whatever basket we may have in mind. The initiative of each individual child is thus called out, making the work true self expression. The development of any human being always corresponds, as it were, with the accomplishment of his work, his work being the material manifestation of his inner state."[28] This description demonstrates that the Modern School did *not* offer hands-on learning for the same reasons many other schools *did*, such as habituating students' bodily movements to repetitive manual labor or training children for future occupations. In fact, the end goal of this basketry class was not even necessarily to produce a usable basket: "There are straight ones and crooked ones, there are those of a strong and firm weave, while others are loose and shapeless; there are the big ones and the tiny ones intended for dolls."[29] Ana Koch-Riedel emphasizes how both teacher and students use basketry as a medium for learning the art of self-expression. Elizabeth Ferm explains how she and her husband judged the students' progress in crafts such as basketry according to "how they handle their material, how self-reliant they are, how they make their own designs, how they control themselves in trying to accomplish something, how or if they make their designs without expecting help from the staff and how much they have observed of the shortcomings of their own work."[30] As Ferm's comment illustrates, the school valued independence of thought and originality over the student's ability to imitate the teacher's knowledge, skill, or larger educational objectives. Moreover, in keeping with the child-centered spirit of the school, Koch-Riedel aligns herself with the children by claiming that "the teacher knows but little more than the pupils."

Not only did the Modern School eschew the idea of a fixed curriculum, but it also approached the question of discipline with a libertarian sensibility. As Paul Avrich describes,

> There was no segregation of the sexes either in the boarding house or the school. Attendance was voluntary. The children came and went as they pleased, pursuing what interested them, ignoring the rest. There was no discipline, no punishment, no formal curriculum. . . . A central assumption of the colonists was that the anarchist ideal of a free society without formal authority or economic oppression would be realized through the education of a generation of children uncorrupted by the commercialism and selfishness of the capitalist system and undisturbed by political repression and indoctrination in religion or government as taught in traditional schools.[31]

This commitment to cultivating the child's individuality and freedom is evident in photos taken at Stelton. In figure 10, for instance, a group of children wanders through a field. Because the children are holding hands and dressed alike, we can assume they are engaged in some kind of formal performance or activity.[32] In spite of the group nature of this activity, the children exhibit freedom of movement, individual poses, and free-spirited happiness. In this respect, the children pictured here contrast markedly with images of children who attended less progressive educational institutions during this period (as earlier chapters of this book illustrate).

Figure 11 also exemplifies the radical form of individuation encouraged by the Modern School. As in many other photos taken at the school, the students are naked, symbolizing the school's rejection of the conformist trappings of mainstream society. The children are also engaged in a variety of parallel but separate activities. One boy looks at the camera while another practices an exercise; several other children play a game, while a boy in front examines something on his arm. Though the only child wearing clothes in the photo is a girl, this fact probably speaks to her individual choice, as other Stelton photos picture naked boys and girls alongside each other. Whereas both figures 10 and 11 evidence the school's lack of strict discipline, figure 10 emphasizes the child's ability to maintain a free spirit in the midst of a structured activity.

FIGURE 10 Children posing in a field at Stelton, undated photograph, ca. 1915. (Modern School Collection, Special Collections and University Archives, Rutgers University Libraries, Box 15.)

A comparison of the Modern School's approach to discipline with that of the Wirt school, as the Deweys describe it, lends further insight into the degree of freedom that Modern School students exercised. According to the Deweys, the Wirt school increased retention by adapting its course of study to the particular needs of each child; as they explain, the child who is losing interest in the school program "is not punished for this lack of interest. . . . His teachers find out in what he is good and give him plenty of time to work at it, and to get ahead in it so that his interest in his work is stimulated."[33] If the child still does not respond with increased interest to the school's program, he or she is "kept in school until he or she learned some one thing . . . instead of leaving or failing entirely by being held back in everything until even the one strong faculty died and the pupil was without either training or the moral stimulus of success."[34] Retention of students was paramount for the Wirt program, given its commitment to teaching children something useful, even if that meant side-stepping its central goal of giving students a small degree of training in a variety of fields so as to make them intelligent about how the outside world operated.

Conversely, the Modern School demanded that initiative emerge from the students themselves. As Alexis C. Ferm notes when discussing the necessity for self-directed activity to accompany physical culture:

FIGURE 11 Naked boys and a clothed girl engaging in a variety of activities at Stelton, undated photograph, ca. 1915. (Modern School Collection, Special Collections and University Archives, Rutgers University Libraries, Box 15.)

> When an adult is able to initiate his activities . . . we hail him as great. . . . But we do not relate this back to the boy or girl. We expect the boy or girl to become physically strong by exercising his or her muscles, but we overlook the fact that it is necessary to begin in childhood to exercise initiative if it is to be developed. If so eminent a schoolman as ex-President Hadley of Yale, in reviewing the work of our schools, states very decidedly that we are not turning out men who can initiate or plan anything, but that we are turning out energetic followers, why do we not sit up and take notice?[35]

Ferm distinguishes the Modern School's approach to cultivating initiative through physical activity from the mainstream school's institution of repetitive muscular exercises. As this book has demonstrated, most citizenship education programs implemented repetitive muscular exercises to inculcate students with specific ideological perspectives. The Modern School rejected such conformistic training of children's bodies and minds.

The Modern School extended its respect for individual autonomy and initiative even to students who were not happy with its program. As Leonard Rico recalls, when, at thirteen years old he told his father that he wanted to leave the Modern School and enroll in public school, "We didn't fight about it; my father just said, 'Okay, I'll take you to the public school and we'll see what you can do.'"[36] Likewise, Maurice Hollod exemplifies this attitude when he describes his tutelage, in 1913, under Cora Bennett Stephenson at the New York Modern School:

> The third day I'm in school I acted a little smart-alecky. [Cora] said to me: "I don't think you're ready for class yet. I think you want to play. So why don't you go out in the yard today?" She said this calmly, without any hostility. I thought, what kind of school is this where they punish you by letting you play? I played in the yard all day. And the next day too. The day after that I told Mrs. Stephenson that I didn't want to go into the yard again. She said, "Do you feel ready to sit down and work with the rest of the class?" I said yes. "All right, come in." Can you imagine the difference between this type of discipline and that in the public schools of that day, a military type of discipline, a barracks discipline?[37]

The philosophy behind Stephenson's method is straightforward: if children want to learn, they will be much more likely to learn if they have a desire to know. Hollod's comments evidence the school's libertarian policy of allowing children to develop as a result of internal motivation, rather than from adult compulsion or the prejudiced viewpoints of their teachers. Alexis Ferm emphasized as much when he objected to militants (such as Hippolyte Havel) at the school, who claimed that the school was falling short of its mission to be "a lever of social transformation, a means of altering social foundations."[38] In order to revolutionize society, Ferm believed, the school first had to give children complete freedom to develop on their own terms: "To become a radical, an anarchist, a free man" was "a matter of inner experience."[39] By raising a generation of children in this way, Modern School educators such as Ferm hoped they would create the conditions for a complete transformation of society.

What is particularly impressive about Hollod's anecdote is his attention to the Modern School's politics. He does not recall the facts he learned in Stephenson's class but rather displays awareness of the school's radical methodology and its relation to the dominant educational landscape. In other words, he does not just attend school; he attends school and reflects on the nature of schooling itself. Even though Hollod may be filtering this memory through knowledge he acquired later in life, he nonetheless claims to have been aware of the material and ideological conditions of his experience. In itself, this speaks to the school's success in teaching students that they were part of a movement that sought to upend the institutions central to mainstream US society. Moreover, Hollod's experience of discipline mirrors the ideology articulated by Modern School educators. This was an unusual concurrence during a period when most citizenship education programs were marked by gaps between educators' stated goals, the schools' curricular realities, and the students' autobiographical accounts of their experiences.

Though Goldman was not involved with the day-to-day operations at the Stelton Modern School, her educational writing—about both her own experiences and the Modern School—embodies her objection to institutions that trained students to reenact their historical conditions. In *Living My Life*, Goldman depicts her own family as one such institution when she complains that her father threw her French grammar book into the fire as a symbolic rejection of her desire to study rather than marry (12).[40] This scene exemplifies Goldman's early encounters with an authority figure who not only valued economic stability over intellectual advancement but also associated economic stability with a gendered set of objectives. In her adult life, Goldman decided to leave her dreary factory job and loveless marriage in a New Jersey suburb to begin a life of economic hardship and political activism in New York City. Narrating this decision and countless others in her autobiography, Goldman demonstrates a willingness to exchange material stability for intellectual freedom and insight.

Recounting her family's lack of support after she leaves her husband, Goldman indicts the traditional family structure for being incompatible with personal freedom. After Goldman's aunt and uncle give her a "cruel reception" for abandoning her husband, she decides to travel to New York. Even though Goldman shows up, uninvited, to the house of A. Solotaroff, a fellow anarchist whom she barely knows, he shows her great hospitality. Reflecting on her treatment by Solotaroff—a man who later would become a good friend—Goldman writes, "I forgot my bitterness that had filled my soul over the cruel reception given to me by my own kin" (4). In narrating these events, Goldman emphasizes her choice to reject "kin" and the safety of the biological family in favor of a less dependable future, but one that meets her need for understanding and justice.[41]

Goldman extended her critique of the family to her critical writing as well. In "The Social Importance of the Modern School," Goldman explains that traditional schools reproduce a restrictive model of the family. In this article, Goldman aligns educators and parents as she critiques schools and families that keep children ignorant about their sexuality. Goldman writes, "Educators . . . are like parents who, having been maltreated in their childhood, now ill-treat and torture their children to avenge themselves upon their own childhood. In their youth the parents and educators had it dinned into their ears that sex is low, unclean, and loathsome. Therefore, they straightaway proceed to din the same things into their children."[42] These comments suggest that most parents have children without first reflecting on the conditions of their own childhood: a process that might have caused them to reject inappropriate parenting styles. In the passage above, Goldman uses *din* as both a verb and a metaphor to describe the cycle of ignorance reproduced by individuals and institutions alike. A "din" is a loud noise, and Goldman's use of it aptly conveys her sense that parents and schools deafen their children as they teach them false truths about sexuality. Education, in this sense, keeps children from understanding what is happening to their bodies and what will happen to them as they begin to engage with members of the opposite sex.

In the same article, Goldman further aligns the school with the family when she describes how the Board of Education, in cooperation with a Catholic family, punished a public school teacher who taught her students the history of George Eliot and George Lewes. This couple lived together without being married and openly admitted to their relationship (a scandalous act for their time). Goldman admonishes the school system for its reaction to the New York high school teacher, Henrietta Rodman, who shared the story of this couple with her students: "In her literature class, [Rodman] explained to her girls the relation of George Eliot to Lewes. A little girl raised in a Catholic home, and the supreme result of discipline and uniformity, related the classroom incident to her mother. The latter reported it to the priest, and the priest saw fit to report Miss Rodman to the Board of Education . . . [which] called Miss Rodman to account and made it very clear to her that if she were to permit herself any such liberties again she would be dismissed from her post."[43] Despite the clear violation of the separation of church and state evidenced by this anecdote, the school and the family here work together to keep children from knowing about historical figures who, like Goldman, challenged traditional family structures.

Goldman also enacted her objection to traditional family structures in her private life. Not only did she live openly with several lovers, without ever marrying, but, as she confesses in her autobiography, at one point she also lived with two lovers simultaneously. Describing her live-in relationship with Alexander (Sasha) Berkman and Fedya Stein in *Living My Life*, Goldman writes, "It had grown clear to me that my feelings for Fedya had no bearing on my love for Sasha. Each called out different emotions in my being, took me into different worlds. They created no conflict, they only brought fulfillment" (61). Juxtaposing Goldman's rejection of monogamy with her later birth control activism—for which she was twice arrested—one can begin to see how she articulated and lived out a queer politics of the family. Goldman posed alternatives to the nuclear family by pursuing an unconventional love life (and writing about it) and by supporting women in their desire to forgo or delay having children.[44]

The Modern School also mirrored Goldman's objection to the nuclear family. By refusing to maintain a distinction between individual family units and the school as an institution, Goldman and other Modern School educators realized their vision of education. According to this vision, school should be part of life rather than training for life, even though the results could be messy.[45] When Charlotte Perkins Gilman came to lecture at the Modern School, she incisively echoed this vision, describing an ideal form of schooling that would begin in babyhood. Gilman stated, "There would never be a parting when the unfortunate infant was sent to school. I wouldn't have them know when they were sent to school, wouldn't have them realize when they were being educated, but would have the educational machinery so surrounding them that they couldn't help being educated at every moment they were awake."[46] Stelton put this vision into practice by maintaining a fluidity between the community and the school, particularly through its support of Elizabeth and Alexis Ferm, who lived and taught there from 1920 to 1925.[47]

In one of the few comments she makes about the Modern School in *Living My Life*, Goldman emphasizes how the Ferms enacted her objection to the traditional school: "The Ferms were the first Americans I ever met whose ideas on education were akin to mine; but while I merely advocated the need of a new approach to the child, the Ferms translated their ideas into practice. In the Playhouse, as their school was called, the children of the neighborhood were bound by neither rules nor text-books. They were free to go or come and to learn from observation and experience" (335). The Ferms, who had no children of their own, envisioned the school as a communal alternative to family and the reproductive educational concept that one's elders should pass on a body of knowledge or a particular point of view to their children. Victor Sacharoff, who began attending kindergarten at the Living House in 1921, recalls, "The lady in charge introduced herself to me as 'Auntie' and explained to me that she was everybody's aunt."[48] As Sacharoff describes it, Auntie Ferm restipulated the family in terms of community. This philosophy, which also characterized the Modern School more generally, parallels Goldman's rejection of the idea that one's values must emerge out of and mimic those held by the members of one's nuclear family.

In a direct rejection of the nuclear family structure, when the Ferms taught at the Modern School they resided with a handful of their students at the Living House, which "remained their exclusive preserve"; this isolation allowed the Ferms to avoid interference from outside sources, particularly parents.[49] The Ferms "deplored all external interference from parents or teachers" because they prized above all "the cultivation of initiative and self-expression" in children and hoped to create an atmosphere in which the children could learn to develop themselves as individuals.[50] Rhya (Levine) Seligman, who came to Stelton in 1920 or 1921 and probably boarded in the Living House, later lovingly recalled the Ferms' rules, one of which stated that "bed wetting (in the dormitory for live-in boarders) [was] punishable by *having to wash your own sheets!*"[51] This rule, like others that shaped life at the Living House, speaks to the Ferms' insistence that children take responsibility for themselves and exercise independence. Seligman's positive recollection of such rules attests to the fact that students appreciated being taken seriously.

The Ferms did encounter some resistance from parents. In recollecting a parent who worried that her son would become "an ignorant farmhand" because he "did not spell his words correctly," Alexis Ferm writes, "What then are we to expect from the parents who are trying to work towards a better state of society? . . . Should we not expect from them that [they] should be more concerned about better men and women than that their children should be able to make a living as professional men, who are mostly parasites?"[52] This comment evidences the Ferms' objection to the modern family as an institution that primed children for their roles in capitalist society. Whether or not a child's parents objected to capitalism, the child's membership in the family would, the Ferms believed, expose him or her to dominant social structures and modes of thought that would undermine the Modern School's libertarian objectives.

In a sense, the Living House, and the Modern School more generally, represent an alternative to Goldman's unhappy experience of the nuclear family and embody her politics of reproduction. As Joseph

Cohen notes, when Goldman visited Stelton to celebrate its first successful year, she "referred to the 'birth control' struggle, in connection with which she had just been imprisoned, and she said that if there were many schools of the kind established at Stelton she would not feel it so necessary to preach family limitation."[53] In other words, she would be happy to encourage parents to bring children into a world if they could attend a school such as Stelton. In this ideal future, parents need not worry about losing control of their child's education, because rather than being a training-ground for life, school would be inseparable from life. The Modern School was able to realize this ideal future in a small way, in part because it was situated in an intentional community. In other words, because students did not have to encounter the outside world on a daily basis, they rarely experienced challenges to the school's libertarian philosophy.[54] The Modern School maintained its independence from mainstream society and therefore avoided reproducing mainstream social and economic structures.

The memories of former Modern School students testify to the school's success in transforming lived experience into education. Many of these students recall that their most satisfying learning experiences happened during the very mundane act of walking. As Ray Porter Miller writes in his essay, "My Teachers at Stelton," "School at Stelton in those days was not something that started at 9 a.m. and ended at 3. It began when we got up in the morning and finished when we went to bed . . . a five-mile hike was just time enough in which to discuss Egypt, the pyramids and slave labor; or to sing French folksongs by way of learning the language."[55] Here, Miller recalls how the school cultivated an embodied form of learning based on freedom rather than constraint. Jon Thoreau Scott also recollects this sense of freedom: "There were no programmed classes in any sense other than the hikes that we used to take."[56] Hiking trips would often emerge in response to students' curiosity; for instance, when Scott asked his father where the Ambrose River went "after it flowed over the dam at Lake Nelson," his father replied, "Let's find out," which led to one such hike. Scott recalls, "At places the going was tough making our way through forests and brush that grew along the banks of the stream. I was completely exhausted by the time we found the end of the Ambrose and, after some rest and a lunch that we had packed, we took a bus to New Brunswick and another back to School Street. It was a remarkable learning experience for a twelve year old. My father was an expert on birds and plants and I learned much about them on such trips."[57] Trips like this constitute a form of education that is long-lasting because of the child's physical immersion in the experience. In retelling this story, Scott reveals how the lessons he learned on the hike (about birds and plants, for instance) are inseparable from his recollections of the embodied experience of hacking through "forests and brush." Moreover, the experience teaches him, in an Emersonian vein, to find out answers to his questions literally by searching for them himself.

At Stelton walking represented an alternative to the constraint that Francisco Ferrer associated with mainstream education. Ferrer argued, "The school imprisons children physically, intellectually, and morally, in order to direct the development of their faculties in the paths desired. It deprives them of contact with nature in order to model them after its own pattern."[58] Walking at Stelton did precisely the opposite; not only did walks take place in nature, but teachers encouraged the children to choose their own destinations and their objectives for walking in the first place. At Stelton, walking was a form of learning that allowed the child to discover what he wanted to know, to find answers by observing the world around him, and to interact with teachers in a nonrestrictive manner. In this respect, the hikes that former students recall exemplify one way Stelton successfully realized its radical interpretation of "learning by doing." Stelton's form of embodied learning thus shared a commitment to "learning by doing" with the assimilationist education programs this book has examined. Both types of schools created learning environments in which students would remember their lessons because their bodies would be immersed in repetitive activities. Yet assimilationist educators required students to engage in activities they often did not choose—such as making beds or operating a printing press—with the objective of learning preordained lessons. By contrast, Stelton depended on students first to discover what they wanted to learn and then to exercise free will in seeking that knowledge. Education, in this case, both depended on and strengthened free will.

Miller's and Scott's memories of hiking and conversing also attest to the school's instantiation of a balance between individual and community. Zachary Schwartz calls attention to this balance in his essay about Stelton, "Not Just a School":

> The School made no robot of me. I had my own problems, troubles,
> interests, talents, and no one else had them quite the same way. . . . I
> was a unit unto myself, and so were the other children, and we
> were given the opportunity to work things out in a way best suited
> to each of us. We learned that each one had a responsibility to the

others in the school, children and teachers alike. We got to know the meaning of discipline, although it came from within rather from without, and we learned that cause and effect went hand in hand and one could not be separated from the other.[59]

Schwartz depicts education as achieving an ideal balance between the child's needs and the needs of the community. His and other students' memories of Stelton exemplify the Modern School's success—both in realizing this balance and in creating the ideal conditions for self-motivated learning.

The *Voice of the Children*, the Modern School's student magazine, further illustrates the school's success in eradicating the gaps between its ideals, methods, and results. Modern School students wrote, edited, and printed this magazine on the school's printing press with little or no supervision. A story titled "The Girl Full of Wonder," by fourteen-year-old Anna Cohen, conveys the school's embrace of education that is inseparable from life, and the Ferms' particularly Emersonian rejection of inherited knowledge. In this story, an unnamed protagonist awakes one morning in a "beautiful wood" and realizes that every one of her thoughts and actions is new to her. Because she has no names for her activities or feelings, the girl must figure out how to live, think, and feel as she moves through the world. The girl benefits from this ignorance because her lack of an inherited language means that she has no fears, hesitations, prejudices, or preconceived ideas: the girl "was not frightened for she did not know what fright meant."[60] With a tone that is more mythical than didactic, this story promotes the Modern School's commitment to letting students discover knowledge by themselves. In this respect, it echoes Elizabeth Ferm's embrace of a truly student-centered form of learning and her simultaneous objection to the pedagogue who "is interested in the history of human affairs, but not in the affairs of the humans who form the class room."[61]

Though the "girl full of wonder" might have learned more quickly with a teacher present, she experiences joy in the free and independent learning that typified the Modern School's pedagogical approach. The story ends when its protagonist has learned as much as she needs to in a process that has given her pleasure: "When she awoke next morning the first thing she saw was the sun. . . . Then she saw the pool and forgot all about the sun and went to play in the water. But not to get clean, but to get cool and comfortable. Later she learned to keep clean, to swim, to talk animal talk, and had many good adventures."[62] This conclusion suggests not only that activity can be an end in itself (the girl goes to the water, but not to get clean) but also that life lessons—such as keeping clean—should not be rushed or prioritized in favor of learning for its own sake.

These examples of the Modern School's success are not meant to suggest that the school faced no difficulties, particularly in its early years. When the early Stelton pioneers arrived at the school, there were no buildings and they spent their first winter with little shelter from the elements.[63] Poor soil made farming difficult. There was a lot of turnover in the educational staff, not only because of the school's isolation, but also because teachers rarely maintained control over their curriculum. Because some of the community's inhabitants were anarchists while others were communists, political infighting about how the school should be run was practically a daily challenge at Stelton. Paul Avrich writes that it was not unusual for parents to barge into classrooms to object to how the students were being taught. He also explains that because Stelton's founders would not force people to do work they did not want to do, the community was often overrun with trash.[64]

While the educators who operated Stelton blurred the line between school and community, its antecedent in New York—with which Goldman was more actively involved—instead blurred the line between family and community. One might even conclude that the Ferrer Center was an institution that wanted to replace the structure of the nuclear family with a radical educational community. This center, which offered classes for children and adults, was "for a long time . . . the only progressive school in America that deliberately sought working-class pupils and attempted to fuse cultural and educational radicalism with a spirit of militant class consciousness."[65] Here was a place where children and their parents could be educated—or re-educated—to imagine themselves as part of a community that was larger and more than a family.

In an early (undated) issue of the *Modern School Bulletin*—probably from 1914, when the school was still at its Manhattan location—the *Bulletin*'s editor, Harry Kelly, rejected criticism that the school was diverging from Francisco Ferrer's focus on the child's education. Kelly objected to those who criticized the Ferrer Center's commitment to teaching children and adults alongside each other and instead suggested, "Let us devote more time to our adult classes and make them attractive that we will in time build up a real peoples [*sic*] university, where the taint of business and success may forever be absent—unless by success we mean the opening of new worlds to the visions of man, and who shall dare say when a man is too old to discover new worlds—and ultimately create as a reality what we now dream of?"[66] Kelly not only hopes that adults will keep their minds open to learning new things but also insists that an ideal educational institution—one that sees itself as part of life, rather than preparation for life—cannot abandon the child once he or she becomes an adult. In a similar vein, Goldman begins her autobiography with an account of the important education she acquired not as a child but as an adult.

Rebirth, Reproduction, and the Martyred Body

Late in *Living My Life*, Goldman suggests that an inverted womb may be the source of the bodily pain that she has experienced throughout her life (and has complained about throughout the text). In *Living My Life*, Goldman weaves together the tale of her bodily pain—which persists because she has refused the operation that might have cured her—with a confession of the physical, verbal, and emotional abuse that her father inflicted on her. Goldman describes her move to New York in terms of being reborn as a political subject.[67] She situates the motivation for this rebirth in an earlier moment, when she contemplated the hanging of the Haymarket martyrs.[68] As she writes, "Their death gave me life. [My life] now belongs to their memory—to their work" (31). Similarly, after hearing the anarchist leader Johann Most speak, Goldman notes, "I had a distinct sensation that something new and wonderful had been born in my soul. A great ideal, a burning faith, a determination to dedicate myself to the memory of my martyred [Haymarket] comrades" (10). Johann Most offers an alternative interpretation of Goldman's political awakening, which Goldman recounts to provide a subtext for her own rebirth narrative: "It was the influence of my childhood that had made me what I was" (69). With these two explanations, Goldman interprets her rebirth as a simultaneous embrace and rejection of the United States: an embrace of the mobility, anonymity, and possibility that allowed her to gain freedom from the model of family into which she was born, and a rejection of the failed realization of US democratic ideals as they affected her directly (exemplified not only by the Haymarket hangings but also by the state's continual suppression of Goldman's freedom to speak, which led eventually to her deportation).[69]

The twinned discourses of family and poverty, which Goldman unites under the rubric of reproduction, infuse volume 1 of *Living My Life*. Goldman explains that her rejection of marriage stems in part from her knowledge that children born into poverty often suffer from unhappy family lives as a result. After becoming a nurse in 1900, and then working as a midwife, Goldman experiences firsthand the dread that many poor women experience when they became pregnant: "Having a large brood of children, often many more than the weekly wage of the father could provide for, each additional child was a curse" (186). Those children who lived, observes Goldman, "were sickly and undernourished . . . ill-born, ill-kept, and unwanted" (186).[70] Goldman explains that she herself would not perform the abortions that women begged her to do: "I would not undertake the task." But this was only because she did not have proper training: "It was not any moral consideration for the sanctity of life; a life unwanted and forced into abject poverty did not seem sacred to me" (186). This discussion reveals Goldman's support of abortion and promotion of birth control.

For Goldman, these reproductive issues were as much personal as political. This dualism explains why Goldman threads her discussion of reproduction with memories of her painful childhood and expressions of disappointment with her conservative lovers. Early in the autobiography, Goldman articulates her objection to having children: "[M]y tragic childhood had been no exception. . . . There were thousands of children born unwanted, marred and maimed by poverty and still more by ignorant misunderstanding. No child of mine should ever be added to those unfortunate victims" (61). Despite this stance, Goldman experiences a crisis when her longtime lover Ed demands that she prioritize their domestic life over her political commitments.[71] Goldman intertwines the narrative of this personal challenge to her reproductive politics with the story of her initiation into midwifery; at one moment she confesses she has to leave Ed because "he would have [her] forswear [her] interests in the movement, sacrifice everything for love of him," (184) and a moment later she expresses sympathy for the women who would invent "fantastic methods" to "get rid of their expected offspring" (185). Goldman has more than a poor childhood in common with these mothers, which she reveals when she recalls Ed's view that "nature has made [woman] for motherhood. All else is nonsense, artificial and unreal" (151). Despite Ed's obvious antipathy to her views, Goldman tries for a time to avoid his "disapproval" by focusing on her home life at the expense of her political commitments. Though she does not explicitly say that this decision leads to "strange nervous attacks," she suggests as much by juxtaposing Ed's increasing demands with the onset of what seem to be panic attacks (187).

Goldman seamlessly weaves together a discourse of illness and pain with the story of her struggle to find a love relationship based on gender equality. This section of the autobiography represents her pain as an over-determined symptom. From one perspective, the pain symbolizes her objection to the reproductive norms Ed imposes on her. It also reminds her that she needs to abandon this otherwise fulfilling love relationship because it threatens to undermine her reproductive politics. At the same time, the pain reads as an unconscious embodiment of Goldman's struggle between wanting to stay and needing to leave. Even though Goldman states unequivocally on several occasions that she would not bring children into the world because of her own miserable childhood, she also acknowledges the ongoing struggle she has between this decision and her desire to have children (which, ironically echoing Ed, she represents as a biologically informed desire). Goldman identifies this desire as her "mother-need" but also justifies ignoring it in favor of the "newfound ideal" she has discovered as a result of her political rebirth (61).[72] Rejecting biological birth in favor of political rebirth, Goldman determines to serve her "newfound ideal . . . completely" and to "find an outlet for [her] mother-need in the love of *all* children" (61, emphasis in original). In this respect, we can see how Goldman might have found an outlet for her "mother-need" not only in her birth control activism and her midwifery but also in her support of education at the Ferrer Center and the Modern School.[73]

Though Goldman frames her rejection of motherhood as a feminist choice, she simultaneously suggests that this refusal is an inevitable consequence of childhood physical abuse, which traumatized her body so indelibly that she could not even permit herself to imagine having an operation that would make it possible to bear children. Goldman introduces this narrative by embedding her confessions of bodily pain in the story of her father's abuse and returns to the same narrative when she discusses her work as a midwife and her inability to stay with Ed. The first of these two scenes begins as Goldman recalls the circumstances under which she left Russia. Goldman describes her approach toward the brook that separated the German and Russian frontiers, and her plunge into the water: "The sudden chill froze my blood; then I felt a stinging sensation in my spine, abdomen, and legs, as if I were being pierced with hot irons. I wanted to scream, but terror of the soldiers checked me. Soon we were over, and the stinging ceased; but my teeth kept chattering and I was in a hot sweat. . . . I was laid up for weeks, and my spine remained weak for years afterwards" (57–58). Following immediately after Goldman's narration of her father's physical abuse, this river scene metonymically connects the very real "stinging" and "piercing" Goldman experienced upon entering the water with her memory of "the whip and the little stool [that] were always at hand" (59). Earlier Goldman had explained that the whip and the stool "symbolized [her] shame and [her] tragedy"; in this scene, she associates the experience of "stinging" pain with the legacy of a weak spine—which, read symbolically, represents the inescapable embodiment of shame. Instead of experiencing border crossing as a moment of exhilarating freedom, Goldman associates it with an experience of bodily pain that recalls her childhood abuse, and, laden with heavy symbolism, remains simultaneously acute and ongoing for her.

This scene dramatizes not only the way the body remembers trauma but also the way the mind frames its injury. Goldman leaves her home in Russia to escape her father, both because of his insistence that she marry and because of his persistent violence. Itemizing the types of paternal violence she experienced, Goldman writes that her father "pounded" and "pulled [her] about," or whipped her for spilling a drop of water from a glass she was forced to carry "back and forth," a process that "used to unnerve [her] and make [her] ill for hours after" (59). As a child, sometimes Goldman would fantasize while she observed children playing happily in the field behind her house: "A strange thought came to me: how wonderful it would be if I were stricken with some consuming disease! It would surely soften father's heart. . . . Perhaps if I should become very ill, near death, he would become kind and never beat me again or let me stand in the corner for hours" (59). Goldman tries to compensate for her feelings of shame and weakness by envisioning her father's regret, but in this fantasy his regret is tied to Goldman's imaginary illness. Here, Goldman figures illness as a vector of empowerment, but one that is tied to the unpleasant memory of physical pain. This psychic structure of pain continues to inform Goldman's depiction of future illnesses.[74] Moreover, because Goldman experiences her father's abuse in an embodied form, she can never fully abandon her unpleasant childhood. Home, Goldman writes, was "a prison" that followed her "from St. Petersburg to America, from Rochester to [her] marriage" (60). In other words, home exists for her as a psychic reality that is simultaneously lodged, like a dormant virus, within her physical self.[75]

In this same section of the autobiography, Goldman simultaneously describes her attachment to pain and her self-image as a political martyr. Goldman explains that after arriving in America she explored and then rejected the possibility of having an operation to remedy the illness from which she suffered: "In America I had consulted [a friend]

Solotaroff about my trouble, and he took me to a specialist, who urged an operation. He seemed surprised that I could have stood my condition so long and that I had been at all able to have physical contact. My friends informed me that the physician had said I would never be free from pain, or experience full sexual release, unless I submitted to the operation" (58). Goldman does consider the operation; surprisingly, however, she evaluates it only as a remedy for her inability to bear children and not as a means to relieve her pain. She reminisces, "I loved babies passionately, and now—now I might have a child of my own and experience for the first time the mystery and wonder of motherhood! I closed my eyes in blissful day-dreaming. A cruel hand clutched at my heart. My ghastly childhood stood before me, my hunger for affection, which Mother was unable to satisfy. Father's harshness toward the children, his violent outbreaks, his beating my sisters and me" (58–59). Despite the promise of relief from pain, Goldman refuses to undergo the surgery. It seems she does so not only because she is unwilling to have children but also because she cannot even allow herself to be capable of having them.

In this scene, Goldman depicts herself as a martyr by transforming the memory of abuse into a social ideal. Throughout the text, Goldman expresses guilt about the fact that she was not convicted for her complicity in the attempted assassination of Henry Frick. Goldman planned the assassination attempt with her lover and political comrade, Alexander (Sasha) Berkman, but Berkman carried it out alone and went to jail for it. Goldman explains that she is eager to relieve this guilt by finding another way to martyr herself for the anarchist cause: "I had determined to serve [my newfound ideal] completely. To fulfil that mission I must remain unhampered and untied. Years of pain and of suppressed longing for a child—what were they compared with the price many martyrs had already paid? I, too, would pay the price, I would endure the suffering, I would find an outlet for my mother-need in the love of *all* children. The operation did not take place." Goldman goes on to compare her sacrifice with Sasha's: "Like Sasha I now felt that I, too, could overcome every difficulty and face every test for my ideal. Had I not overcome the strongest and most primitive craving of a woman—the desire for a child?" (61). Ironically, though Goldman represents her ability to overcome the biological craving for motherhood as a strength, refusing the operation leads to her debilitating experience of bodily pain.

Goldman's representation of this pain simultaneously evokes her painful, personal experiences and her political objection to the ideologies and practices that informed those experiences. In this respect, these scenes recall Arthur and Joan Kleinman's theory about how individual and communal experience can find simultaneous expression in the body.[76] As the Kleinmans argue, the "memory of bodily pain" can evoke "social complaints . . . [that are] lived and relived (remembered) in the body."[77] At the same time, bodily pain can exist "as a form of resistance against local sources of oppressive control."[78] In other words, the physically embodied memory of trauma can function simultaneously as a form of social criticism and resistance to oppression. The Kleinmans' theory offers one framework for understanding Goldman's contradictory explanations for refusing to have the operation. At one moment, Goldman explains that her refusal is a form of resistance to reproducing child poverty; at another, she claims it is a response to personal trauma; at a third moment, she concludes that her life "would never know harmony in love for very long, that strife and not peace would be [her] lot. In such a life there was no room for a child" (187).[79] But the question remains: Why does Goldman refuse to have an operation that promises to alleviate her acute and ongoing pain? Moreover, why doesn't she consider the alleviation of pain as a compelling reason to have the operation? These ellipses suggest that Goldman's martyrdom requires a physical reminder not only of the historical pain she associates with her experience of child abuse but also of an associative pain that arises from her identification with the women she encounters as a midwife.

It does not seem coincidental that one of the scenes through which Goldman triangulates her personal history, social commitments, and bodily pain occurs in the midst of her discussion of abortion, and of women who mutilate their own bodies in attempting to miscarry. She writes: "Jumping off tables, rolling on the floor, massaging the stomach, drinking nauseating concoctions, and using blunt instruments . . . it was harrowing, but it was understandable" (186). With this description, Goldman aligns her bodily pain with the problem of unwanted children among New York's working-class community. She complicates this discussion of unwanted children by juxtaposing it with a confession that she could not continue to stay home to please Ed, "[refusing] invitations to lecture because [she] sensed Ed's disapproval" (187). Goldman then twines a description of her panic attacks into this narrative, as if to hint that these attacks emerge as a form of embodied resistance to pressure from Ed: "I developed strange nervous attacks. Without preliminary warning I would fall to the ground as if knocked down by a heavy blow. I did not lose consciousness . . . but I was not able to utter a word. My chest felt convulsed, my throat compressed; I had agonizing pain in my legs as if the muscles were being pulled asunder. This condition would last from ten minutes to an hour and leave me utterly exhausted" (187). Because she does not lose consciousness during these attacks, Goldman is forced to observe what is happening to her. Yet the attack immobilizes her, preventing her from speaking or controlling her body. The stark violence of this description symbolizes Ed's successful pressure to keep Goldman from giving public lectures, Goldman's (temporary) capitulation to his desire, and her awareness that this dilemma aligns her with the women who are pressured to birth and raise unwanted children.

Goldman further reflects on the significance of her panic attacks by juxtaposing her discussion of them with a memory of her father's violence. Goldman recalls that as a young child, as she sat quietly considering her ambivalent feelings toward her father—her fear of him and her desire for his love—she was shocked by "a terrific pain in [her] head . . . as if I had been struck with an iron bar. It was Father's fist that had smashed the round comb I wore to hold my unruly hair" (60). During this particular attack, Goldman's father also repudiates his biological link to her, claiming that she could not possibly be his daughter because she neither looks nor acts like him. In juxtaposing this scene with a description of the panic attacks she suffered as an adult, Goldman evokes the psychic interconnectedness of her memory of pain and her ongoing experience of it. Goldman describes panic attacks that come on suddenly and unexpectedly, making her feel as if she is being "knocked" or "struck" down by sudden violence. Though she explains logically that the panic attacks are probably an effect of her inverted womb, her explanation does not account for the narrative parallels that she draws between her past and present. Goldman therefore leaves the reader wondering if her pain might not exist simultaneously on physical and psychological registers.

Goldman's symbolic articulation of embodied pain demonstrates the interconnectedness of the personal and the social in her life. Though the Kleinmans are discussing another cultural context, their comments offer useful insight into these connections: "We mean that pain and inner resentment, outer suffering and social resentment, merged. Each complaint, elaborated in the context of a story that integrated social and bodily suffering, was a moral commentary, first about a delegitimated local world, ultimately about the delegitimation of Chinese society."[80] Like the survivors whom the Kleinmans discuss, Goldman integrates the memory of family trauma and the social problem of unwanted children in describing her embodied pain. As the historical record proves, however, Goldman was not incapacitated by this experience of victimization. True, she suffered moments in which pain immobilized her, but she moved past those moments and ultimately channeled her pain into a commitment to social change. Because she could not escape from her embodied memories, Goldman decided that she needed them. In this respect, they became a symbol of her political martyrdom.

Though she represents herself as a martyr, Goldman also comes across as a Jeremiah. In *Living My Life*, Goldman continually seeks to reinvigorate what she sees as fallen democratic ideals. For instance, she attributes her ongoing legal troubles to the US government's unconstitutional attacks on her right to exercise free speech. Exposing her mistreatment at the hands of the US police and the legal system, Goldman insists that her experience of injustice belies the media's claim that US institutions are threatened from the outside—from "foreign riff-raff and criminals who came to our country to destroy its democratic institutions" (79). On the contrary, Goldman argues, foreigners like her were attempting to rehabilitate democratic ideals by invoking international principles, in her case the anarchist and libertarian ideals of non-Americans such as Kropotkin and Ferrer. In other words, Goldman suggests that the United States might begin to revitalize its own democratic structures by embracing international influence. This is not to say that Goldman blindly idealizes the "foreign"—her exodus from her biological family attests to that. Rather, her experience in America teaches her that the family is one institution whose problematic nature crosses borders. Through her autobiographical writing and her educational activism, Goldman exemplifies the necessity of transforming the family by simultaneously transforming individuals, schools, and communities.

Conclusion

This book has examined the role that progressive educational practices played in cultivating US citizenship between 1880 and 1920. Focusing on both educational archives and autobiographical accounts of citizenship education, the book illustrates how the practices of citizenship education did not always reflect the theories articulated by citizenship educators. The book also identifies commonalities and differences within the progressive approach to citizenship education. Though citizenship educators across the political spectrum adopted hands-on education in place of an outdated method of rote learning, they invariably yoked these methods to different ideas about success and citizenship.

As the dominant citizenship ideology during this period, civic republicanism influenced the operation of assimilationist education programs. When these programs were effective, their principles informed the narratives through which new citizens filtered their experiences of education and national belonging. Charles Eastman, Booker T. Washington, and Abraham Cahan illustrate the success of such programs in their citizenship autobiographies. These texts feature the genre characteristics of the realist or (more usually) idealist bildungsroman. As such, they conclude with their protagonists' adaptation to mainstream society and usually narrate this adaptation as a "dialectical process of mutual consent" between the protagonist and society.[1]

Liberal and cosmopolitan models of citizenship exerted a more minor but still palpable influence on the education of new citizens. Because these discourses had limited circulation at the institutional level, they materialize most forcefully in the educational autobiographies of progressive, cosmopolitan educators such as W. E. B. Du Bois and Jane Addams. In keeping with their validation of cultural pluralism, these educators write within the tradition of the dissensual bildungsroman, a subgenre that foregrounds the gradual incorporation into society of individuals who have been excluded from the universalist categories of liberal democracy.[2] Libertarian ideas about schooling represented an even more radical approach to progressive education than liberal and cosmopolitan models of citizenship did. These ideas influenced both the Modern School and the autobiography of Emma Goldman, an educator and activist who refuses to portray her development in terms of adaptation to mainstream US society. Goldman's autobiography fits within the tradition of the antibildungsroman; it not only depicts Goldman's refusal to be incorporated into a society that she views as having distorted principles but also dramatizes her embrace of a political identity influenced by international intellectual traditions.

It is not within the scope of this book to fully trace contemporary interpretations of terms like *success, citizenship*, and *autobiography*. I can, however, draw a few broad conclusions about citizenship education in the contemporary United States. First, I will demonstrate that civic republicanism and liberalism continue to circulate, as ghosts of their former selves, in our current moment. Next, I will identify different models of transnational citizenship that have emerged to characterize the global experiences of political activists, capitalist managers and elites, and migrants. Finally, I will discuss a handful of symbolic moments from contemporary texts that represent the new literature of citizenship: Eric Liu's essayistic memoir *The Accidental Asian: Notes of a Native Speaker* (1999); Jhumpa Lahiri's story "Nobody's Business" (2001); and Zhang Zhen's poetic autobiographical account "The Jet Lag of a Migratory Bird: Border Crossings toward/from 'the Land That Is Not'" (2013). These texts offer self-conscious reflections on the inevitable translation of experience that happens when authors adopt narrative structures influenced by dominant discourses of citizenship.

The latter half of the twentieth century was dominated by a cultural pluralist model of citizenship, which was intensified by the civil rights movement and the multiculturalist decades that followed.[3] In the twenty-first century, however, US citizenship has been marked by a concurrence of civic republican and transnational discourses, both of which testify to the increasingly global nature of US life (as reaction and reflection, respectively). In the educational sphere, civic republicanism functions as both a rhetorical mode and a formative influence. Rhetorically, civic republicanism marks the language of educators who lament its absence in US life. For example, in his introduction to the 2005 essay collection *Civic Education and Culture*, Bradley Watson worries that a diverse population, emboldened by the dominant discourse of multiculturalism, has made it impossible to achieve a civic republican ideal in the post-9/11 era. In Watson's view, this objectionable status quo has produced educational institutions that promote "regime transformation" rather than (the preferable goal, in his view) "regime transmission."[4]

Conversely, Kathleen Knight Abowitz and Jason Harnish suggest that the embrace of diversity may not be the dominant discourse in US education, especially since the terrorist attacks of 9/11 have contributed to a resurgence of nationalist sentiment and a subsequent increase in civic republicanism at US educational institutions. Knight Abowitz and Harnish made a comprehensive study of "scholarly and curricular English-language" educational texts published between 1990 and 2003. Examining public school standards and curricula, as well as documents produced by private foundations, teachers' unions, and independent nonprofit groups, they identified the presence of the following civic republican features in US schools: an emphasis on "personal responsibility and the common good," reflected for instance in community service requirements; lessons on the history of democratic institutions; promotion of civic virtues such as "self-sacrifice, patriotism, loyalty, and respect"; and the cultivation of "loyalty to nationalist symbols and icons."[5] Citing Chester Finn's 2001 study, Knight Abowitz and Harnish identify 9/11 as the direct cause of an increased pressure on students to recite the Pledge of Allegiance; Finn writes, one month after 9/11, "Kids are pledging allegiance in Pennsylvania, singing 'God Bless the U.S.A.' in Arkansas, wearing red, white and blue to school (for a 'Patriotism Day' assembly) in Maryland."[6]

Linda Bosniak corroborates the position that civic republicanism has regained authority in recent decades. Like Knight Abowitz and Harnish, Bosniak argues that this discourse coexists with a liberal, rights-based model of citizenship. However, Bosniak argues that in the contemporary United States civic republicanism manifests centrally through an activist populace that has demonstrated a "revitalized interest in citizenship's political dimension."[7] Contemporary political activists do not, in Bosniak's view, represent a single political position; they are variously motivated, usually by civic republican or communitarian ideals, and in this respect pose a challenge to the dominance of liberal (or rights-based) citizenship.[8] Though Bosniak's discussion predates the Tea Party movement, this movement perfectly exemplifies the type of activism that she has identified in a contemporary US context.

While Bosniak does not comment on the presence of this activist sensibility in an educational context, we can identify its influence on the form of standardized testing that has developed since January 2002, when George W. Bush signed the No Child Left Behind Act into law. Since that time, leaders of both political parties have embraced an activist approach to reforming education through the measurement of outputs. This approach limits teacher autonomy in an attempt to increase teacher accountability, tying federal funding for schools to student performance on knowledge-based tests.[9] By encouraging the acquisition of standardized knowledge, as well as a mastery of test-taking skills, these tests devalue individual knowledge, abilities, and intellectual qualities. They instead favor the capacity to select the allegedly best answer from a limited set of options. In this respect, they not only exemplify civic republican ideology but also have hastened a return to rote memorization, the nineteenth-century methodology so misguided that opposition to it united nineteenth-century educators of all political persuasions.[10] Some have argued that because the Common Core standards emphasize critical thinking skills, their recent adoption by almost all of the US states will replace the trend in which schools spend an enormous amount of time drilling their students with practice tests to prepare for the real thing.[11] This possibility, however, comes with its own irony, since instituting the Common Core standards requires the transformation of critical thinking—an ostensibly nonquantitative activity—into a testable skill, characterized by the selection rather than generation of ideas.[12]

Another ironic element marking the trend in standardized testing is that, despite its civic republican qualities, both its proponents and its opponents have measured its value in global terms. A decade before No Child Left Behind was passed into law, the elder President Bush sought to implement America 2000, which "aimed to achieve the world's best math and science test scores by the turn of the twentieth century."[13] From then until the present moment (when the testing regime has been revalidated by Barack Obama's Race to the Top), supporters of standardized testing have continued to link the ostensible accountability created by standardized tests to the maintenance of the United States as a global power.[14] In "The Role of Education Quality in Economic Growth," for example, Eric Hanushek and Ludger Wößmann cite a number of US studies that link substantial "earnings advantages to higher achievement on standardized tests."[15] Though their argument does not necessarily prove that standardized testing directly results in higher earnings, their study nonetheless validates the use of standardized tests, which (they say) can prove a correlation between high academic performance and higher earnings. Exemplifying the popular concern with student performance in highly competitive fields, these authors cite mathematics testing as their primary example, arguing that "when test scores are standardized . . . one standard deviation in mathematics performance at the end of high school translates into 12 percent higher annual earnings."[16] This mode of reasoning justifies the transformation of schools into laboratories for producing globally competitive workers who are judged by their performance on tests and resulting income levels.

Those who oppose standardized testing also invoke a global context, arguing that testing has not helped Americans compete successfully with high-performing international students from countries as diverse as China and Finland.[17] These critics also focus on US students' performance in the globally competitive fields of math and science. For instance, a recent University of Missouri study found that American students "score significantly lower than students worldwide in mathematics achievement"; it also suggested that this trend could be reversed if educators adopted the integrated mathematics curriculum often used to teach better-performing students.[18] Other critics suggest that Finland should serve as a model for the transformation of US schools. In Finland, unlike the United States, high-performing schools mandate "gateway exams" (rather than the "grade-by-grade standardized tests" used in the United States); more importantly, Finnish schools "set a high bar for entry into the teaching profession and make sure that the institutions that train teachers do it exceedingly well."[19] Finally, there are critics who oppose testing because it undermines the individuality and diversity of students.[20] Yong Zhao, for instance, rejects testing not only because in his view, it puts the US worker at a global disadvantage but also because it devalues creative, independent thought—which he nostalgically believes was valued in a previous period of US history.[21] Zhao calls attention to the crisis in which technology is replacing traditional jobs, while jobs that "cannot be computerized" are being "outsourced to other countries with lower labor costs."[22] Citing Daniel Pink's 2006 book, *A Whole New Mind: Why Right-Brainers Will Rule the Future*, Zhao argues that we no longer need the standardized workers required by the industrial and information ages; we now need "creators and empathizers" suited for the conceptual age that we are in.[23] Creative thinkers, he reassures us, cannot be produced by an educational field dominated by standardized testing.

Though civic republicanism undergirds the dominance of standardized testing and exists as a rhetorical framework for public conversations about citizenship education, it is far from the only citizenship discourse circulating in the contemporary United States. Liberal citizenship discourse continues to validate cultural pluralism, but it also has taken on an expanded function, pluralizing the social spaces in which citizenship practices are thought to occur. As Linda Bosniak argues, the new pluralism has challenged the tripartite classification of the private, civil, and civic spheres (of family, work, and politics, respectively); it has done so by redefining the practice of citizenship as something that happens not only in the political sphere but also in the workplace, the economy, the neighborhood, professional associations, and the family.[24] Paul Wapner further argues that civil society is no longer limited to the nation-state; it also exists as an "associational space" in transnational civil society, "above the individual and below the state, but also across national boundaries."[25]

Whereas at the turn of the twentieth century civic republicanism, liberalism, and cosmopolitanism coexisted as the three central citizenship discourses, today the first two persist—albeit in the changed forms that I have identified—alongside a new, global sensibility. Contemporary understandings of global citizenship, however, refer to a number of disconnected transnational communities with varying socioeconomic standings and objectives. Global citizenship is not a twenty-first-century correlative to the Kantian cosmopolitical tradition—with its embrace of universalist ideals—that W. E. B. Du Bois and Jane Addams embraced.[26] Rather, it comprises a range of "cross-border identities, relationships, and allegiances" organized around transnational activism, capitalism, or migration.[27] Obviously, the deterritorialized transnational activists working on behalf of human rights, environmentalism, or other causes are not likely to have much in common with the denationalized "business and financial elite" that has little sense "of global civic responsibility."[28] Likewise, this capitalist elite has interests and needs different from those of the global managerial and laboring classes that also participate in transnational capitalism.

One way that the discourse of global citizenship affects the educational terrain is through educators who call for schooling that will prepare students for competition in the global sphere. In *World Bank Education*, Evan Watkins rejects the (traditional, civic republican) objective of schools that focused on the "preservation and transmission of some cultural heritage that ostensibly has given the Euro-American world its long global preeminence."[29] Though Watkins rejects the school's reproductive function as a transmitter of a common culture, he does not instead embrace cultural pluralism. Rather, he calls for the repurposing of schools as training grounds for global workers. He articulates the need for "a specifically national workforce that would allow the United States to continue to occupy its appropriately vanguard position in a global economy" and proposes achieving this goal with "job training" and "credentializing" programs.[30]

A turn to the sphere of literature can help elucidate how contemporary US immigrants—and their children—adopt, reimagine, or reject discourses of belonging. We can observe the narrative treatment of these discourses in the work of three authors: Eric Liu, who was born in the United States to Taiwanese immigrant parents; Jhumpa Lahiri, an immigrant whose family migrated from London to the United States when she was two years old; and Zhang Zhen, a US resident who was born in China, migrated to Sweden, and came to the United States only as an adult. A comparative analysis of these three texts demonstrates that a broad diversity exists even within this narrow sampling of authors that we can categorize as "successful" (in the fields of politics, literature, and academia, respectively). Despite their diversity, all three authors invoke civic republican ideology as they tell their stories and foreground the different aspects of their identities that emerge as they occupy varying social spaces.

* * *

The Accidental Asian: Notes of a Native Speaker is a set of autobiographical reflections on Asian American identity by Eric Liu, a political commentator and former speechwriter for Bill Clinton.[31] In the book's first chapter, Liu reflects on the symbolism of another book, a memory book that he keeps by his bedside, which tells one version of his (deceased) father's life story. The book, made by his father's best friends, frames his father's experience of immigration and Americanization as a progress narrative, one that Liu both accepts and challenges. This memory book symbolizes the pressure that contemporary immigrants to the United States often experience: to tell their stories through a conventional set of narrative demands informed by the realist or idealist bildungsroman. As Liu explains, his father's friends produced this Americanization narrative in the "familiar idiom of progress—the steady sense of climbing, and climbing higher; of forgetting, and forgetting more."[32] Liu's discussion implies that these friends were motivated by what William Boelhower describes as the "ritual requirements of American behavior codes"; a book like Liu's suggests that these codes continue to influence US life, even though Boelhower locates them in an earlier, nativist period of US history.[33]

On one level, Liu identifies with this narrative of loss, which has an alienating effect on his own identity. Reflecting on the memory book, Liu expresses sadness about all that he does not know about his father's history. The book includes photos and memories that tell the story of his father's life, but the stories are written in Chinese, a language, Liu confesses, he "once could read and write with middling proficiency but [has] since let slip into disuse."[34] Liu knows what the book says because his mother has translated it for him, but he is not sure whether to blame himself for his ignorance. He wonders, is it typical for second-generation immigrants to "accept without comment what few recollections the first generation offers," or is his own lack of curiosity the cause of his ignorance?[35] Liu's alienation recalls the alienation that Charles Reznikoff experienced from his family and culture and expressed in "Early History of a Writer." As the American-born children of immigrants, both Liu and Reznikoff are nostalgic for identities they know only through reminders of what they don't know. Just as Reznikoff has the uncanny experience of saying good-bye to a grandfather he hardly knows because they don't speak the same language, Liu experiences the memory book— which promises to impart a feeling of closeness—as a symbol of how little he really knows about his father. With the memory book in hand, Liu senses just "how opaque an inheritance one's identity truly is."[36]

Though Liu's experience of alienation is very real, as his own memoir progresses it begins to reveal a story about his father's cosmopolitanism, which is quite different from the story emblematized by the memory book. Liu explains that despite the memory book's progress narrative, he knows that his father maintained two identities, one represented by English and the other by Mandarin. Not only did Liu's father excel in his English classes as a teenager in Taiwan, but "once he came to the states he picked up jargon, slang, and idiom with a collector's enthusiasm."[37] As a philosophy student at the University of Illinois, in his master's program in mathematics, and through his twenty-seven years working for IBM, Liu's father was known for his "facility with English."[38] On the other hand, at home he spoke with his wife only in Mandarin Chinese, with a mastery of the language that was "as good as that of any

Confucian gentleman-scholar": so good that it enabled him to read and study the Chinese classics.[39] This evidence of the linguistic identities that Liu's father shifted between speaks not only to the difference between first- and second-generation immigrants but also to the complex realities of identity that often get buried beneath narratives of assimilation (represented here by the memory book).

A similar tension between experience and narrative demands characterizes Jhumpa Lahiri's story "Nobody's Business." This story is ostensibly about Sangeeta (Sang), a Harvard dropout struggling through a bad relationship. However, the story offers less insight into Sang's identity than into the fascination that the story's white, American protagonist has with the exotic markers of Sang's life: markers with which Sang herself does not even identify. Sang is either the Americanized child of Indian immigrants or a member of the 1.5 generation (children who immigrated before adolescence). Though the story doesn't say where Sang was born, the narrator implies that it doesn't matter; what really matters is that Sang is alienated from her parents' culture: "She spoke Bengali infrequently—never to her sister, never to her suitors, only a word here and there to her parents, in Michigan, to whom she spoke on weekends."[40] The reader never learns why Sang is reluctant to speak Bengali—if she cannot speak it or will not speak it. This obfuscation parallels the narrator's unwillingness to reveal where Sang was born. Are these facts unimportant to our understanding of Sang's identity, or are we kept ignorant of them to suggest that outsiders (like the reader, and the story's point-of-view character, Paul) base their reactions to other people on uninformed assumptions about their identities?

On one level, "Nobody's Business" is about the awkward relationship between Sang and Paul, the white, point-of-view character who is a graduate student in English at Harvard and also Sang's housemate. Through Paul—who is neither lover nor friend to Sang but only an acquaintance—Lahiri offers us a portrait of Sang that is at once intimate and distanced by Paul's outsider perspective. Through watching Paul watch Sang, the reader learns that Sang is continually subjected to Indian suitors seeking an arranged marriage. Sang rejects this path, just as she has dropped out of Harvard and taken a job at a local bookstore, despite her parents' shock and disappointment. Paul watches as Sang fields calls from potential suitors and gets hurt by her philandering fiancée; but because Paul filters his perceptions of her through his own expectations, he never gets to know Sang very well at all. Perhaps the closest Paul ever gets to Sang is through a visit to her bedroom while she is away in London. In the bedroom, Paul "undid his belt buckle, but suddenly the desire left him, absent from his body just as she was absent from the room."[41] Paul's action reveals that his desire for Sang is symptomatic of a false intimacy, which Paul acquires through watching Sang and filtering what he sees through a set of expectations.

Paul's relationship with Sang, which symbolizes the shallow intimacy produced by one-sided desire, parallels Sang's experience of the arranged marriage, an Indian custom that she experiences only as a reminder of her distance from that culture. Paul is fascinated by the frequent calls from suitors, who (like Paul) imagine an intimacy with Sang that is merely a product of their desire. The narrator explains, "Every so often a man called for Sang, wanting to marry her. Sang usually didn't know these men. Sometimes she had never even heard of them. But they'd heard that she was pretty and smart and thirty and Bengali and still single, and so these men, most of whom also happened to be Bengali, would procure her number from someone who knew someone who knew her parents, who, according to Sang, desperately wanted her to be married." The fact that these potential suitors know Sang only as a set of statistics reminds the reader how falsely appealing it can be to think we know someone through the concrete details of his or her life. The telephone calls—and Sang's reaction to them—also evidence the difficulty of translating an Indian marriage tradition to a US context. Sang takes the calls, presumably because not doing so would show disrespect to her parents. But the narrator portrays these scenes satirically: on one date, the suitor "had driven her north up I-93, pointing from the highway to the corporation he worked for. Then he'd taken her to a Dunkin' Donuts, where, over crullers and coffee, he'd proposed."[42] The incompatibility of a marriage proposal at a Dunkin' Donuts shop becomes a metaphor for the incompatibility of Sang's American life and the tradition of the arranged marriage.

The suitors' phone calls that Sang regularly fields also symbolize how written language can reify the processual nature of identity. Sang's habitual reaction to these calls was to "take notes . . . on the message pad kept next to the phone," on which she would "write down the man's name, or 'Carnegie Mellon,' or 'likes mystery novels.'" Sang's notes would inevitably devolve into doodles, signifying how useless her note taking was, because concrete details about a person's life in fact tell us very little about that person. It is only after she hangs up after each phone call that Sang explains to her housemates how little these men really know her: "These men weren't really interested in her. They were interested in a mythical creature created by an intricate chain of gossip, a web of wishful Indian-community thinking in which she was an aging, over-looked poster child for years of bharat natyam classes, perfect SATs."[43]

In "Nobody's Business," Lahiri creates parallels between the story's many elements: the lack of intimacy between the potential groom and bride of an arranged marriage, Sang's alienation from her family's cultural traditions, and the story of Paul's failure to pass his PhD exams. The reader learns that when Paul took his first oral exam, "he had not been able to reply to the first question, about comic villainy in *Richard III*. He had read the play so many times he could picture each scene, not as it might be performed on a stage but, rather, as the pale printed columns in his Pelican Shakespeare."[44] Paul knows the play in its written form only—not as it might have been performed—a fact that recalls Sang's ironic lists of her suitors' statistics (she and her suitors can know about each other on paper, but this is no substitute for the real thing). The incommensurability between knowing a person through experience and knowing a person through statistics is akin to the incommensurability between Shakespeare's plays as most people experienced them in Elizabethan England and the plays as Paul knows them, on paper. These portraits of incommensurability could also be commenting allegorically on the failed project of canonizing the immigrant experience. This process necessarily entails an exclusion of lived experiences that one cannot fairly reduce to the formal demands of Americanization narratives.

Zhang Zhen, a Chinese poet and professor of cinema studies at New York University, instead attempts to sidestep the conventional demands of the immigrant autobiography. In "The Jet Lag of a Migratory Bird," Zhen chooses not to focus on her experiences living in China, Sweden, Russia, or America. Instead, she foregrounds her moments of arrival to and departure from these places. Portraying the continuous demands of adapting to new countries, Zhen reveals the transnational nature of her identity. As someone who has lived a "life of incessant border crossings" (Zhen attended five universities and nine short- or long-term language programs around the world), she has an identity marked by transition and translation.[45] With every crossing, Zhen has to reconfigure her role vis-à-vis the world around her, which she experiences viscerally.[46] When she arrives, jet-lagged, in foreign airports, Zhen wonders what language she should speak; this dilemma gives her the "sensation of a swelling and clumsy tongue."[47] In these moments, Zhen's tongue seems to embody her experience of dislocation: of existing between, rather than in, cultures. Zhen also experiences this embodiment as one of "regenerating amputated limbs."[48] With this image, which she borrows from Norma Field, Zhen suggests that the different aspects of her self are located in her body (her limbs); with each migration, she has to undergo the physically painful and yet creative experience of reorienting herself to a new culture.

Though these continual shifts can be difficult, Zhen ultimately embraces her experience of being a "migratory bird": she does not feel nostalgic for an isolated, nationalized identity—as an American or Chinese woman. Rather, she understands that she can experience her transnationalism as the source of epiphanies, which mark themselves on her body and become part of her multilayered consciousness. Zhen explains that the first of these epiphanies happened while she was "dreaming on a train to Moscow"; it was "as though something invisibly slashed your skin but not until much later that you found a scar, a souvenir, of that experience so profound it almost amounted to a paradigm shift."[49] What is interesting about this passage is that Zhen shifts into the second person as she describes her epiphany, as though speaking from the centered position of an "I" would not make sense when describing such radical shifts in her sense of self. Rather, as Zhen literally crosses national borders, she experiences her consciousness simultaneously as an out-of-body experience (represented by her consciousness of what is happening) and as an embodied experience (because the memory of the experience persists as an image of a body literally transformed). At the same time, Zhen confesses that despite all her schooling and language training she is unable to communicate with her illiterate grandmother in rural China, who speaks a difficult dialect that Zhen knew a bit of as a child but subsequently forgot. Zhen's embrace of a transitional identity makes her an outsider to any single national culture; and her experience as an American is accompanied by a sense of loss and alienation from her grandmother. This grandmother represents the culture Zhen left behind so she could encounter new languages, ideas, and experiences, gleaned from a migratory life.

In his 1915 essay "Democracy versus the Melting-Pot," Horace Kallen argues that every human "lives and moves and has his being" through the medium of ancestors who persist within him.[50] As Sarah Wilson notes, this passage assumes that the immigrant "is cut off from 'the' past externally, but retains 'his' grandfather internally—presumably primarily biologically, but to some degree also psychically."[51] But what if our ancestry is either consciously lost to us or known—as was Liu's— only in a partial way that is ultimately unsatisfactory? When I was in college, and researching my own ancestors, I heard a story about my great-aunt Rose, whom I never knew. Apparently Rose was a wonderful cook, but if

someone asked her for a recipe she would leave out one important ingredient so the finished product would come out wrong. As a result, the
person who had requested the recipe would have to come to Rose's house
to eat her food. When I told my eight-year-old son this story, he asked
for a specific example: What was the recipe, what ingredient was left out?
But I could not answer, for the story I told him was the only part of the
story that I knew. In other words, what I knew was that there were very
specific things (the recipe, the ingredients) that I did not know.

As a second-generation American descended from eastern European Jews, I have experienced an alienation similar to that evoked by
Liu, Lahiri, and Zhang. Paradoxically, this alienation feels like loss, even
though it is loss of something I never really had. My grandparents, and
their parents, immigrated to New York City from eastern Europe at the
turn of the twentieth century. My grandfather—a devout Orthodox Jew
and cantor—began working in the garment industry but ended up moving to California and becoming a successful real estate investor. His many
sisters—also immigrants—continued to speak Yiddish and got involved
in leftist political and artistic communities: one worked with Margaret
Sanger, another joined the communists, and a third acted in the Yiddish theater before becoming a Rockette. My grandparents' generation
experienced internal divisions that echo the rift between German and
Yiddish Jews that I discuss earlier in this book. My grandfather and his
male siblings embraced capitalism, and with it assimilation. As a result,
my grandfather, and in turn my immediate family, became increasingly
isolated from my great-aunts. When I became old enough to ask why I
didn't know my great-aunts or their children, my grandmother told me
that they always asked for handouts and would complain, during the
Jewish holidays, about my grandfather's never-ending religious sermons
(capitalist success did not interfere with my grandfather's religiosity). I
therefore grew up without a living memory of my great-aunts, whereas
I have "known" the world of my grandfather through the values and
practices that were passed on to me through my father and his immediate family. I cannot say that I have lost the living knowledge of my
great-aunts, because I never knew it. What my experience suggests is that
assimilation to the United States does not necessarily silence the immigrant's past, but it can silence elements of it that are out of keeping with,
or threatening to, a mainstream US ideology of success and assimilation.

Notes

Introduction

1. Walt Whitman, "When I heard the Learn'd Astronomer," in *Leaves of Grass* (1900; repr., New York: Bartleby.com, 1999), www.bartleby.com/142/180.html.

2. Emily Dickinson, "If the foolish call them 'flowers,'" in *Complete Poems* (1924; repr., New York: Bartleby.com, 2000), www.bartleby.com/113/1094.html.

3. Derek Heater, *A History of Education for Citizenship* (London: Routledge Falmer, 2004), 113. Most also supported Horace Mann's proposal that students should be taught the basic principles of the US Constitution (105).

4. David B. Tyack, *The One Best System: A History of American Urban Education* (Cambridge, MA: Harvard University Press, 1974), 44–45.

5. Ibid., 180.

6. Ibid., 196. As David Tyack, Lawrence Cremin, and Derrick Alridge have noted, the diversity within educational progressivism has made it a difficult term to define. I share Alridge's response to critics who unfairly challenge Cremin's characterization of progressivism; see Derrick Alridge, *The Educational Thought of W. E. B. Du Bois* (New York: Teacher's College Press, 2008), 152 n. 14.

7. Tyack, *One Best System*, 197.

8. Ibid., 197.

9. See Lawrence Cremin, *The Transformation of the School: Progressivism in American Education, 1876–1957* (New York: Vintage, 1964). For explanation of my reliance on Cremin, cf. note 6 above. With reference to my use of civil and civic rights, see Karl Marx, "On the Jewish Question," where he elaborates on this distinction in post-Revolutionary France and America. The civil sphere, Marx writes, is a "realm of needs, labor, private interests, and private right," while the civic sphere constitutes the realm of politics. Karl Marx, "On the Jewish Question," in *The Marx-Engels Reader*, ed. Robert C. Tucker, 2nd ed. (New York: Norton, 1978), 113. Linda Bosniak notes that while most liberal theorists agree that civil society "represents aspects of social life not

encompassed by the state," those influenced by Gramsci view civil society as separate from both the state and the economy. Other critics identify the private sphere (represented by the home/family) as a category separate from the civil sphere. See Linda Bosniak, "Citizenship Denationalized," *Indiana Journal of Global Legal Studies* 7, no. 2 (Spring 2000): 476–77 n. 119.

10. In the US context, as Michael Carnoy argues, turn-of-the-century progressivist reformers established a school differentiation system that subjected "working class and immigrant children [who] could not meet the difficult regimen of the middle-class oriented program" to a stratified curriculum "so that working-class children would not drop out, but neither would they receive academic instruction." Michael Carnoy, *Education as Cultural Imperialism* (New York: David McKay, 1974), 248.

11. For an excellent study of citizenship education as it affected African Americans and Native Americans in Kansas, see Kim Warren, who both distinguishes between the types of training directed at these groups and demonstrates that both groups were subject to "Christian indoctrination, strict discipline, and displays of patriotism"; Kim Cary Warren, *The Quest for Citizenship: African American and Native American Education in Kansas, 1880–1935* (Chapel Hill: University of North Carolina Press, 2010), 57. Warren also emphasizes how members of these groups developed approaches to national membership that reflected their cultural and historical particularities.

12. As Painter demonstrates, evolutionary and genetic ideologies, which often contradicted each other in their logic and proposed solutions, coexisted in American public thought during this period. See Nell Irvin Painter, *The History of White People* (New York: Norton, 2011), chaps. 20–24.

13. Carl Degler, *In Search of Human Nature: The Decline and Revival of Darwinism in American Social Thought* (New York: Oxford University Press, 1991), 42.

14. Chip Rhodes notes that such "internal contradictions" were constitutive of the progressive educational movement, such that one of its central innovations, the Gary Plan, could be "hailed (and attacked) for its supposed challenge to the status quo" even as it was recognized for promoting a "nationalist celebration of sameness." Chip Rhodes, *Structures of the Jazz Age: Mass Culture, Progressive Education, and Racial Disclosures in American Modernism* (London: Verso, 1998), 147.

15. Jeffrey Mirel has produced a wonderful study of citizenship education directed at European immigrants in Chicago, Cleveland, and Detroit. Mirel focuses on Americanization efforts at public schools and adult education programs, as well as on the foreign-language newspapers through which these immigrants influenced US civic culture. Jeffrey Mirel, *Patriotic Pluralism: Americanization Education and European Immigrants* (Cambridge, MA: Harvard University Press, 2010).

16. I have not examined the experience and literature of Mexicans, Chinese, and other groups of new Americans in this study. Most citizenship education programs geared toward Mexican Americans operated in the 1920s and 1930s, much later than the programs I have examined. Some schools did exist for Chinese Americans at the turn of the twentieth century, but not for the purpose of Americanizing them (given the anti-immigrant legislation targeting Chinese immigrants). Though Americanization programs existed in US colonies, such as the Philippines and Hawaii, I could not do justice to that topic within the confines of this monograph.

17. For classic studies of Native American education, see Frederick Hoxie, *A Final Promise: The Campaign to Assimilate the Indians, 1880–1920* (Lincoln: University of

Nebraska Press, 1984); and David Wallace Adams, *Education for Extinction: American Indians and the Boarding School Experience, 1875–1928* (Lawrence: University Press of Kansas, 1995); on African American education, see James D. Anderson, *The Education of Blacks in the South, 1860–1935* (Chapel Hill: University of North Carolina Press, 1988); and on Jewish immigrant education, see Stefan F. Brumberg, *Going to America, Going to School: The Jewish Immigrant Public School Encounter in Turn-of-the-Century New York City* (New York: Praeger, 1986).

18. Cremin, *Transformation of the School*, 129.

19. Larry Cuban, *How Teachers Taught: Constancy and Change in American Classrooms, 1890–1990* (New York: Teacher's College, Columbia University), 26.

20. John and Evelyn Dewey, *Schools of To-morrow* (New York: E. P. Dutton, 1915), 232.

21. Ibid., 257.

22. Ibid., 134.

23. Cuban, *How Teachers Taught*, 25. According to Cuban, Barbara Finkelstein coined these terms.

24. Ibid.

25. This text comes from a 1789 Massachusetts law passed on June 25, 1789, titled "An Act to Provide for the Instruction of Youth, and for the Promotion of Good Education." The law outlines the ideal objectives for establishing school districts; cited in Rhodes, *Structures*, 154.

26. Cremin, *Transformation of the School*, 132–36.

27. Rhodes, *Structures*, 141. *One-sided thought* is Dewey's term, cited by Rhodes.

28. Ibid.

29. Ibid., 143. In this respect, we can place Dewey squarely within the tradition of the American jeremiad that I discuss later in this introduction.

30. Cremin, *Transformation of the School*, 150.

31. Rhodes, *Structures*, 143.

32. Ibid., 140–41.

33. Cremin, *Transformation of the School*, 24.

34. Emerson White, quoted in Cremin, *Transformation of the School*, 29; see also 26, 34.

35. Ibid., 155–57.

36. Ibid., 22.

37. Ronald D. Cohen and Raymond A. Mohl, *The Paradox of Progressive Education: The Gary Plan and Urban Schooling* (Port Washington, NY: Kennikat Press, 1979), 24.

38. Cremin, *Transformation of the School*, 34.

39. Cohen and Mohl, *Paradox of Progressive Education*, 20.

40. Ibid., 46.

41. For the Dewey quote, see Rhodes, *Structures*, 141. With the argument that individuals associate habits with objects rather than ideas, James moved away from the dominant, associationist school of thought, represented in the nineteenth century, for instance, by Alexander Bain. For an extended discussion of the long trajectory of habit theory, beginning with Aristotle, see Michael G. Johnson and Tracy B. Henley, *Reflections on the Principles of Psychology: William James after a Century* (Hillsdale, NJ: Lawrence Erlbaum Associates, 1990).

42. William James, *Principles of Psychology*, vol. 1 (Cambridge, MA: Harvard University Press, 1983), 122.

43. Francesca Bordogna, *William James at the Boundaries: Philosophy, Science, and the Geography of Knowledge* (Chicago: University of Chicago Press, 2008), 268.

44. Ibid., 259.

45. Ibid.

46. Charles Darwin, "General Principles of Expression," in *The Expression of the Emotions in Man and Animals*, Kindle ed. (CreateSpace Independent Publishing Platform, 2012).

47. As Carl Degler demonstrates, Darwin "raised no objection to the idea that the behavior of parents, under certain circumstances, might be inherited by their offspring." Given Darwin's acceptance of the "principle of acquired characters," it makes sense that Darwinian social scientists might also believe "that behavior, or habits, to use Darwin's term, might be inherited." Degler, *In Search*, 21.

48. Though the British philosopher Herbert Spencer published his theories before Darwin, he is commonly associated with social Darwinism, which became popular in the late nineteenth-century United States. Though the ideas of social Darwinists such as Spencer, William Graham Sumner, and E. A. Ross differed in significant ways, in general these figures represented a conservative trend that defended "the social and economic hierarchy of nineteenth-century America." See Degler, *In Search*, 13.

49. In response to the critical debate about whether James was a social Darwinist, Lucas McGranahan opines that we can see him as one only "in the sense of having a theory influenced by Darwin, and also in the sense of believing in the reality and importance of time and change in nature and society." In McGranahan's view, with which I agree, James was *not* a social Darwinist in the "most pernicious, familiar, and Spencerian sense of the term, which involves gleaning a substantive ethnical or political position directly from facts about nature or natural processes." Lucas McGranahan, "William James's Social Evolutionism in Focus," *Pluralist* 6, no. 3 (2011): 84.

50. See Degler, *In Search*, 21.

51. Ibid., 24.

52. Writing about the preparation of workers *and* consumers at educational institutions during the Progressive Era, Chip Rhodes explains that while we usually locate the production of workers through schools and the production of consumers through mass culture, schools in fact felt they could construct "the needs and desires of subjects." Rhodes, *Structures*, 149–50. My book also illustrates how educational institutions sought to train new citizens simultaneously to identify and operate as capitalist workers and consumers.

53. Edward Casey, "Habitual Body and Memory in Merleau-Ponty," in *A History of Habit: From Aristotle to Bourdieu*, ed. Tom Sparrow and Adam Hutchinson (Lanham, MD: Lexington Books, 2013), 190.

54. Ibid., 211.

55. Ibid., 212.

56. Steven G. Matthews, "The Instantiated Identity: Critical Approaches to Studying Gesture and Material Culture," paper presented at the annual meeting of the Theoretical Archaeology Group, University of Glasgow, Scotland, December 17–19, 2004, Semioticon.com, www.semioticon.com/virtuals/archaeology/instantiated.pdf, p. 4.

57. Sue Ellen Henry, "Bodies at Home and at School: Toward a Theory of Embodied Social Class Status," *Educational Theory* 63, no. 1 (February 2013): 4. Explaining the relationship between Bourdieu's ideas and Chris Shilling's theory of corporeal

realism, Henry explains how they both demonstrate that "society does not only write itself upon the body, the body also changes society as a result of its actions and reactions" (4).

58. Stephen Macedo, *Diversity and Distrust: Civic Education in a Multicultural Democracy* (Cambridge, MA: Harvard University Press, 2000), 89.

59. Ibid., 92.

60. Ibid., 94.

61. Theodore Roosevelt, "A Square Deal for All Americans," in *Roosevelt in the Kansas City Star: War-Time Editorials* (Boston: Houghton Mifflin, 1921), Internet Archive, Library of Congress, https://archive.org/details/rooseveltinkansa01roos, 143–44.

62. J. A. Banks, quoted in Kathleen Knight Abowitz and Jason Harnish, "Contemporary Discourses of Citizenship," *Review of Educational Research* 76, no. 4 (Winter 2006): 653–90, 670.

63. Kimberly Hutchings, "Political Theory and Cosmopolitan Citizenship," in *Cosmopolitan Citizenship*, ed. Kimberly Hutchings and Roland Dannreuther (Basingstoke: Palgrave Macmillan, 1999), 3–34, 8.

64. Ibid.

65. Ibid., 8.

66. See Knight Abowitz and Harnish, "Contemporary Discourses," for a useful general discussion of this.

67. Linda Bosniak, "Citizenship Denationalized," *Indiana Journal of Global Legal Studies* 7, no. 2 (Spring 2000): 471.

68. When I use the term *civic republicanism* in my discussions of assimilationist education, I am referring to its ideological emphasis on uniformity, rather than its practical promotion of political action.

69. My work, alongside that of Kim Warren and Jeffrey Mirel, attests to the failure of assimilationist educators to prevent alternate articulations of US citizenship in the public sphere. See Warren, *Quest for Citizenship*, and Mirel, *Patriotic Pluralism*.

70. Hutchings, "Political Theory," 5.

71. Ibid., 7.

72. Ibid.

73. Bosniak examines contemporary discussions of this trend in work by Judith Shklar, Rogers Smith, Charles Black, and Kenneth Karst. Bosniak cites Black's discussion of the Warren court to identify the central features of this trend, and I also cite it because it captures perfectly what Black calls "the positive content and worth of American citizenship. . . . First, citizenship is the right to be heard and counted on public affairs, the right to vote on equal terms, to speak, and to hold office when legitimately chosen. . . . Second, citizenship means the right to be treated fairly when one is the object of action by that government of which one is also a part. . . . Thirdly, citizenship is the broad right to lead a private life. . . . [Finally, the Warren Court] affirmed, as no Court before it ever did, that this three-fold citizenship is to be enjoyed in all its parts without respect to race. Charles L. Black, *The Unfinished Business of the Warren Court*, 46 Wash.L. REV. 3, 8–10 (1970), quoted in Bosniak, "Citizenship Denationalized," 464–65 n.60.

74. Knight Abowitz and Harnish, "Contemporary Discourses," 653–90.

75. Renato Rosaldo and Juan Flores, quoted in Knight Abowitz and Harnish, "Contemporary Discourses," 669.

76. In a challenge to Horace Kallen's concept of cultural pluralism, Jeffrey Mirel uses the term *patriotic pluralism* to characterize the immigrant's simultaneous commitment to his or her ethnic particularity and intense "emotional attachment" to "American democracy"; Mirel argues that Kallen undervalued the latter. Mirel, *Patriotic Pluralism*, 105. Of particular interest is Mirel's discussion of immigrant journalists who represented important US historical events "in ways that legitimated [the presence of these groups] in the United States"; ibid., 120.

77. Knight Abowitz and Harnish, "Contemporary Discourses," 677.

78. Hutchings, "Political Theory," 12.

79. Carl Levy, "Anarchism and Cosmopolitanism," *Journal of Political Ideologies* 16, no. 3 (October 2011): 266.

80. Gavin Kendall, Ian Woodward, and Zlatko Skrbis, *The Sociology of Cosmopolitanism: Globalization, Identity, Culture, and Government* (London: Palgrave Macmillan, 2009), 67.

81. Bryan Turner, quoted in Kendall, Woodard, and Skrbis, *Sociology of Cosmopolitanism*, 67, 69. Kendall, Woodward, and Skrbis stress that cosmopolitanism is not a static entity but an ethical stance, which, in its ideal manifestation, takes the "form of ironic, detached, but fundamentally ethical concern for the other" (98).

82. Hansen, *Lost Promise*, 67.

83. Ibid., 70. Hansen describes both Addams and Du Bois as cosmopolitan patriots who "embrace a social-democratic ethic that reflected the interconnected and mutually dependent nature of life in the modern world" (8).

84. Knight Abowitz and Harnish, "Contemporary Discourses," 673. In this respect, one can see the mutual compatibility of reconstructionist discourse and the genre of the American jeremiad, which I examine later in this introduction.

85. Pheng Cheah, "Given Culture: Rethinking Cosmopolitical Freedom in Transnationalism," in *Cosmopolitics: Thinking and Feeling beyond the Nation*, ed. Pheng Cheah and Bruce Robbins (Minneapolis: University of Minnesota Press, 1998), 171.

86. Particularly with Du Bois, we can see how a global morality can be limited as a result of its embodiment by a privileged cosmopolitan philosopher, whose particular point of view "masquerades as universal." Hutchings, "Political Theory," 18.

87. Todd Kontje, *Private Lives in the Public Sphere: The German Bildungsroman as Metafiction* (University Park: Pennsylvania State University Press, 1992), 9. Kontje makes this statement in describing the canonical German bildungsroman.

88. Stephen Greenblatt, *Renaissance Self-Fashioning*, quoted in Kontje, *Private Lives*, 8.

89. Kontje, *Private Lives*, 9.

90. Ibid., 11.

91. Paul Jay, "What's the Use? Critical Theory and the Study of Autobiography," *Biography* 10, no. 1 (Winter 1987): 39–54, 44.

92. Ibid., 44.

93. Joseph Slaughter, *Human Rights, Inc.: The World Novel, Narrative Form, and International Law* (New York: Fordham University Press, 2007), 113.

94. Ibid., 115.

95. Todd Kontje, *The German Bildungsroman: History of a National Genre* (Columbia, SC: Camden House, 1993), 8.

96. Ibid., 35. Kontje thus praises Lukács's reading of *Wilhelm Meister's Apprenticeship*, which recognizes the irony with which Goethe "offers only an *attempted* synthesis between the individual and society, one that necessarily falls short of its goal" (35).

97. Slaughter, *Human Rights*, 180.

98. Ibid., 94.

99. Ibid., 181.

100. Ibid., 182.

101. Ibid., 184.

102. Ibid., 182.

103. Jer. 7:18. I cite this passage from the *Tanakh: A New Translation of The Holy Scriptures According to the Traditional Hebrew Text* (Philadelphia: Jewish Publication Society, 1985).

104. Sacvan Bercovitch, *The American Jeremiad* (Madison: University of Wisconsin Press, 1978), 160.

105. Nancy Fraser, "Rethinking the Public Sphere: A Contribution to the Critique of Actually Existing Democracy," *Social Text* 25/26 (1990): 56–80, 66.

106. Dana Nelson, *National Manhood: Capitalist Citizenship and the Imagined Fraternity of White Men* (Durham, NC: Duke University Press, 1998), 6.

107. Horatio Alger, *Ragged Dick, or, Street Life in New York* (1868; repr. New York: Collier Books, 1962), 130.

108. Michael Moon, "'The Gentle Boy from the Dangerous Classes': Pederasty, Domesticity, and Capitalism in Horatio Alger," *Representations* 19 (Summer 1987): 87.

109. The Horatio Alger stories were not the only nineteenth-century texts for children promoting the fantasy that financial success and stability were open to all. For instance, the popular *McGuffey's Newly Revised Eclectic Third Reader* (1853) promised that "the road to wealth, to honor, to usefulness, and happiness, is open to all, and all who will, may enter upon it with the almost certain prospect of success." Quoted in Richard M. Huber, *The American Idea of Success* (New York: McGraw-Hill, 1971), 25.

110. In his excellent comparative discussion of Alfred Stieglitz and Lewis Hine, Alan Trachtenberg presents, but also challenges, the dichotomy between documentary and pictorialist photography. Alan Trachtenberg, "Camera Work/Social Work," in *Reading American Photographs: Images As History, Mathew Brady to Walker Evans* (New York: Hill and Wang, 1990).

111. The Modern School photos I discuss, collected at Rutgers University Libraries Special Collections, are not explicitly categorized as Steckbardt's; while interviews with students and histories of the school note that Steckbardt took most of the photos of life at the school, he did not sign any of his photos. The Steckbardts were at Stelton as early as 1921. E-mail correspondence with Modern School Archivist Fernanda Perrone, 26 February 2014.

1 / On Autobiography, Boy Scouts, and Citizenship

A shorter version of this chapter appeared in *Arizona Quarterly*: Tova Cooper, "On Autobiography, Boy Scouts, and Citizenship: Revisiting Charles Eastman's *Deep Woods*," *Arizona Quarterly* (Winter 2009): 1–35.

1. Erving Goffman coined the term *total institutions* in his essay "On the Characteristics of Total Institutions," in *Asylums: Essays on the Social Situation of Mental Patients and Other Inmates* (New York: Doubleday, 1961).

2. Cathleen Cahill's excellent book *Federal Fathers and Mothers* shares my methodological approach. Cahill draws extensively on archival materials and compares federal policy with the quotidian realities of schools and other institutions through

which the US government realized its assimilation policy. Likewise, Cahill and I both address parallels between the status of African Americans and American Indians during this period and discuss the complex position of white women who taught in the Indian schools. Cahill's central focus, however, is on the intimate relationships between colonial agents and colonized American Indians in what she and others have termed the "maternalist welfare state"; in particular, Cahill focuses on the government's efforts to transform the Indian's family, home, and daily occupations. Cathleen D. Cahill, *Federal Fathers and Mothers: A Social History of the United States Indian Service, 1869–1933* (Chapel Hill: University of North Carolina Press, 2011), 6–7.

3. Joseph Slaughter, *Human Rights, Inc.: The World Novel, Narrative Form, and International Law* (New York: Fordham University Press, 2007), 180. One such assimilationist autobiography is Luther Standing Bear's *My People, the Sioux*, first published in 1928. For an extended discussion of Native American boarding schools and assimilationist autobiography, see David Wallace Adams, *Education for Extinction: American Indians and the Boarding School Experience, 1875–1928* (Lawrence: University Press of Kansas, 1995).

4. As I discuss in this book's introduction, Kontje characterizes the bildungsroman as a "metafictional" genre that not only transforms literature through its reflexivity but also "examines this transformation." Todd Kontje, *Private Lives in the Public Sphere: The German Bildungsroman as Metafiction* (University Park: Pennsylvania State University Press, 1992), 11.

5. Diana Fuss, *Identification Papers* (New York: Routledge, 1995), 148, 152.

6. Slaughter, *Human Rights*, 94.

7. Among the critics of *From the Deep Woods* is Warrior, who views Eastman's "blinding progressivistic optimism" as a characteristic of his alignment with US educational policies. Robert Allen Warrior, *Tribal Secrets: Recovering American Indian Intellectual Traditions* (Minneapolis: University of Minnesota Press, 1995), 6. Brumble puts forth the most extended critique of social Darwinism in chap. 7 of *Indian Boyhood*. David Brumble III, *American Indian Autobiography* (Lincoln: University of Nebraska Press, 1988). Some recent writing about Eastman's autobiographical work has, however, has looked more favorably on his challenges to dominant discourses. See Tony Dykema-VanderArk, "'Playing Indian' in Print: Charles A. Eastman's Autobiographical Writing for Children," *MELUS* 27, no. 2 (Summer 2002): 9–30; and Lucy Maddox, *Citizen Indians: Native American Intellectuals, Race, and Reform* (Ithaca, NY: Cornell University Press, 2005). Amelia Katanski offers an excellent analysis of how Eastman uses irony to critique dominant US culture. Amelia Katanski, *Learning to Write "Indian": The Boarding School Experience and American Indian Literature* (Norman: University of Oklahoma Press, 2007).

8. Arnold Krupat, *Red Matters: Native American Studies* (Philadelphia: University of Pennsylvania Press, 2002), ix. Krupat adds a third term, *indigenism*, to this configuration; this term references another set of critics who compare indigenous knowledges and experiences, emphasizing values that derive from indigenous peoples' relationship with the land. Krupat, *Red Matters*, 12.

9. Gerald Vizenor, *Manifest Manners: Postindian Warriors of Survivance* (Hanover, NH: University Press of New England, 1994), 12.

10. Lopenzina argues that after caring for the victims of the US government's massacre at Wounded Knee, Eastman became increasingly politicized and critical of the

government's anti-Indian policies. Drew Lopenzina, "Good Indian: Charles Eastman and the Warrior as Civil Servant," *American Indian Quarterly* 27 (2003): 727–57.

11. Raymond Wilson, *Ohiyesa: Charles Eastman, Santee Sioux* (Urbana: University of Illinois Press, 1983), 142.

12. Raymond Wilson, introduction to *From the Deep Woods to Civilization: Chapters in the Autobiography of an Indian*, by Charles Eastman, ed. Raymond Wilson (Lincoln: University of Nebraska Press, 1977), vi–vii.

13. After two years at the mission school in Flandreau, near his father's house, Eastman transferred to the Santee Normal School, a religious institution that offered instruction in Sioux. There Eastman developed a close relationship with Alfred Riggs, the school's superintendent and son of the missionary Stephen Riggs. In 1876, Eastman transferred to Beloit, a state college in Wisconsin, where he studied for three years before transferring to Knox College in Illinois (1879–81). After receiving a BS from Dartmouth in 1887, Eastman entered Boston University School of Medicine, graduating as a doctor in 1890. For a detailed biography of Eastman, see Raymond Wilson, *Ohiyesa*.

14. Because the Dawes Act weakened tribal relations and allowed white settlers to acquire valuable Indian lands, Eastman's support for it is troublesome. Nonetheless, Eastman later criticized the Burke Act of 1906 (Wilson, *Ohiyesa*, 139). This revision of the Dawes Act made it more difficult for Indians to become citizens by creating a delay of twenty-five years between the government's issuing of patents for land and the actual distribution of land titles and citizenship. Francis Paul Prucha, *The Great Father: The United States Government and the American Indians*, vol. 2 (Lincoln: University of Nebraska Press, 1997), 668.

15. Eastman could be described as a "bicultural activist," the term Kim Warren uses to describe Ella Deloria, who sought to build "a bridge between Native American and white societies" by "modeling a bicultural identity" and "preserving Sioux languages," and Henry Roe Cloud, who lobbied for Native American legal equality and founded the American Indian Institute to prepare Native Americans "for higher education and national leadership"; Kim Cary Warren, *The Quest for Citizenship: African American and Native American Education in Kansas, 1880–1935* (Chapel Hill: University of North Carolina Press, 2010), 162–70.

16. The texts through which Eastman retold Sioux myths and stories include *Indian Boyhood; Red Hunters and the Animal People; Old Indian Days; Wigwam Evenings*; and *Indian Heroes and Great Chieftains*.

17. During the education campaign's early years, many children were abducted or otherwise coerced into attending government schools; increasingly, however, new laws required school officials to obtain parent approval before transferring children to on- or off-reservation boarding schools.

18. By 1900, there were 153 boarding schools (many of them on reservations) with a total of 17,708 students, and 154 day schools with 3,860 students. Adams, *Education for Extinction*, 58; for a chart of specific schools and their opening dates, see 57.

19. Ibid., 63. Congress did give parents the authority to keep their children from attending off-reservation schools.

20. Ibid., 65–66.

21. As social Darwinism gave way to eugenics, and many educators began to doubt that education could produce total assimilation, the popularity of off-reservation

schools declined (in favor of reservation schools); at the same time, these schools began to teach Indian arts and crafts, whereas up until that point the schools had prohibited all forms of native culture. These developments intensified with the tenures of commissioners William Jones (1897–1905) and Francis Leupp (1905–9).

22. As Prucha explains, the Dawes Act was the work of "eastern humanitarians who deeply believed that communal landholding was an obstacle to the civilization they wanted the Indians to acquire and who were convinced that they had the history of human experience on their side." Prucha, *Great Father*, 669. Reformers worried that if the Dawes Act were not passed the Indians would lose everything, because white settlers were rapidly encroaching upon Indian land, and the government was not adequately defending their rights to it (669).

23. For discussions of the degree to which boarding schools effected tribal dis-identification, see Adams, *Education for Extinction*; Brenda Child, *Boarding School Seasons: American Indian Families, 1900–1940* (Lincoln: University of Nebraska Press, 1998); and Tsianina Lomawaima, *They Called It Prairie Light: The Story of Chilocco Indian School* (Lincoln: University of Nebraska Press, 1994).

24. 24 U.S. Stat. 388–91.

25. There was a delay of twenty-five years between the government's issuing of patents for the land and the actual distribution of the allotment. Prucha, *Great Father*, 668. Cf. note 14.

26. According to Rogers Smith, the Dawes Act instituted a form of American Indian citizenship that relied on birth status but also required consent (the adoption of American principles). The introduction of consent to birthright citizenship led to the creation of ascriptive hierarchies that qualified the inclusiveness implied by consent. In other words, even though consensual belonging meant that "all [an individual] had to do was to commit himself to the political ideology centered on the abstract ideals of liberty, equality, and republicanism," certain groups—such as American Indians—were deemed more or less capable of or ready to adopt such ideals. Gleason, quoted in Rogers Smith, *Civic Ideals: Conflicting Visions of Citizenship in U.S. History* (New Haven, CT: Yale University Press, 1997), 14.

27. Despite his shortcomings, Marshall did provide a much-needed counterbalance to the "renewed ascendancy of state-centered Republicanism" during this era; moreover, he distinguished himself from nativistic federalists by arguing that the rights of native and naturalized citizens should be considered indistinguishable—a decision that benefited immigrants to the United States. Smith, *Civic Ideals*, 191.

28. *Cherokee Nation v. Georgia*, 30 U.S. 1 (1831). Justice Smith Thompson wrote the dissenting opinion for this case, on behalf of himself and Justice Story, arguing, in favor of the Cherokees' sovereignty, that the Cherokees "have never been, by conquest, reduced to the situation of subjects to any conqueror, and thereby lost their separate national existence, and the rights of self-government, and become subject to the laws of the conqueror."

29. A year later, in a decision more sympathetic to Indian rights (*Worcester v. Georgia*), Marshall firmly "rejected all state regulation of Native American affairs or acquisition of tribal lands . . . promising that national power would be used to protect the tribes against state and private encroachments." Smith, *Ideals*, 239. However, Marshall still left the tribes "dependent on, and arguably subject to, the dominion of the United States, though they were not American nationals" (239). Moreover, Marshall's

landmark decision was not enforced by President Jackson, leading to the Cherokees' ultimate expulsion from their lands during the Trail of Tears.

30. Civil Rights Act of 1866, 14 Stat. 27–30 (Apr. 1866). Moreover, section II of the Fourteenth Amendment was more specific in its exclusion of Indians from citizenship status, as it excluded "Indians not taxed" from eligibility for being counted in the selection of congressional representatives. Prucha, *Great Father*, 683.

31. Smith, *Civic Ideals*, 308.

32. Ibid., 309, emphasis added.

33. Ibid.

34. *Ex Parte Crow Dog*, 109 U.S. 556 (1883).

35. Smith, *Civic Ideals*, 393.

36. *Elk v. Wilkins*, 112 U.S. 556 (1883).

37. Smith, *Civic Ideals*, 395.

38. Prucha, *Great Father*, 679. The seven crimes were murder, manslaughter, rape, assault with intent to commit murder, arson, burglary, and larceny. The constitutionality of the Major Crimes Act was subsequently questioned and upheld by the 1886 Supreme Court case *United States v. Kagama*, in what David E. Wilkins describes as a decision made in complete disregard of "a century of federal legislation, the treaty process[,] . . . early Supreme Court precedents," and the Constitution. David E. Wilkins, *American Indian Sovereignty and the U.S. Supreme Court: The Masking of Justice* (Austin: University of Texas Press, 1997), 73. In a federalist decision that blatantly disregarded tribal sovereignty, Justice Samuel Miller declared that the US government had jurisdiction over a crime committed by one Indian against another.

39. Quoted in Prucha, *Great Father*, 677.

40. Ibid.

41. According to Thayer, the Dawes Act didn't provide state and federal legal protection to Native Americans either immediately or completely enough. However, Thayer's proposed bill never made it through Congress—primarily because of vocal opposition from Dawes himself. Prucha, *Great Father*, 681.

42. As Samuel Kirkwood writes in his 1881 report to Congress, "Education in English is the primary impediment to their becoming citizens, and this question, and the question of work, go hand in hand." Samuel Kirkwood, *Report of the Secretary of the Interior*, US 47th Congress, 1st sess. (Washington, DC: Government Printing Office, 1881–83), iv.

43. Kirkwood, *Report*, i. This attitude reflects a larger, late nineteenth-century trend in public conversations about the role of education in cultivating citizens. For instance, in an 1862 statement about the role of public schools, the Illinois superintendent of public instruction argued, "The chief end is to make GOOD CITIZENS. Not to make precocious scholars . . . not to impart the secret of acquiring wealth . . . not to qualify directly for professional success . . . but simply to make good citizens." Quoted in Smith, *Ideals*, 217. US education commissioner John Eaton also "echoed many educators when he wrote in 1874 that unless public schools 'elevated and harmonized' the citizenry—especially poor, ignorant blacks and whites in the South, as well as immigrants—the 'existence of a republic' would be an 'impossibility'" (322).

44. One particularly striking example of this occurs in an 1899 comment made by T. J. Morgan, commissioner of Indian affairs: "All school girls should be supplied with proper pocket handkerchiefs. A handkerchief as a civilizer comes before the primary

reader. If we wish to civilize these girls we must teach them the use of the pocket hand-kerchief and give them such ones as civilized girls carry." Quoted in Genevieve Bell, "Telling Stories Out of School: Remembering the Carlisle Indian Industrial School, 1879–1918" (PhD diss., Stanford University, 1996), 345.

45. Merrill Gates, quoted in Adams, *Education for Extinction*, 18.

46. Ibid., 22.

47. Ibid., 23, emphasis added. This sentiment later manifests itself at the curricular level, when Estelle Reel writes that Indians needed to be taught to "have a *desire* and ambition to irrigate more land" alongside "*the ability to carry out their desires.*" Estelle Reel, *Course of Study for the Indian Schools of the United States, Industrial and Literary* (Washington, DC: Government Printing Office, 1901), 10.

48. Cahill also addresses the federal government's attempts to instill capitalist val-ues into American Indians, particularly in the context of the Indian Service's transfor-mation of native ideas of domestic space. See Cahill, *Federal Fathers and Mothers*, 49.

49. Dawes had another view of the relationship between absorption and assimila-tion; he thought that absorption preceded assimilation and was realized through the mere immersion of foreigners into mainstream America. Assimilation would come later, after "time and contact . . . individual effort and social force . . . education and religion." This gradated process of absorption and assimilation was not limited, in his view, to American Indians, for "the Bohemians in Chicago, the Polish Jews in New York, are absorbed into our civilization, though they speak no English or live in squalor. Assimilation is another and a better thing, but it is the step that follows absorption." Quoted in Bell, *Telling Stories*, 42.

50. For useful discussions of the role of clothing and the before-and-after photos in the government schools, see Michael C. Coleman, *American Indian Children at School, 1850–1930* (Jackson: University Press of Mississippi, 1993); Adams, *Education for Extinction*; and Laura Wexler, *Tender Violence: Domestic Visions in an Age of U.S. Imperialism* (Chapel Hill: University of North Carolina Press, 2000).

51. Slaughter, *Human Rights*, 113.

52. Minnie Braithwaite Jenkins, *Girl from Williamsburg* (Richmond, VA: Dietz Press, 1951), 4. As David Wallace Adams writes, "By 1900 the Indian Office reported that of the 347 teachers employed [at such boarding schools], 286 were women." Adams, *Education for Extinction*, 82.

53. In her memoir, one teacher, Estelle Aubrey Brown, bitterly describes a woman's limited options: "If a girl failed to get a husband, she could teach at a rural school—if she could spell. She could be a country dressmaker—if she could sew. Failing these, she could be a burden, for which no qualifications were necessary. But she could not be employed in the office of a businessman or professional man. . . . For a girl, life in the hamlet was a dreary business that made even the threat of Indian atrocities in distant lands seem preferable." Estelle Aubrey Brown, *Stubborn Fool: A Narrative* (Caldwell, ID: Caxton Printers, 1952), 15–16.

54. See "The Women and Men of the Indian Service," Part Two of Cahill's *Federal Fathers and Mothers*, for a thorough discussion of the Indian Service as a "maternalist agency" (65).

55. Jenkins, *Girl from Williamsburg*, 318.

56. Ibid., 324–25, 325.

57. Ibid., 294.

58. During the years of its operation (1879–1918), Carlisle published both weekly and monthly newspapers whose names continually changed. The *Indian Helper* was published during Pratt's superintendency, while the *Indian Craftsman* appeared during the superintendency of Moses Friedman—who was particularly active in both sending copies of the *Arrow* (the weekly newspaper at the time) to former students and corresponding with said students. Genevieve Bell notes that while Pratt sent copies of the school papers to "every member of Congress, all Indian agencies and military posts, and most prominent American newspapers" (66), reaching a circulation of ten thousand paid subscribers in 1896, it was not until Friedman's superintendency that former students were eligible to join the subscription audience (325–26). Bell, *Telling Stories*.

59. *Indian Helper: A Weekly Letter* (Carlisle, PA: US Indian Industrial School), September 11, 1891, 1.

60. For evidence supporting the claim that the MOTBS was Marianna Burgess, see Jacqueline Fear-Segal, "Eyes in the Text: Marianna Burgess and *The Indian Helper*," in *Blue Pencils and Hidden Hands: Women Editing Periodicals, 1830–1910*, ed. Sharon Harris and Ellen Gruber Garvey (Boston: Northeastern University Press, 2004). While Jessica Enoch, Jacqueline Fear-Segal, Joel Pfister, and others have done wonderful examinations of the MOTBS, my purpose in discussing this figure is to emphasize the way he represents the intersection of material and psychological embodiment of the school's ideology. See Jessica Enoch, "Resisting the Script of Indian Education: Zitkala Ša and the Carlisle Indian School," *College English* 65, no. 2 (2002); Fear-Segal, "Eyes in the Text"; and Joel Pfister, *Individuality Incorporated: Indians and the Multicultural Modern* (Durham, NC: Duke University Press, 2004).

61. Fear-Segal, "Eyes in the Text," 130.

62. Ibid., 124.

63. When I was reading these columns at the NYPL, I found them compellingly addictive for this reason.

64. Enoch, "Resisting the Script," 12. I agree with Barbara Landis's view, quoted by Bell, that "the 'Man in the Bandstand' or 'MB' was probably Marianna Burgess, the director of the printing press. It seems to [Landis] that the persona of the 'Man in the Bandstand' was meant to evoke the watchful gaze of Pratt [the school's founder], but that the column itself was often authored by others, mostly [sic] commonly Marianna Burgess." Bell, *Telling Stories*, 66 n. 21.

65. *Indian Helper*, March 9, 1888.

66. Ibid., October 4, 1891, and October 16, 1981. Though I draw on Jessica Enoch's Foucaultian reading of the MOTBS, I extend her analysis by identifying how the panopticon effect also manifests materially in the structure of the newspaper. As students read the paper, they no doubt internalized the exhortations of the MOTBS and likely were motivated to self-regulate their bodies accordingly.

67. We can judge the weekly newspaper's success by perusing letters from former Carlisle students, whose closing lines almost invariably, and sometimes desperately, request subscriptions to the school's newspaper.

68. This would have involved instruction and practice in mock trials, the use of ballots, and other forms of democratic government. For further discussion of this debate, see Frederick E. Hoxie, *A Final Promise: The Campaign to Assimilate the Indians, 1880–1920* (Lincoln: University of Nebraska Press, 1984); Smith, *Civic Ideals*; and Kirkwood, *Report*.

69. Kirkwood, *Report*, vii.

70. Georges Bataille, *The Accursed Share*, vol. 1, trans. Robert Hurley (New York: Zone Books, 1991), 68.

71. Prucha, *Great Father*, 647.

72. Christopher Bracken, *The Potlatch Papers: A Colonial Case History* (Chicago: University of Chicago Press, 1997), 21. Bracken is paraphrasing from chap. 5 of Locke's 1690 text, *The Second Treatise of Government*.

73. Bracken, *Potlatch Papers*, 39.

74. John Locke, quoted in ibid., 21.

75. Prucha, *Great Father*, 651. This reasoning was not new: for example, Puritans had adopted similar arguments to justify their cooptation of Indian lands in the seventeenth century. See Ronald Takaki, *A Different Mirror: A History of Multicultural America* (Boston: Little, Brown, 1993), 35.

76. Bracken, *Potlatch Papers*, 45.

77. Michael Rogin, quoted in Dana D. Nelson, *National Manhood: Capitalist Citizenship and the Imagined Fraternity of White Men* (Durham, NC: Duke University Press, 1998), 62.

78. Wilson calls Eastman an acculturated rather than an assimilated Indian. Wilson, *Ohiyesa*, 36.

79. Not all SAI members were equally enthusiastic about assimilating, which caused dissension within the organization. Zitkala Ša was one SAI member who not only returned to her reservation after leaving a government boarding school but also wrote stories and articles critical of US policies toward American Indians.

80. Eight of the original eighteen SAI members were educated at Carlisle, including Thomas L. Sloan (Omaha), Albert Hensley (Winnebago), Louis McDonald (Ponca), and Cleaver Warden (Arapaho).

81. Hazel W. Hertzberg, *The Search for an American Indian Identity: Modern Pan-Indian Movements* (Syracuse, NY: Syracuse University Press, 1971), 114.

82. Sean Teuton, "A Question of Relationship: Internationalism and Assimilation in Recent American Indian Studies," *American Literary History* 18 (2006): 173.

83. Warrior, *Tribal Secrets*, 6.

84. Maddox, *Citizen Indians*, 134.

85. While Maddox and I similarly reconsider Eastman's contributions to American Indian intellectual history by drawing on his overlooked texts, Maddox's analysis focuses on how Eastman figures his body, both visually and verbally, as a symbol of the spiritual health toward which he strives and which he imagines for the nation.

86. Maddox, *Citizen Indians*, 133.

87. Warrior, *Tribal Secrets*, 8.

88. Quoted in ibid., 6.

89. Ibid.

90. Quoted in Hertzberg, *Search*, 68.

91. Quoted in ibid., 69.

92. SAI member and Indian activist Carlos Montezuma illustrates such differences in the 1919 issue of his journal *Wassaja*, where he explains that "at the birth of the great Society of American Indians, a majority of the charter members thought that the society could harmonize and work with the Indian Bureau for one common cause. . . . [But by 1919] the REAL INDIANS of the S.A.I. turned the tide against the

Indian Bureau." Quoted in Peter Iverson, *Carlos Montezuma and the Changing World of American Indians* (Albuquerque: University of New Mexico Press, 1982), 148. Also see Prucha, *Great Father*, 782, for a summary of why the SAI (under Eastman's leadership) staunchly opposed the Indian Office.

93. See this chapter's introductory comments for a discussion of Krupat; look to the Introduction for a description of Rosaldo and Flores's theory of cultural citizenship.

94. Hertzberg, *Search*, 97.

95. Ibid.

96. Fayette McKenzie, quoted in Hertzberg, *Search*, 133.

97. Quoted in Elizabeth Hutchinson, *The Indian Craze: Primitivism, Modernism, and Transculturation in American Art, 1890–1915* (Durham, NC: Duke University Press, 2009), 218.

98. Renato Rosaldo and Juan Flores, quoted in Kathleen Knight Abowitz and Jason Harnish, "Contemporary Discourses of Citizenship," *Review of Educational Research* 76, no. 4 (Winter 2006): 669.

99. Eastman's comments here suggest that when he invokes "Indian" values he may be using the term interchangeably with "Sioux."

100. Prucha, *Great Father*, 783.

101. Hertzberg, *SAI*, 180, 219.

102. Prucha, *Great Father*, 782.

103. Iverson, *Carlos Montezuma*, 151.

104. Ibid., 188.

105. Even though American Indians served as consultants and leaders to the Boy Scouts and Campfire Girls, the majority of the children who attended these camps were white. There were, however, a number of African American Boy Scout troops throughout the South. For a discussion of the Boy Scouts, including Eastman's involvement in it, see Philip J. Deloria, *Playing Indian* (New Haven, CT: Yale University Press, 1998), 122–25.

106. Wilson, *Ohiyesa*, 151.

107. Charles Eastman, *Indian Scout Talks: A Guide for Boy Scouts and Campfire Girls* (Boston: Little, Brown, 1914), 170. Katanski makes a similar point in her discussion of Eastman's adoption of the term *savagery*. Katanski, *Learning to Write "Indian,"* 153.

108. Eastman, *Indian Scout Talks*, 190. The communal ideal that Eastman presents in this passage directly articulates the values that he dramatized in his Indian myths and stories published as early as 1904: for instance, *Red Hunters and the Animal People*. In this earlier text's depiction of plains animal communities, also aimed at young white children, Eastman aligns "Red men" with animals as he presents an alternative model to the white man's selfish and wasteful mode of life.

109. Kimberly Hutchings, "Political Theory and Cosmopolitan Citizenship," in *Cosmopolitan Citizenship*, ed. Kimberly Hutchings and Roland Dannreuther (Basingstoke: Palgrave Macmillan, 1999), 7.

110. Ibid.

111. Eastman, *Indian Scout Talks*, 170.

112. Deloria, *Playing Indian*, 102.

113. As Clifford Putney explains, the embrace of primitiveness in white boys' camps recalls both evolutionary and educational ideologies, which assumed that

white children might experience primitiveness, but only as a phase of development. Clifford Putney, *Muscular Christianity: Manhood and Sports in Protestant America* (Cambridge, MA: Harvard University Press, 2003), 6. Putney also reminds us that the idealization of preindustrial values, which Eastman evokes in this passage, was central to the Christian masculinity movement (6).

114. Gayatri Spivak first introduced the idea of the "*strategic* use of positivist essentialism"; see Gayatri Spivak, "Subaltern Studies: Deconstructing Historiography," in *Selected Subaltern Studies*, ed. Ranajit Guha and Gayatri Spivak (New York: Oxford University Press, 1988), 13.

115. Eastman, *Indian Scout Talks*, 170.

116. Deloria, *Playing Indian*, 102.

117. Eastman, *Indian Scout Talks*, 6.

118. Ibid., 33, 41.

119. Ibid., 137. These types of ceremonies were also practiced in the Eastmans' summer camp for girls, which they started in July 1915 (and expanded in 1916 to accommodate boys). In this popular camp, which had become economically unviable by 1921, the Eastmans "set out to create in their campers a sense of appreciation for the out-of-doors and the folk and woodlore of the Native American." David Reed Miller, "Charles Alexander Eastman, The 'Winner': *From the Deep Woods to Civilization*," in *American Indian Intellectuals: 1976 Proceedings of the American Ethnological Society*, ed. Margot Liberty (St. Paul, MN: West, 1978), 67.

120. Eastman, *Indian Scout Talks*, 102.

121. Ibid., 43.

122. Ibid.

123. Charles Eastman, "The North American Indian," in *Papers on Inter-racial Problems, Communicated to the First Universal Races Congress Held at the University of London, July 26–29* (London: P. S. King and Son, 1911), 375.

124. Ibid.

125. Quoted in Iverson, *Carlos Montezuma*, 148, emphasis in original.

126. Wong writes that Eastman builds an "uneasy alliance" between "Christian and Sioux values." Hertha Wong, *Sending My Heart Back across the Years: Tradition and Innovation in Native American Autobiography* (New York: Oxford University Press, 1992), 142. Peterson invokes Gloria Anzaldúa's concept of the borderlands to argue that Eastman establishes continuity with his Sioux past but ultimately articulates his identity within the framework of social Darwinism. Erik Peterson, "An Indian, an American: Ethnicity, Assimilation, and Balance in Charles Eastman's *From the Deep Woods to Civilization*," *Studies in American Indian Literature* 4, nos. 2–3 (1992): 145–60. Powell suggests that while Eastman acknowledges his status as the object of a Euro-American gaze, he challenges that gaze with a decidedly Sioux perspective. Malea Powell, "Imagining a New Indian: Listening to the Rhetoric of Survivance in Charles Eastman's *From the Deep Woods to Civilization*," *Paradoxa* 15 (2001): 211–25.

127. Fuss, *Identification Papers*, 148.

128. Wilson, introduction to Eastman, *From the Deep Woods*, xviii.

129. Charles Eastman, *From the Deep Woods to Civilization: Chapters in the Autobiography of an Indian*, ed. Raymond Wilson (Lincoln: University of Nebraska Press, 1977), 125. All subsequent page citations to this work are to this edition and are given parenthetically in the text.

130. This discussion of Eastman in terms of Boelhower's autobiographical theory does not purport to minimize the historical differences between the Americanization experiences of American Indians and eastern European immigrants. I agree with Alan Trachtenberg when he writes, "Both Indians and immigrants were subjected to a process called 'Americanization,' a set of institutional devices and regimes that operated with an a priori notion of what and who an American was supposed to be, an essentialist idea of a presumed cultural nationality." Alan Trachtenberg, *Shades of Hiawatha: Staging Indians, Making Americans, 1880–1930* (New York: Hill and Wang, 2004), xxii.

131. William Boelhower, *Autobiographical Transactions in Modernist America: The Immigrant, the Architect, the Artist, the Citizen* (Verona: Del Bianco Editore Udine, 1992), 126.

132. Ibid., 71–72.

133. Ibid., 60.

134. Ibid., 69.

135. Even after a series of bad experiences with "civilized Christians," Eastman renews his faith in Christianity, which, he explains, "is not at fault for the white man's sins" (149).

136. Henry Lewis Morgan, Ancient Society "Arts of Subsistence," 1877, www .marxists.org/reference/archive/morgan-lewis/ancient-society/ch02.htm, para. 1.

137. The chief was "glad that [Eastman] was apparently satisfied with the white man's religion and his civilization. As for them, he said, neither of these had seemed good to them. The white man had showed neither respect for nature nor reverence toward God, but, he thought, tried to buy God with the by-products of nature. He tried to buy his way into heaven, but he did not even know where heaven is" (ibid., 148–49).

138. Nelson, *National Manhood*, 88.

139. Charles Eastman, *The Soul of the Indian: An Interpretation* (1911; repr., Lincoln: University of Nebraska Press, 1980), 24.

140. Charles Eastman, "The Indian's Plea for Freedom," *American Indian Magazine* 6, no. 4 (1919): 162.

141. With these lines, Eastman alludes to Thoreau's *Walden*: "I went to the woods because I wished to live deliberately . . . and reduce [life] to its lowest terms." Eastman, *From the Deep Woods*, 172. Eastman is, of course, punning on what Thoreau meant, because he is suggesting that white civilization is in many respects degraded when it is reduced to trade alone. Though Bercovitch faults the transcendentalists for being too complicit with American capitalism, Eastman's sentiments here and elsewhere are in keeping with the central tenets of American transcendentalist writers like Thoreau.

142. Eastman's objection to US nationalism might also stem from the traumatic experiences of his early childhood, when his exile to Canada separated him from his father.

143. Charles Eastman, "Opening Address," *American Indian Magazine* 7, no. 3 (1919): 145. The journal in which this article appeared was edited by Zitkala-Ša and published by the SAI; it contains the proceedings of the organization's annual conferences.

144. Ibid., 146. See Cheryl Walker for a discussion of American Indian contributions to US political culture. Cheryl Walker, *Indian Nation: Native American Literature and Nineteenth-Century Nationalisms* (Durham, NC: Duke University Press, 1997).

145. See Peterson, "Indian, an American," for another discussion of Eastman as an American Indian Jeremiah.

146. See, for example, Charles Eastman, "A Review of the Indian Citizenship Bills," *American Indian Magazine* 6, no. 4 (1919): 182–83.

147. Eastman, "Indian's Plea," 162.

148. Ibid., 164.

149. Critiquing the Burke Act (which changed the provisions of the Dawes Act to delay the distribution of land titles for patented land), Eastman accused the government of "[using] our money and our property for their own benefit" (ibid., 164).

150. Charles Eastman, *The Indian To-Day: The Past and Future of the First American* (Garden City, NY: Doubleday, Page, 1915), 63. Subsequent page citations to this work are to this edition and are given parenthetically in the text.

151. Eastman, "Indian's Plea," 164.

152. Eastman's comments here recall Thomas Jefferson's 1808 speech to a group of Delawares, Mohicans, and Munries as he tried to convince them to adopt agriculture and Anglo-American laws. Jefferson told them, "You will mix with us by marriage, your blood will run in our veins, and will spread with us over this great island." Quoted in Robert S. Tilton, *Pocahontas: The Evolution of an American Narrative* (New York: Cambridge University Press, 1994), 24.

153. Pfister, *Individuality Incorporated*, 46–47.

154. This exemplifies the tendency of assimilationist educators to adopt civic republicanism in a qualified manner: promoting its unified vision of national culture but not its corresponding valuation of political participation.

155. Fear-Segal, "Eyes in the Text," 135.

2 / The Scenes of Seeing

An earlier version of this essay appeared in American Literature. "The Scenes of Seeing: Frances Benjamin Johnston and Visualizations of the 'Indian' in Black, White, and Native Educational Contexts." *American Literature* (September 2011). 509–545.

1. This photo references the public anxiety that resulted from an increase in women's bicycling at the turn of the twentieth century, a trend that caused many conservatives to worry about women's adoption of masculine dress, their increased independence, and the possibility that bicycling might lead to sexual stimulation. See Julia Christie-Robin, Belinda Ordaza, and Dilia López-Gydosh, "From Bustles to Bloomers: Exploring the Bicycle's Influence on American Women's Fashion, 1880–1914," *Journal of American Culture* 35, no. 4 (December 2012): 315–31.

2. Joseph Slaughter, *Human Rights, Inc.: The World Novel, Narrative Form, and International Law* (New York: Fordham University Press, 2007), 181.

3. Ibid., 180.

4. Thomas J. Morgan, commissioner of Indian affairs from 1889 to 1893, instituted this curriculum.

5. For excellent discussions of this topic, see Elizabeth Hutchinson, *The Indian Craze: Primitivism, Modernism, and Transculturation in American Art, 1890–1915* (Durham, NC: Duke University Press, 2009); see also Barbara Babcock, "'Maids of Palestine': Pueblo Pots, Potters, and the Politics of Representation," in *Art and the Native American: Perceptions, Reality, and Influences*, ed. Mary Louise Krumrine and Susan C. Scott (University Park: Department of Art History, Pennsylvania State University, 2001), 246–67.

6. Johnston also contributed to two other exhibitions at the Paris Expo: a representation of the "new education" and an exhibit on American women photographers. Rebecca Ruth Bergman, "Visions of American Progress: The Photographs of Frances Benjamin Johnston at the Paris Exposition of 1900" (MA thesis, University of Missouri–Kansas City, 2006), 4.

7. As Du Bois explains in his review of the event, he and Calloway "collected and installed" the exhibit. W. E. B. Du Bois, "The American Negro at Paris," *American Monthly Review of Reviews* 22 (November 1900): 575, 577.

8. Rebecka Rutledge Fisher, "Cultural Artifacts and the Narrative of History: W. E. B. Du Bois and the Exhibiting of Culture at the 1900 Paris Exposition Universelle," *Modern Fiction Studies* 51, no. 4 (Winter 2005): 756. The quotation is from Du Bois, "American Negro," 591, in Fisher, "Cultural Artifacts," 759.

9. Fisher, "Cultural Artifacts," 761.

10. Robert Rydell, "Gateway to the 'American Century': The American Representation at the Paris Universal Exposition of 1900," in *Paris 1900: The "American School" at the Universal Exposition*, ed. Diane P. Fischer (New Brunswick, NJ: Rutgers University Press, 1999), 141.

11. Thomas Calloway, quoted in Rydell, "Gateway," 141. Even though the philosophical approach to progressive education resulted from "the application of pragmatism to education," in practice educators often both aligned themselves with and misread the views of men such as Dewey, who advocated hands-on learning as a starting point for increasingly abstract forms of intellectual inquiry. George F. Kneller, *Introduction to the Philosophy of Education* (New York: John Wiley and Sons, 1964), 94, 100. Howard Rogers, the director of the Paris Expo's Department of Education and Social Economy, claimed that US educational institutions trained "the citizen, not the artisan . . . [so that] every boy between the ages of 5 and 18 is offered an education which may fit him to be the president of the republic"; yet the exhibit featured the curricula at Hampton and Tuskegee, institutions that solidified, rather than equalized, class divisions in US society. *Report of the Commissioner-General for the United States to the International Universal Exposition, Paris, 1900*, vol. 2 (Washington, DC: Government Printing Office, 1901), 366.

12. Ruth Spack, *America's Second Tongue: American Indian Education and the Ownership of English, 1860–1900* (Lincoln: University of Nebraska Press, 2002), 61.

13. Spack cites Hampton's reproduction of Swinton's "racial paradigm" from Hampton's paper, the *Southern Workman*, February 1885, 20, quoted in Spack, *America's Second Tongue*, 72.

14. Elaine Goodale, "Anniversary Exercise of the Hampton Normal and Agricultural Institute," quoted in Spack, *America's Second Tongue*, 65.

15. Spack, *America's Second Tongue*, 72–73.

16. Joel Pfister, *Individuality Incorporated: Indians and the Multicultural Modern* (Durham, NC: Duke University Press, 2004), 20.

17. Francis La Flesche, *The Middle Five: Indian Schoolboys of the Omaha Tribe* (Lincoln: University of Nebraska Press, 1978), 22, quoted in Spack, *America's Second Tongue*, 125.

18. Ibid., 126.

19. For another account of linguistic resistance by American Indian boarding school students, see Kim Cary Warren, *The Quest for Citizenship: African American and Native American Education in Kansas, 1880–1935* (Chapel Hill: University of North Carolina Press, 2010).

20. Lincoln Kirstein, *The Hampton Album: 44 Photographs by Frances B. Johnston from an Album of Hampton Institute* (New York: MoMa, 1966). This book contained 44 of the 159 photos from a leather-bound album that art critic Lincoln Kirstein found in a Washington, D.C., bookstore during the Second World War. The entire collection of Johnston's Hampton photos numbers in the hundreds and is housed at the Library of Congress.

21. Berch particularly attacks Wexler for "[basing] much of her analysis on MOMA's captions" and argues that Johnston "consistently resisted the use of the caption as commentary." Bettina Berch, *The Woman behind the Lens: The Life and Work of Frances Benjamin Johnston, 1864–1952* (Charlottesville: University Press of Virginia, 2000), 54. In my examination of Johnston's photographs at the Library of Congress, however, I found that Johnston often described her photographs with captions and in many cases used evocative titles such as *The Dawn of Civilization, Children of Uneducated Parents,* or *House of Thrifty Indian.* Library of Congress, Lot 11051-5, Box 2 of 2.

22. Berch, *Woman behind the Lens,* 47.

23. Laura Wexler, *Tender Violence: Domestic Visions in an Age of U.S. Imperialism* (Chapel Hill: University of North Carolina Press, 2000), 151.

24. Shawn M. Smith, *American Archives: Gender, Race, and Class in Visual Culture* (Princeton, NJ: Princeton University Press, 1999), 170.

25. Judith Fryer Davidov, *Women's Camera Work: Self/Body/Other in American Visual Culture* (Durham, NC: Duke University Press, 1998), 167.

26. Jeannene Przyblyski's analysis of the Hampton photos emphasizes moments in which the students exist as "seeing" subjects rather than "seen" objects. Jeannene M. Przyblyski, "American Visions at the Paris Exposition 1900: Another Look at Frances Benjamin Johnston's Hampton Photographs," *Art Journal* 57, no. 3 (Fall 1998): 63.

27. One exception is Eric Margolis's wonderful examination of Johnston's Carlisle photographs in the context of assimilative education. Eric Margolis, "Looking at Discipline, Looking at Labour: Photographic Representations of Indian Boarding Schools," *Visual Studies* 19, no. 1 (April 2004): 72–96.

28. Berch calls attention to the fact that Johnston did not write about her views on race and uses this absence to justify our seeing her as a "neutral outsider." Berch, *Woman behind the Lens,* 54.

29. John Dewey, *Democracy and Education: An Introduction to the Philosophy of Education* (New York: Free Press, 1967), 302. See my conclusion to chapter 2 for an alternative reading of Johnston's silence.

30. Ibid., 297.

31. Ibid., 318.

32. Laura Wexler notes that "the Native American, black, and white drama of the schoolroom is encoded within a set of symbols of our national identity, and of personal identity, that situates us, the viewers, in the ministerial and powerful place." Wexler, *Tender Violence,* 170. See also Smith, *American Archives,* 170.

33. Berch, *Woman behind the Lens,* 54.

34. Margolis, "Looking at Discipline," 86.

35. Ibid., 93.

36. Ibid., 77.

37. James Guimond, *American Photography and the American Dream* (Chapel Hill: University of North Carolina Press, 1991), 38.

38. Ibid., 37–38.

39. Wexler, *Tender Violence*, 139–40.

40. The Hampton album's title is *Whittier School Students on a Field Trip Studying Plants, Hampton, Virginia*, but *A Seed Lesson* is the caption that Johnston penciled on the back of the photo.

41. The kind of hands-on learning that we associate with progressive education was linked with the increasing popularity of industrial education. By the 1890s, Lawrence Cremin explains, public schools across the United States were adopting industrial education in areas inhabited by white, working-class populations. Lawrence Cremin, *American Education: The Metropolitan Experience, 1876–1980* (New York: Harper and Row, 1988), 29. The inclusion of manual and vocational training in public schools for all races was accepted as a "vision of popular schooling suitable to the demands of the industrial age" (33). This development was ultimately solidified by the 1917 Smith-Hughes Act, which provided "federal aid for vocational secondary education" (52).

42. Dewey, *Democracy and Education*, 302.

43. Edith Westcott and Frances Benjamin Johnston, *New Education Illustrated (Primary)* 1 (August 1, 1901): n.p., Frances Benjamin Johnston Collection, Library of Congress, Prints and Photographs Division, Lot 2749 (G).

44. Dewey, *Democracy and Education*, 302.

45. Westcott and Johnston, *New Education Illustrated*, 1900, n.p.

46. Dewey, *Democracy and Education*, 302.

47. Peter Schmidt, *Sitting in Darkness: New South Fiction, Education, and the Rise of Jim Crow Colonialism* (Jackson: University Press of Mississippi, 2008), 121.

48. Spack, *America's Second Tongue*, 73.

49. James Anderson, *The Education of Blacks in the South, 1860–1935* (Chapel Hill: University of North Carolina Press, 1988), 39–40.

50. Ibid., 34, 36.

51. Spack, *America's Second Tongue*, 70.

52. Mike Hawkins, *Social Darwinism in European and American Thought, 1860–1945: Nature as Model and Nature as Threat* (Cambridge: Cambridge University Press, 1997), 84.

53. Though industrial and manual labor training represented the dominant approach to African American education during this period, alternatives did thrive. For excellent discussions of the role of African American educators in providing such alternatives, particularly as they used schools to instill racial pride, see Warren, *Quest for Citizenship*, chap. 5, and Adam Fairclough, *A Class of Their Own: Black Teachers in the Segregated South* (Cambridge, MA: Harvard University Press, 2007).

54. Dewey, *Democracy and Education*, 318.

55. Schmidt, *Sitting in Darkness*, 109, 118.

56. Ibid., 118.

57. Ibid. Progressivist racial discourse imagined civic belonging for nonwhites as a set of rights *"that could be managed by racial superiors until the distant future moment when they could be understood and claimed."* Schmidt, *Sitting in Darkness*, 114, italics in original.

58. Clifford Putney, *Muscular Christianity: Manhood and Sports in Protestant America* (Cambridge, MA: Harvard University Press, 2003), 6.

59. Eva Cherniavsky, *Incorporations: Race, Nation, and the Body Politics of Capital* (Minneapolis: University of Minnesota Press, 2006), xix.

60. Other Johnston photos, many unpublished, evoke individuality, interiority, and equality of opportunity through their architecture or subject matter. A few such examples include Hampton students reciting *The Merchant of Venice* (Lot 11051-1); Hampton students both holding and wearing American flags (Lot 2749); and a series of Carlisle photos from Lot 12369, including girls making fruit cookies, with one half-smiling directly at the camera, a smiling girl working the printing press, and a group of native students in a nature scene, some watching the teacher lecture about a pine cone, some looking off into the distance.

61. Henry Lewis Morgan, *Ancient Society* (New Brunswick, NJ: Transaction, 2000), 12.

62. George Stocking, "The Turn-of-the-Century Concept of Race," *Modernism/Modernity* 1, no. 1 (1994): 14. In this essay, Stocking argues that the four central strains of race theory at the turn of the twentieth century—the ethnological, Lamarckian, polygenist, and evolutionist—often overlapped with each other as they articulated relationships between "physical and cultural heredity" (10). He identifies a paradox by which the "antagonistic traditions of polygenism and Lamarckianism could coexist without apparent tension . . . because the fourth tradition, evolutionism . . . made possible an accommodation between them" (12). In Chapter 4, I explore a manifestation of this phenomenon through my analysis of embodied training at the Educational Alliance and the Hebrew Orphan Asylum.

63. Robert Francis Engs, "Red, Black, and White: A Study in Intellectual Inequality," in *Region, Race, and Reconstruction: Essays in Honor of C. Vann Woodward* (Oxford: Oxford University Press, 1982), 252. However, the largest number of historical and literary narratives that validated intermarriage between natives and whites occurred during the eighteenth century, a trend that makes sense given white settlers' desires to validate their sense of national belonging during that period. As a trope, intermarriage did not serve to validate nineteenth-century attitudes and policies toward Native Americans. See Edward J. Gallagher, "Pocahontas Time Line," *The Pocahontas Archive*, n.d., http://digital.lib.lehigh.edu/trial/pocahontas/time.php, accessed March 11, 2014. Lewis Henry Morgan, as cited in *Encyclopedia of American Indian History*, Vol. 1, ed. Bruce Johansen and Barry Pritzker, (Santa Barbara: ABC-CLIO, 2007), p. 51.

64. In her comparative study of citizenship education for African Americans and Native Americans in Kansas, Kim Warren explores this issue, arguing, "While Native Americans were supposed to use their education to assimilate, and even disappear, into white society . . . African Americans were to use their education to learn how to be hard workers who maintained a distinct position on the margins of white society"; Warren, *Quest for Citizenship*, 14.

65. Stocking, "Turn-of-the-Century Concept," 12.

66. Even if this is only a lifelike reproduction of a man, its hyperrealism supports my view that placing this simulation of living activity in a display case partakes of reification.

67. Both sets are in the Frances Benjamin Johnston Collection, Lot 11051-5, Box 2 of 2, Library of Congress.

68. Of course, Hampton and Tuskegee emphasized progress, represented both by advances in agricultural techniques and by the goal of encouraging African Americans to own their own farms or at least use their education to fare better in the marketplace.

69. Booker T. Washington, *Working with the Hands: Being a Sequel to Up from Slavery Covering the Author's Experiences in Industrial Training at Tuskegee* (New York: Doubleday, Page, 1904), 89.

70. This contrasts with texts, such as success manuals, directed at white farmers, which encouraged them to take advantage of mechanical reapers, steam-driven tractors, and extended railroad lines so they could profit from the modernization of US life while still maintaining a moral high ground associated with "rural and small-town life." Judy Hilkey, *Character Is Capital: Success Manuals and Manhood in Gilded Age America* (Chapel Hill: University of North Carolina Press, 1997), 103–5.

71. Kim Warren has an excellent discussion of the differences that marked educators' approaches to assimilation, work, and intermarriage for African Americans and Native Americans; Warren, *Quest for Citizenship*, chap. 1.

72. Berch, *Woman behind the Lens*, 53.

73. Hutchinson, *Indian Craze*, 202.

74. Quoted in ibid. Echoing my discussion in chapter 1 of the way that mainstream educators increasingly aligned the American Indian with his clothing, here Leupp invokes an image of the school as a washing machine and the Indian student's identity as identical to his clothing.

75. Tsianina K. Lomawaima, "Estelle Reel, Superintendent of Indian Schools, 1898–1910: Politics, Curriculum and Land," *Journal of American Indian Education* 35, no. 3 (May 1996): sec. 2, subsec. 2, para. 2, http://jaie.asu.edu/v35/V35S3es.htm.

76. Reel's remarks throughout the curriculum suggest that she intended it primarily for younger children attending reservation schools, but there is ample evidence that the curriculum was used as a template for activities at nonreservation schools. For instance, Genevieve Bell demonstrates how William Mercer, Carlisle's superintendent from 1904 to 1908, "brought Carlisle's curriculum into line with" Reel's *Course of Study*. Genevieve Bell, "Telling Stories Out of School: Remembering the Carlisle Indian Industrial School, 1879–1918" (PhD diss., Stanford University, 1996), 82. What this means is that a course of study geared toward elementary school children was being consulted as a guide for the education of high school age (and older) students.

77. Hutchinson has a wonderful chapter on Estelle Reel's development of a native craft tradition in Indian boarding schools, titled "The White Man's Indian Art: Teaching Aesthetics at the Indian Schools." Hutchinson, *Indian Craze*, 51–90.

78. Lomawaima, "Estelle Reel," sec. 2, subsec. 2, para. 4.

79. Cited in Lomawaima, "Estelle Reel," sec. 3, para. 3.

80. David Wallace Adams, *Education for Extinction: American Indians and the Boarding School Experience* (Lawrence: University Press of Kansas, 1995), 310.

81. Estelle Reel, *Course of Study for the Indian Schools of the United States, Industrial and Literary* (Washington, DC: Government Printing Office, 1901), 56.

82. Hutchinson, *Indian Craze*, 69.

83. Reel, *Course of Study*, 57.

84. Georg Lukács, *History and Class Consciousness: Studies in Marxist Dialectics*, trans. Rodney Livingstone (Cambridge, MA: The MIT Press, 1971), 91.

85. Hutchinson, *Indian Craze*, 80.

86. Reel, *Course of Study*, 145.

87. See Robert Francis Engs, *Educating the Disenfranchised and Disinherited: Samuel Chapman Armstrong and Hampton Institute, 1839–1893* (Knoxville: University of Tennessee Press, 1999); see also Donal Lindsey, *Indians at Hampton Institute, 1877–1923* (Chicago: University of Illinois Press, 1995). These books offer well-documented

discussions of how Samuel Chapman Armstrong used American Indians and African Americans to represent the benefits of Americanization to each other at Hampton.

88. Engs, *Educating the Disenfranchised*, 248–49.

89. Ruth Spack writes, "In 1880 [Booker T.] Washington reported that [Native American] students longed to attend study hour and to have 'a pile of books,' just as the African American students did, but had not yet been 'permitted' to do so." Booker T. Washington, "Incidents of Indian Life at Hampton," *Southern Workman*, December 1880, 125, quoted in Spack, *America's Second Tongue*, 66.

90. Edith Westcott, *New Education Illustrated (Geography)* 3 (1900): n.p., Frances Benjamin Johnston Collection, Library of Congress, Prints and Photographs Division, Lot 2749 (G).

91. Comparing the proliferation of Indian myths such as Hiawatha in schools for immigrants and American Indians in the late nineteenth century, Rayna Green and John Troutman write: "Most immigrants in American schools in the latter part of the nineteenth century were given new stories to replace their cultures' traditional ones, and Indian students were no exception. These stories served to Americanize Indians, to force them into sharing a partly invented mutual history and culture." Green and Troutman, "By the Waters of the Minnehaha: Music and Dance, Pageants and Princesses," in *Away from Home: American Indian Boarding School Experiences, 1879–2000*, ed. Margaret Archuleta, Brenda Child, and K. Tsianina Lomawaima (Phoenix, AZ: Heard Museum, 2004), 61.

92. These letters are collected at the National Archives, Record Group [RG] 75, Entry 1327 (Carlisle Student Records) or RG75, Records of the Education Division (Records Concerning Former Students, Industries Section, 1910–25, Box 1).

93. Nez Perce, National Archives, Record Group [RG] 75, Entry 1327, letter 892. It is important to remember that letters that were directly critical of Carlisle may not have been saved—and that the students represented by these letters are a self-selected group and exclude the large number of students who did not finish Carlisle because of sickness, death, or running away (a frequent problem). Genevieve Bell writes that only 761 of approximately 10,000 students actually graduated from Carlisle. Bell, *Telling Stories*, 331. Likewise, only 158 of the 1,230 native students who attended Hampton between 1878 and 1912 actually graduated. Spack, *America's Second Tongue*, 73.

94. Stephen's explanation that he didn't "want to get punished again" is most likely a reference to the afterlife, since by this time he had become extremely religious, as other letters from him testify.

95. See Tsianina Lomawaima, *They Called It Prairie Light: The Story of the Chilocco Indian School* (Lincoln: University of Nebraska Press, 1995); see also Brenda Child, *Boarding School Seasons: American Indian Families, 1900–1940* (Lincoln: University of Nebraska Press, 2000). These two scholars have documented students' evasions and rebellions of attempts by school authorities to micromanage their behavior.

96. Priscilla La Mote to Charles Dagenett, Supervisor of Indian Employment, National Archives, Group RG75, Records of the Education Division (Records Concerning Former Students, Industries Section, 1910–25, Box 1).

97. See Pfister for an analysis of the multiple valences of the term *Indian* at Carlisle, both as it was wielded in the service of the school's assimilationist agenda and as it was used by students who, Pfister argues, often performed "Indianness" in order to parody (rather than parrot) the "Carlisle line." Pfister, *Individuality Incorporated*, 70.

98. Again, Pfister extensively demonstrates how students performed "Indianness" to challenge the savagery-civilization time line. Ibid., 47.

99. Sara Hoxie, "The American Indian," *Indian Craftsman* 2, no. 4 (December 1909), in *The Red Man* (New York: Johnson Reprint, 1971).

100. Ibid.

101. In her examination of Hampton student records, Ruth Spack cites the graduation speech of Zallie Rulo to make a similar argument. Rulo aligns savagery with acts rather than racial identities, testifying to the fact that not all students accepted imputations of savagery quietly: "During last year in Dakota, there was one man killed by the Indians.... There were six Indians killed by the white men. Of which savage out West do you think you would be most afraid, the red savage or the white savage?" Quoted in Spack, *America's Second Tongue*, 76.

102. Gerald Vizenor, *Manifest Manners: Postindian Warriors of Survivance* (Hanover, NH: University Press of New England, 1994), 12–13.

103. Ibid., 12.

104. In *White Man's Club: Schools, Race, and the Struggle of Indian Acculturation*, Jacqueline Fear-Segal explores manifestations of students' self-definition within the total institution.

3 / Curricular Cosmopolitans

1. "The Tuskegee Machine" was Du Bois's term for Booker T. Washington and his coterie of white philanthropists who catered to and shaped public opinion, promoted work as a central educational goal for African Americans, and sanctioned the use of public and private educational institutions to engender his vision of African American citizenship.

2. Deegan argues that Jane Addams and W. E. B. Du Bois shared a "community-based" sociological practice influenced by the British sociologist Charles Booth, whose work "mapped the relationship between poverty, work, community, and social life." Mary Jo Deegan, "W. E. B. Du Bois and the Women of Hull-House, 1895–1899," *American Sociologist* 19, no. 4 (Winter 1988): 303.

3. Ibid., 305.

4. Ibid., 308. In *The Lost Promise of Patriotism*, Jonathan Hansen describes both Addams and Du Bois as cosmopolitan patriots who "embrace a social-democratic ethic that reflected the interconnected and mutually dependent nature of life in the modern world." Jonathan Hansen, *The Lost Promise of Patriotism: Debating American Identity, 1890–1920* (Chicago: University of Chicago Press, 2003), 8.

5. In *Lines of Activity*, Shannon Jackson describes Addams's embrace of immigrant cultures as "immigrant cosmopolitanism." Shannon Jackson, *Lines of Activity: Performance, Historiography, Hull-House Domesticity* (Ann Arbor: University of Michigan Press, 2000), 116. My chapter focuses more centrally on the simultaneous presence of pragmatism and social Darwinism in Addams's cosmopolitan philosophy and practice.

6. Ross Posnock, *Color and Culture: Black Writers and the Making of the Modern Intellectual* (Cambridge, MA: Harvard University Press, 1998), 23.

7. Hansen, paraphrasing Dewey's ideas from *Democracy and Education* in *Lost Promise*, 63.

8. Though I borrow the adjective *idealist* from Joseph Slaughter, this is the dominant form of the bildungsroman to which Moretti's claim refers. Franco Moretti, *The*

Way of the World: The Bildungsroman in European Culture (Brooklyn, NY: Verso, 2000), viii. As Moretti also notes, the private sphere is the place where the bildungsroman was usually read.

9. Joseph Slaughter, *Human Rights, Inc.: The World Novel, Narrative Form, and International Law* (New York: Fordham University Press, 2007), 184.

10. Shannon Jackson also discusses Addams's pragmatist approach to education at Hull-House, particularly as Addams sought to realize her theories through action. Jackson, *Lines of Activity*, 15.

11. William James, "Habit," in *Principles of Psychology*, vol. 1 (Cambridge, MA: Harvard University Press, 1983).

12. Nonetheless, beginning in the twentieth century, African American men and women (as administrators at segregated schools and community organizers) helped to develop an African American middle class equipped "with the pride and strategies needed to sustain the twentieth-century fight for legal and social equality"—propelling their students into "direct involvement in mainstream society that white reformers had never intended to allow." Kim Cary Warren, *The Quest for Citizenship: African American and Native American Education in Kansas, 1880–1935* (Chapel Hill: University of North Carolina Press, 2010), 125. Also see Warren's discussion of Sumner High School, which offered a predominantly classical education to its African American students (chap. 5).

13. While African Americans in northeastern cities (of whom only 23 percent worked in agriculture) took advantage of "tax-supported public education" and industrial training, southern agricultural laborers (40 percent of whom were black) were systematically denied educational opportunities by the white planter class. James D. Anderson, *The Education of Blacks in the South, 1860–1935* (Chapel Hill: University of North Carolina Press, 1988), 21.

14. Ibid., 27. Historians of public education both during and after Reconstruction agree that even schools purporting to train African Americans for political citizenship were in fact focused on producing an efficient workforce. See Robert C. Morris, *Reading, 'Riting, and Reconstruction: The Education of Freedmen in the South, 1861–1870* (Chicago: University of Chicago Press, 1981).

15. Morris, *Reading, 'Riting, and Reconstruction*, 49.

16. Ibid., 220.

17. Ibid., 153.

18. Quoted in ibid., 206.

19. Ibid., 150.

20. Industrial education increased in the 1880s, when the John F. Slater Fund began earmarking its donations to southern schools for "low-level industrial training." Anderson, *Education of Blacks*, 66.

21. Edward Ayers, *The Promise of the New South: Life after Reconstruction* (New York: Oxford University Press, 1992), 419.

22. Adam Fairclough, *A Class of Their Own: Black Teachers in the Segregated South* (Cambridge, MA: Harvard University Press, 2007), 178.

23. Ibid., 182–83. Fairclough makes this claim but bases it on statements made by Atkins rather than curricular evidence.

24. Ibid., 178.

25. Ibid., 190–220.

26. W. E. B. Du Bois, introduction to *The Common School and the Negro American* (Atlanta, GA: Atlanta University Press, 1911), n.p.

27. Ibid., 131.

28. Even up through the 1940s, Du Bois's attempts to improve education for southern blacks, such as his plan to institute history, anthropology, and sociology courses at southern land-grant colleges, were systematically cancelled or undermined. Du Bois, introduction to *Common School*, n.p.

29. David Levering Lewis, *W. E. B. Du Bois: Biography of a Race, 1868–1919* (New York: Henry Holt, 1993), 245.

30. Washington's contemporaries generally praised him for providing a solution to the race problem in America through his emphasis on industrial education for African Americans. Nonetheless, black intellectuals besides Du Bois—for instance, William Trotter and Ida Wells Barnett—critiqued Washington for popularizing a pedagogy that intended "to keep Blacks in a menial position and perpetuate the caste system." Booker T. Gardner, "The Educational Contributions of Booker T. Washington," *Journal of Negro Education* 44, no. 4 (Autumn 1975): 514.

31. W. E. B. Du Bois, "The Hampton Idea" (1906), in *The Education of Black People: Ten Critiques, 1906–1960*, ed. Herbert Aptheker (New York: Monthly Review Press, 2001), 28.

32. Ibid., 30.

33. W. E. B. Du Bois, *Dusk of Dawn: An Essay toward an Autobiography of a Race Concept* (Piscataway, NJ: Transaction Press, 1983), 217.

34. As far as I know, critics have neither compared *Up from Slavery* and *Working with the Hands* nor analyzed the latter as exemplifying Washington's projection of a path for others that is different from the one he imagines for himself. However, in "The Envy of Erudition," Ernest L. Gibson III does argue that despite Tuskegee's emphasis on industrial training Washington valued the intellectual erudition more commonly associated with Du Bois (evidenced by his participation in debate at Hampton, his hiring of Fisk graduates at Tuskegee, his marriage to Margaret Murray, and his efforts to provide his own children with a liberal arts education). Ernest L. Gibson III, "The Envy of Erudition: Booker T. Washington and the Desire for a Du Boisian Erudition," *Black Scholar* 43, nos. 1/2 (Spring 2013): 52–68.

35. Booker T. Washington, *Up from Slavery: An Autobiography* (1901; repr., Boston: Bedford/St. Martin's, 2003), 176.

36. Carl Pedersen, "Sea Change: The Middle Passage and the Black Imagination," in *Defining Travel: Diverse Visions* (Jackson: University Press of Mississippi, 2001), 263.

37. Washington, *Up from Slavery*, 177.

38. As Paul Gilroy and Carl Pedersen and have argued, representations of the Atlantic Ocean—particularly in trips carrying the African American character away from the United States—have often been deployed to suggest a "freely chosen" dislocation that both counterpoints the forced dislocation of slavery and grants the black man insight and freedom from the *landed* history of oppression. Paul Gilroy, *The Black Atlantic: Modernity and Double Consciousness* (Cambridge, MA: Harvard University Press, 1993), 133.

39. As Washington himself notes, the majority of Tuskegee students became teachers (of agriculture and industry), agricultural laborers, or domestic servants—not

members (like Washington himself) of a highly educated black elite. Booker T. Washington, *Working with the Hands: Being a Sequel to "Up from Slavery" Covering the Author's Experiences in Industrial Training at Tuskegee* (New York: Doubleday, Page, 1904), 200.

40. Ibid., 183.

41. Ibid., 32.

42. Ibid., 152.

43. As Houston Baker argues, *Up from Slavery* evidences Washington's hatred of his body and his efforts to overcome the limitations of embodied experience. Houston A. Baker, *Turning South Again: Re-thinking Modernism/Re-reading Booker T.* (Durham, NC: Duke University Press, 2001).

44. Ibid., 146.

45. Washington, *Working with the Hands*, 139.

46. Judith Shklar, *American Citizenship: The Quest for Inclusion* (Cambridge, MA: Harvard University Press, 1991), 81.

47. Ayers, *Promise*, 208.

48. Ibid., 195. See ibid., chap. 8, for a thorough discussion of agricultural conditions in the postbellum South.

49. Washington, *Up from Slavery*, 81.

50. Henry Lewis Morgan, "Arts of Subsistence," chap. 2 of *Ancient Society* (London: MacMillan, 1877), accessed December 2, 2013, www.marxists.org/reference/archive/morgan-lewis/ancient-society/cho2.htm, para. 1.

51. Gilroy writes that Du Bois viewed progress, or "the logical momentum of historical development," as being incompatible with the interests of the southern black laborer. Gilroy, *Black Atlantic*, 129.

52. Du Bois, *Dusk of Dawn*, 217. One way that *The Souls of Black Folk* promotes intellectual education is through Du Bois's construction of himself as one in a long line of black leaders (stretching back to his grandmother through Douglass, Crummell, and others) who were "made," rather than "born," to lead. Du Bois leaves open the possibility that his fellow African Americans might also achieve such "talent" (217).

53. In *Dusk of Dawn*, for example, Du Bois claims that everything he says about his own life is filtered through the lens of race: "Had it not been for the race problem early thrust upon me and enveloping me, I should have probably been an unquestioning worshipper at the shrine of the social order and economic development into which I was born" (27).

54. Posnock, *Color and Culture*, 5, 13.

55. W. E. B. Du Bois, *The Autobiography of W. E. B. Du Bois: A Soliloquy on Viewing My Life from the Last Decade of Its First Century* (New York: International Publishers, 1968), 156–57.

56. Gilroy, *Black Atlantic*, 121.

57. Ibid., 133.

58. Du Bois, *Autobiography*, 176.

59. Ibid. In chap. 1 of *The Souls of Black Folk*, Du Bois famously tells the story of the moment he discovered he was black. W. E. B. Du Bois, *The Souls of Black Folk* (1903; repr., New York: Dover, 1994).

60. Maria Diedrich, Henry Louis Gates Jr., and Carl Pedersen, eds., *Black Imagination and the Middle Passage* (New York: Oxford University Press, 1999), 6–7.

61. W. E. B. Du Bois, "Diary of My Steerage Trip across the Atlantic," in *Papers of W. E. B. Du Bois*, 1894, reel 87:510, n.p.

62. Du Bois, *Autobiography*, 180–81.

63. Du Bois, "Diary," n.p.

64. Ibid. Du Bois might not have included these comments in the final *Autobiography* because he had been accused of expressing anti-Semitic sentiments in some of his writings.

65. Ibid.

66. Posnock, *Color and Culture*, 5.

67. Du Bois, "Diary," n.p.

68. Posnock, *Color and Culture*, 10.

69. Du Bois, "Diary," n.p.

70. In her analysis of Du Bois's children's literature, Michelle Phillips insightfully argues that *The Souls of Black Folk* evokes the simultaneity of double consciousness and the end of childhood innocence; she also suggests that through his children's literature Du Bois sought to intervene in the black child's development at this very moment, "at once to be a source for the black child's entry into double consciousness and to repurpose double consciousness as a model for a resilient black subjectivity beginning in childhood." Michelle Phillips, "The Children of Double Consciousness: From *The Souls of Black Folk* to the *Brownies' Book*," *PMLA* 128, no. 3 (May 2013): 590, 592.

71. Ibid., 591.

72. Though Katharine Capshaw Smith emphasizes the centrality of Jessie Fauset's editorial voice in the *Brownies' Book*, Du Bois nonetheless exerted a strong editorial voice in shaping the magazine and used it to promote cosmopolitan citizenship. Katharine Capshaw Smith, *Children's Literature of the Harlem Renaissance* (Bloomington: Indiana University Press, 2006), 25.

73. W. E. B. Du Bois, *Crisis*, 1919, quoted in Diane Johnson-Feelings's introduction to *The Best of the Brownies' Book*, ed. Diane Johnson-Feelings (New York: Oxford University Press, 1996).

74. In an early discussion of the *Brownies' Book* in 1965, Elinor Sinnette notes that the magazine sought to "counter racial stereotypes and provide black child readers with inspiring images and stories of black history and life." Phillips, "Children of Double Consciousness," 605 n. 5. Violet Harris also argues that the magazine provided an alternative to popular children's literature from the era, which presented African Americans as "inferior, happy-go-lucky, and childlike" and encouraged them to "submit to the paternalistic guidance of whites." Violet J. Harris, "Race Consciousness, Refinement, and Radicalism: Socialization in *The Brownies' Book*," *Children's Literature Association Quarterly* 14, no. 4 (Winter 1989): 192. My emphasis is on the magazine's efforts to cultivate a cosmopolitan sensibility by juxtaposing stories of slave heroes with uplifting narratives about people of color from around the world.

75. Born a slave in 1774, Katy Ferguson became free at the age of eighteen and ultimately founded New York City's first Sunday school. From "Katy Ferguson: A True Story," in Johnson-Feelings, *Best of the Brownies' Book*, 36–37. Betsey Blakesley was a slave in North Carolina who, in the winter of 1849–50, escaped by ship to Boston by cramping her body into a space that was two feet, eight inches wide. Lillie Buffum Chace Wyman, "The Bravest of the Brave: A True Story," in Johnson-Feelings, *Best of the Brownies' Book*, 83.

76. Willie Mae King, "When Bennie Was Fired," in Johnson-Feelings, *Best of the Brownies' Book*, 142.

77. Ibid., 145.

78. Franklin Lewis, letter to the editor, in Johnson-Feelings, *Best of the Brownies' Book*, 25.

79. Ibid.

80. Phillips focuses on early examples of this column in the *Crisis*, in which Du Bois harnesses the "anti-imperial" symbol of the Crow to his indictment of capitalism; Du Bois blames capitalism not only as the "root cause of the First World War" but also as one reason that American democracy failed "to cross the lines of inequality separating races, nations, genders, and (we may now add) generations." Phillips, "Children of Double Consciousness," 602.

81. In this respect, the *Brownies' Book* was like Emma Goldman's *Mother Earth*.

82. *Brownies' Book* 1, no. 10 (October 1920), Library of Congress Digital Collections, Rare Book and Special Collections Division, http://memory.loc.gov/service/rbc/rbc0001/2004/2004ser01351/2004ser01351.pdf, p. 308; PDF p. 328.

83. The *Brownies' Book* also reached the shores of France: in one letter, Gabrielle writes to assure American readers that the French not only valued the efforts of black soldiers in Chambery but also "shall not forget that in America they are unhappy, and on this side of the ocean we shall do all that we can to help them. The old world must help a part of the new to conquer their liberty and rights." *Brownies' Book* 1, no. 2 (February 1920), Library of Congress Digital Collections, Rare Book and Special Collections Division, http://memory.loc.gov/service/rbc/rbc0001/2004/2004ser01351/2004ser01351.pdf, p. 52; PDF p. 56. With a circulation of four thousand, the *Brownies' Book* was not enormously popular, but it did boast a national (and as these examples show, international) audience. Smith, *Children's Literature*, 25.

84. Max Simpson, letter to the editor, in Johnson-Feelings, *Best of the Brownies' Book*, 25.

85. Pocahontas Foster, letter to the editor, in Johnson-Feelings, *Best of the Brownies' Book*, 54.

86. In *Americans All*, Diana Selig notes that the interwar "cultural gifts" movement—a precursor to contemporary multiculturalism—was inspired by John Dewey's and Jane Addams's appreciation of "immigrant gifts" (Addams's phrase); Diana Selig, *Americans All: The Cultural Gifts Movement* (Cambridge, MA: Harvard University Press, 2008), 21.

87. Hansen, *Lost Promise*, 70. We could also use this term to characterize the *Brownies' Book*.

88. Gavin Kendall, Ian Woodward, and Zlatko Skrbis, *The Sociology of Cosmopolitanism: Globalization, Identity, Culture, and Government* (London: Palgrave Macmillan, 2009), 98.

89. Pheng Cheah, "Given Culture: Rethinking Cosmopolitical Freedom in Transnationalism," in *Cosmopolitics: Thinking and Feeling beyond the Nation*, ed. Pheng Cheah and Bruce Robbins (Minneapolis: University of Minnesota Press, 1998), 158.

90. Georg Cavallar, "Cosmopolitanisms in Kant's Philosophy," *Ethics and Global Politics* 5, no. 2 (2012): 97.

91. In contrast to James Clifford's argument that in the "dominant [Victorian] discourses of travel, a "non-white person [could] not figure as a heroic explorer,

aesthetic interpreter, or scientific authority," here Du Bois embodies this persona. James Clifford, "Traveling Cultures," in *The Predicament of Culture: Twentieth-Century Ethnography, Literature, and Art* (Cambridge, MA: Harvard University Press, 1988), 106.

92. In *Sociology of Cosmopolitanism*, Kendall, Woodward, and Skrbis, citing Bryan Turner, stress that cosmopolitanism is not a static entity but an ethical stance, which, in its ideal manifestation, takes the "form of ironic, detached, but fundamentally ethical concern for the other" (98).

93. Jane Addams, *Twenty Years at Hull-House with Autobiographical Notes* (New York: Penguin, 1998), 285. Subsequent citations to this work are to this edition and are given parenthetically in the text.

94. Jane Addams, *Democracy and Social Ethics* (Chicago: University of Illinois Press, 2001), 83.

95. Ibid.

96. James Salazar argues that Addams used "the practices of physical culture" at Hull-House to build "transnational character." James Salazar, *Bodies of Reform: The Rhetoric of Character in Gilded Age America* (New York: New York University Press, 2010), 234. Though Addams undeniably promoted transnationalism at Hull-House, her discussions of physical activity reveal a social Darwinist perspective.

97. See Addams, *Twenty Years*, 17. As Carl Degler explains, Lamarck assumed "that behavior patterns of parents could be inherited by their offspring." Carl Degler, *In Search of Human Nature: The Decline and Revival of Darwinism in American Social Thought* (New York: Oxford University Press, 1991), 20. Darwin viewed this process as accidental and emphasized the long-term quality of such inheritance, writing that "habits . . . followed during many generations probably tend to be inherited." Charles Darwin, *The Descent of Man*, quoted in Degler, *In Search*, 20.

98. Herbert Spencer, *Education: Intellectual, Moral, and Physical* (New York: D. Appleton, 1891), 5.

99. Charles Eastman, *Indian Scout Talks: A Guide for Boy Scouts and Campfire Girls* (Boston: Little, Brown, 1914), 179. In *Lines of Activity*, Shannon Jackson also tracks the "Darwinist evolutionary paradigm" that appears repeatedly in *Twenty Years at Hull-House*. Jackson, *Lines of Activity*, 51–52.

100. Salazar calls attention to the pragmatist elements of physical activity at Hull-House—its role in helping immigrants "[formulate] new habits of action and forms of conduct." Salazar, *Bodies of Reform*, 231.

101. In a similar vein, David E. Bender argues that the presence of spacious gymnasiums in settlement houses was supposed to facilitate the child's transformation from primitivity to civic-mindedness. He cites Addams's statement (to the Playground Association) that "the city streets fostered a primitivism that could only be reversed in the supervised gymnasium." David E. Bender, "The Perils of Degeneration: Reform, the Savage Immigrant, and the Survival of the Unfit," *Journal of Social History* 42 (Fall 2008): 17.

102. In her comparative analysis of Jane Addams and Martha Nussbaum, Carol Hay elucidates Addams's attempts, in *Hull-House*, simultaneously to unify the community and to validate the "singularity of every individual." Carol Hay, "Justice and Objectivity for Pragmatists: Cosmopolitanism in the Work of Martha Nussbaum and Jane Addams," *Pluralist* 7 (Fall 2012): 90.

103. As James Salazar argues, Hull-House "was not simply an industrial or trade school devoted to the integration of bodies into the machinery of industrial capitalism." Salazar, *Bodies of Reform*, 232.

104. Addams, *Democracy and Social Ethics*, 8.

105. Ibid., xix.

106. Ibid., 13.

107. Hansen, *Lost Promise*, 70.

108. Jeffrey Mirel argues that Zangwill's *The Melting Pot* has come to represent an assimilationist position when it more accurately evokes the view of amalgamationists, who "envisioned the melting pot as mixing all the races in the United States as a new, composite people." Jeffrey Mirel, *Patriotic Pluralism: Americanization Education and European Immigrants* (Cambridge, MA: Harvard University Press, 2010), 33. Yet Mirel supports his position by citing the assimilationist imagery with which Zangwill depicts this transformation: "The Great Alchemist melts and fuses them with his purging flame!" Israel Zangwill, quoted in Mirel, *Patriotic Pluralism*, 34. By imagining the "fusing" together of cultures, and the "purging" of their differences, Zangwill evokes an assimilationist aesthetic.

109. Another example of the transformation of space at Hull-House occurred when the Social Extension Committee invited a group of Italian women to an evening event and were surprised when the women sent their husbands; after initially sitting in puzzlement in rows of chairs along the wall, these men spontaneously took over the space, and "untiring pairs of them danced the tarantella . . . sang Neapolitan songs . . . performed some of those wonderful sleight-of-hand tricks so often seen on the streets of Naples . . . explained the coral finger of St. Januarius . . . [and] politely ate the strange American refreshments" (ibid., 231).

110. During this period, southern Italians were not viewed as being white.

111. Addams's 1930 book, *Second Twenty Years at Hull-House*, continues the antiwar trend in Addams's work, addressing peace efforts during the First World War, as well as the concerns and inhibitions of the postwar generation.

112. Jane Addams, *Newer Ideals of Peace* (Chautauqua, NY: Chautauqua Press, 1907), 16, 17, 19.

113. Kendall, Woodward, and Skrbis, *Sociology of Cosmopolitanism*, 67.

114. Ibid., 67, 69; see also note 92 above on cosmopolitanism as an ethical stance.

115. Ibid.

116. Ibid.

117. Hansen, *Lost Promise*, 67.

4 / Educating the *Ostjuden*

1. *Ostjuden* is a term that German Jews in Germany used (perhaps in a derogatory sense) to refer to Jews of eastern European descent. It was later used in the United States to refer to the eastern European Jewish immigrant population. In the chapter, I use this term interchangeably with *eastern European Jews*. Aviva Ben-Ur explains that the category of the "German Jew" arose during the early nineteenth century, "when emerging nation states in Western and Central Europe . . . demanded that Jews wholly identify as French-, German-, or Englishmen." As a result of these pressures, central European Jews who had left urban ghettos and acquired a middle-class status "reidentified as 'German Jews' and labeled their unemancipated brethren as 'Ostjuden'

(Eastern Jews)." Aviva Ben-Ur, "Diasporic Reunions: Sephardi/Ashkenazi Tensions in Historical Perspective," July 25, 2012, www.jewishideas.org/articles/diasporic-reunions-sephardiashkenazi-tensions-histo. Also see Steven E. Aschheim, *Brothers and Strangers: The East European Jew in German and German Jewish Consciousness, 1800–1923* (Madison: University of Wisconsin Press, 1982).

2. Though religious and political Jews generally did not identify with each other, Abraham Cahan offers evidence that some religious Jews numbered among the strikers recruited by the Jewish labor movement. In a July 1898 *Atlantic Monthly* article, "The Russian Jew in America," Cahan describes a scene in which "the sweat-shop striker and the religious enthusiast are found in the same person." Cahan cites one Jew's invocation of both workers' rights and the Old Testament as he explains his presence at a religious Mishnah class *and* his intent to participate in a strike the following day:

> You know the saying, "half for yourselves and half for your God." To-morrow we shall go to the meeting again. Ours is a just cause. It is for the bread of our children we are struggling. We want our rights, and we are bound to get them through the union. Saith the law of Moses: Thou shalt not withhold anything from thy neighbor nor rob him; there shall not abide with thee the wages of him that is hired through the night until morning. So it stands in Leviticus. So you see that our bosses who rob us and who don't pay us regularly commit a sin, and that the cause of our union is a just one.

Abraham Cahan, "The Russian Jew in America," *Atlantic Monthly*, July 1898, 263–87, www.tenant.net/Community/LES/cahan5.html, para. 5.

3. The majority of eastern European Jewish immigrants spoke Yiddish. While some working-class and rural German Jews spoke Yiddish, this was not generally the case for middle- and upper-class German Jews.

4. I am grateful to Sarah Wilson for her articulation of this and other insights.

5. Antin's 1912 autobiography, *The Promised Land*, narrates Antin's enthusiastic embrace of public school and subsequent Americanization. Mary Antin, *The Promised Land* (Boston: Houghton Mifflin, 1912).

6. Anzia Yezierska's novels and stories tend to follow this pattern.

7. *The Rise of David Levinsky* was first serialized in *McClure's* between 1911 and 1915 and was later published as a single novel in 1917.

8. Joseph Slaughter, *Human Rights, Inc.: The World Novel, Narrative Form, and International Law* (New York: Fordham University Press, 2007), 179.

9. This incompatibility recalls Walter Benjamin's comments about translation; as he explains, when original content appears in a foreign language, the language appears "unsuited to its content, overpowering and alien," whereas there is "a certain unity in the original, like a fruit and its skin." Walter Benjamin, "The Task of the Translator," in *Illuminations: Essays and Reflections*, trans. Harry Zohn (New York: Schocken Books, 1968), 75.

10. Slaughter, *Human Rights*, 184.

11. *Bleter Fun Mein Leben* was published by the Forward Publishing Company in five volumes between 1926 and 1931; only the first two of these have been translated into English. This chapter examines the two translated volumes, published in 1969 as *The Education of Abraham Cahan*. Abraham Cahan, *The Education of Abraham Cahan*, trans. Leon Stein, Abraham Conan, and Lynn Davison (Philadelphia: Jewish

Publication Society of America, 1969), originally published as *Bleter Fun Mein Leben*, 2 vols. (New York: Forward, 1926–31).

12. Moses Rischin writes, "In the 1870's, 40,000 East European Jews migrated to the United States, compared to a trickle of 7,500 in the century's first seven decades. . . . In the 1890's over 200,000 crossed the ocean to the United States; in the 1890's another 300,000 followed." Moses Rischin, *The Promised City: New York's Jews, 1870–1914* (Cambridge, MA: Harvard University Press, 1977), 20.

13. Kim Van Alkemade, "Orphans Together: A History of New York's Hebrew Orphan Asylum," paper presented at the 2006 Biennial Scholars' Conference on American Jewish History, June 5–7, 2006, Charleston, SC, www.cofc.edu/jwst/pages/biennialpapers060906.htm, 2.

14. Adam Bellow, *The Educational Alliance: A Centennial Celebration* (Arlington, VA: Educational Alliance, 1990), 42. It wasn't until the first decade of the twentieth century that the EA offered lectures in Yiddish. The institution never embraced the Russian language, which represented the most radical element of the Jewish intelligentsia. Rischin, *Promised City*, 101–3.

15. Stephan Brumberg, *Going to America, Going to School: The Jewish Immigrant Public School Encounter in Turn-of-the-Century New York City* (New York: Praeger, 1986), 66. English was a priority of the Baron de Hirsch Fund, the EA's central supporter. Bellow, *Educational Alliance*, 37–39.

16. Of course this diversity did not bother all Americans; for instance, Horace Kallen "invented cultural pluralism as a plea for tolerance of hyphenated (ethnic) identity" and as a challenge to nativist and assimilationist sentiments. Ross Posnock, *Color and Culture: Black Writers and the Making of the Modern Intellectual* (Cambridge, MA: Harvard University Press, 1998), 23.

17. In 1871, Jews gained legal equality in Germany but suffered from an anti-Semitic backlash. Jack Zipes, "Oskar Panizza: The Operated German as Operated Jew," in *The Operated Jew: Two Tales of Anti-Semitism*, trans. Jack Zipes (New York: Routledge, 1991), 104–5.

18. In his 1941 study, David Efron examined the presence of a complex gestural language in communities of "traditional" eastern European Jews (both in Europe and in the United States). Efron argues that these Jews used "gestural notation" to accompany verbal expression of their "mental activity." David Efron, quoted in Paul Connerton, *How Societies Remember* (Cambridge: Cambridge University Press, 1989), 81.

19. Sander Gilman, *The Jew's Body* (New York: Routledge, 1991), 28.

20. In response to discrimination from the Sephardic community, German Jews began to "[model] themselves in manners, dress, and politics on the leaders of the Protestant society." Bellow, *Educational Alliance*, 7. After the Civil War, despite the assimilated status and economic success of German Jews, upwardly mobile Protestants increased their social discrimination against this group as "a way of preserving their own claims to membership in polite society." Eric L. Goldstein, "'Different Blood Flows in Our Veins': Race and Jewish Self-Definition in Late Nineteenth Century America," *American Jewish History* 85, no. 1 (1997): 32.

21. For an excellent treatment of racial anti-Semitism in the United States, see Goldstein, "'Different Blood,'" and Eric Goldstein, "The Unstable Other: Locating the Jew in Progressive-Era American Racial Discourse," *American Jewish History* 89, no. 4 (December 2001): 383–409.

22. David Blaustein, *Memoirs of David Blaustein: Educator and Communal Worker*, ed. Miriam Blaustein (New York: McBride, Nast, 1913), 134.

23. Gilman, *Jew's Body*, 42–43.

24. Benjamin Ward Richardson, quoted in Gilman, *Jew's Body*, 52–53.

25. Max Nordau, quoted in Gilman, *Jew's Body*, 53.

26. Gilman, *Jew's Body*, 12.

27. This anti-Semitic language included imputations that eastern European Jews were not fully white. Goldstein explains that from the 1870s to the 1890s German American Jews defined themselves as racially different from other whites, while also insisting that they were ideally assimilated as Americans. Goldstein, "'Different Blood,'" 35. At the turn of the century, however, as whiteness increasingly became "a prerequisite for citizenship," eastern European Jews were included in the category of not-quite-white (54).

28. Albert Shiels, introduction to *The School and the Immigrant*, prepared by direction of Thomas Churchill, President of the Board of Education, ed. Albert Shiels (New York: New York City Department of Education, 1915), 12.

29. Bellow, *Educational Alliance*, 72.

30. Rischin cites "miserable darkened Hebrews" from the *Hebrew Standard* (June 15, 1894), "piggish jargon" from the *New York Times* (August 19, 1877), and "dangerous principles" from the *Eighteenth Annual Report, United Hebrew Charities, City of New York*, 11–12. Rischin, *Promised City*, 97.

31. Rischin, *Promised City*, 101–3. The ban on Yiddish was lifted by Blaustein after his appointment as EA director in 1898; at this time he introduced Yiddish books and newspapers into the library and allowed Yiddish societies to meet in the building. Also around this time, Paul Abelson began working for the EA; he incorporated lectures in Yiddish, as well as Yiddish translations of the Declaration of Independence, the Constitution, and Ben Franklin's *Autobiography*, into the ever-expanding adult education program. Bellow, *Educational Alliance*, 84–86.

32. Brumberg, *Going to America*, 80.

33. Ibid., 91, 155.

34. Religious Jews also avoided EA programs because they offered a watered-down form of religious instruction.

35. At the EA, where attendance was voluntary, the student population probably consisted of those who were willing to accept the "emphasis on patriotic exercises and 'acceptable behavior' [and] the weak religious impulse of Reform." Bellow, *Educational Alliance*, 77. For an orphan asylum such as the HOA, attendance and exposure to the German Jewish educational program were less voluntary.

36. According to McNeill, the traditional form of Orthodox prayer—which he calls a "collective muscular-musical path to God"—dates back to the Hebrew prophets, whose "demand for justice and true piety" was achieved as a result of a dancing and singing. William H. McNeill, *Keeping Together in Time: Dance and Drill in Human History* (Cambridge, MA: Harvard University Press, 1995), 71.

37. Cahan, "Russian Jew in America," para. 3.

38. Hebrew Orphan Asylum Papers, Box 11, American Jewish Historical Society.

39. Quoted in Brumberg, *Going to America*, 151–52.

40. Bellow, *Educational Alliance*, 91.

41. Tyack writes, "By 1900 . . . thirty-one states had passed compulsory education laws"; though some communities ignored them, they were nonetheless "useful in

establishing a principle accepted by the law-abiding parents." David Tyack, *The One Best System: A History of American Urban Education* (Cambridge, MA: Harvard University Press, 1974), 71. New York instituted compulsory attendance in 1874. Nonetheless, Orthodox Jews, like many other immigrant groups, preserved their language and religious culture in evening and weekend schools.

42. Horace Mann, for instance, created a powerful coalition of religious Protestants and secularists to advocate for public schools that would support a nonsectarian Protestant viewpoint. John C. Jeffries Jr. and James E. Ryan, "A Political History of the Establishment Clause," in *Religion and the Constitution*, edited by Michael W. McConnell, John H. Garvey, and Thomas C. Berg (New York: Wolters Kluwer Law and Business, 2011), 383–85. After interviewing eastern European Jews educated in New York City schools, Stephan Brumberg concluded that public school education glorified Protestant values and lifestyles. Brumberg, *Going to America*, 126.

43. Brumberg, *Going to America*, 75.

44. Quoted in ibid., 79.

45. Quoted in ibid., 76.

46. Quoted in ibid.

47. Ibid., 114.

48. Ibid., 154.

49. Cahan, *Education of Abraham Cahan*, 229.

50. See Clifford Putney, *Muscular Christianity: Manhood and Sports in Protestant America, 1880–1920* (Cambridge, MA: Harvard University Press, 2001), 38.

51. Gail Bederman writes that "some middle-class men—fearful of working-class men's challenges to their authority—cared more about taming potentially disruptive working-class boys in the public schools than about combating overcivilized effeminacy." Gail Bederman, *Manliness and Civilization: A Cultural History of Gender and Race in the United States, 1880–1917* (Chicago: University of Chicago Press, 1996), 100. By the 1890s, schools in areas inhabited by white, working-class populations adopted manual and vocational training as a method of "popular schooling suitable to the demands of the industrial age." Lawrence Cremin, *The Transformation of the School: Progressivism in American Education, 1876–1957* (New York: Vintage, 1964), 29.

52. This treatise was collected in a volume of essays describing civics and citizenship education in New York City public schools.

53. Henry Jenkins, *Report of the Advisory Committee to the Board of Education of the City of Los Angeles on Certain Aspects of the Organization and Administration of the Public School System (Begun April 17 and Completed May 22 1916)* (Los Angeles: Los Angeles Board of Education Advisory Committee, 1916), 69.

54. Cary Goodman, "(Re)Creating Americans at the Educational Alliance," *Journal of Ethnic Studies* 6, no. 4 (Winter 1979): 22–23.

55. Jenkins, *Report of the Advisory Committee*, 69–70.

56. Ibid., 70.

57. Shannon Jackson explains that the nineteenth-century "physical culture movement advocated a philosophical and practical approach to moral development by unifying the lessons of elocution (the physical apparatus that allowed mental expression) with active exercise." This approach echoed the basic tenets of recapitulation theory. Shannon Jackson, *Lines of Activity: Performance, Historiography, Hull-House Domesticity* (Ann Arbor: University of Michigan Press, 2000), 111–12.

58. James Salazar, *Bodies of Reform: The Rhetoric of Character in Gilded Age America* (New York: New York University Press, 2010), 116–17.

59. Putney, *Muscular Christianity*, 6.

60. Salazar, *Bodies of Reform*, 117.

61. For an excellent account of recapitulation theory in this context, see Bederman, *Manliness and Civilization*.

62. As Bellow argues, German Jews believed that "physical improvement" would lead to the "moral progress" of the *Ostjuden*. Bellow, *Educational Alliance*, 53.

63. For a discussion of the shift away from evolutionism and toward Mendelian genetics and its "fixation upon difference" in the first two decades of the twentieth century, see Sarah Wilson, "The Evolution of Ethnicity," *ELH* 76 (2009): 247.

64. This position is also associated with polygenism, the theory that different races derived from and remained on separate and unequal paths of descent. George Stocking, "The Turn-of-the-Century Concept of Race," *Modernism/Modernity* 1, no. 1 (1994): 12.

65. Carl Degler, *In Search of Human Nature: The Decline and Revival of Darwinism in American Social Thought* (New York: Oxford University Press, 1991), 22. Eugenicist reformers sought to influence racial progress by managing bodies rather than environments, for example through the sterilization of "feeble-minded" or criminal types (42).

66. Ibid., 23–24.

67. This is one explanation for the rapid decline in citizenship education programs beginning in the second decade of the twentieth century.

68. Sarah Wilson writes that they believed in a "Darwinism [that] insistently biologized immigrants. Wilson, "Evolution of Ethnicity," 250.

69. As Sarah Wilson explains, "Evolutionary thinking was often tagged as Darwinian when, in fact, it combined elements from a number of evolutionary theories." Wilson, "Evolution of Ethnicity," 272 n. 14. Wilson also shows how Jewish immigrant authors drew on the "symbolic and metaphorical modes of Darwinian thinking" to "destabilize [race-based] orthodoxies" (250, 257).

70. Cathy Boeckmann writes, "There was never a line drawn between physical evolution and mental evolution in the late nineteenth century, precisely because neo-Lamarckian thought posited that mental factors evolve in tandem with biological ones." Cathy Boeckmann, *A Question of Character: Scientific Racism and the Genres of American Fiction, 1892–1912* (Tuscaloosa: University of Alabama Press, 2000), 26.

71. Quoted in Irving Howe and Kenneth Libo, *How We Lived: A Documentary History of Immigrant Jews in America, 1880–1930* (New York: Richard Marek, 1979), 58.

72. Goodman, "(Re)Creating Americans," 13.

73. Ibid., 13.

74. These materials are located at the American Jewish Historical Society, Baron de Hirsch Fund Papers, "Miscellaneous Items," I-359, Box 2 of 2.

75. E. A. Ross, *The Old World in the New: The Significance of Past and Present Immigration to the American People* (New York: Century, 1914), 289.

76. Ibid., 290.

77. Baron de Hirsch Fund Papers, "Miscellaneous Items."

78. Ibid.

79. Pierre Bourdieu, *The Logic of Practice*, trans. Richard Nice (Palo Alto, CA: Stanford University Press, 1992), 69, 69–70, 73.

80. Pierre Bourdieu, *Distinction: A Social Critique of the Judgment of Taste*, trans. Richard Nice (Cambridge, MA: Harvard University Press, 1984), 191.

81. Bourdieu, *Logic of Practice*, 69, 67–68.

82. In her discussion of Victorian adoption disputes, Sarah Abramowicz demonstrates that although the nineteenth-century "doctrine of freedom of contract" offered individuals a "potentially radical freedom of choice," that choice was qualified by a model of child development that "[emphasized] the formative power of early experiences." Sarah Abramowicz, "Childhood and the Limits of Contract," *Yale Journal of Law and the Humanities* 21 (2009): 37.

83. Maurice Bernstein, "All Still! Life among a Thousand Siblings" (American Jewish Committee Oral History Collection, Dorot Jewish Division, New York Public Library, Box 147a), 19.

84. Ibid., 105–6.

85. James Salazar writes that US involvement in the Spanish-American War and the "'manly exercises' promoted by educational institutions" were separate prongs of US power, equally formative of and "necessary to the nation's muscular health" (*Bodies of Reform*, 118).

86. Displays of patriotism were also required in New York City public schools. In 1914, "the By-laws of the Board of Education were formally amended 'so as to provide that at all assemblies of the schools at least one patriotic song shall be sung, and that at least once a week there shall be a salute to the National Flag' followed by the singing of the 'Star-Spangled Banner.'" Brumberg, *Going to America*, 130.

87. In his discussion of the militaristic nationalism taught at the EA, Cary Goodman reminds us that the German Jewish barons who ran the EA "had a great deal at stake in an aggressive American foreign policy, having invested heavily in international consortiums and cartels." Goodman, "(Re)Creating Americans," 13. Ironically, though students in this photo are supposed to symbolize their benefactors' economic interests, they themselves were not being trained to achieve economic mastery.

88. Charles Reznikoff, "Early History of a Writer," in *By the Well of Living and Seeing, Poems, 1918–1975: The Complete Poems of Charles Reznikoff*, ed. Seamus Cooney (Santa Rosa, CA: Black Sparrow Press, 1989), 167.

89. Ibid.

90. Stephen Fredman, *A Menorah for Athena: Charles Reznikoff and the Jewish Dilemmas of Objectivist Poetry* (Chicago: University of Chicago Press, 2001), 23.

91. Ibid., 315.

92. Ibid., 318–19.

93. Charles Reznikoff and Reinhold Schiffer, "A Poet in His Milieu," in *Charles Reznikoff: Man and Poet*, ed. Milton Hindus (Orono, ME: National Poetry Foundation, 1984), 124. Even though *cheder* students read Hebrew texts, Yiddish was the language of instruction in these schools.

94. Reznikoff, "Early History," 316–17.

95. Reznikoff was associated with the "Objectivists," a group of poets that also included Louis Zukofsky, George Oppen, and Carl Rakosi. These poets made language the central object of their poetry, avoided the confessional and expressive modes, and rejected hierarchy and metaphysics. Like the other Objectivists, Reznikoff privileged ordinary language over symbol and metaphor; by distilling the world into a constellation of facts, events, and details, he imposed responsibility for interpreting meaning onto the reader. For a good

discussion of Reznikoff's Objectivist aesthetic, see Charles Bernstein, "Reznikoff's Nearness," in *The Objectivist Nexus: Essays in Cultural Poetics*, ed. Rachel Blau DuPlessis and Peter Quartermain (Tuscaloosa: University of Alabama Press, 1999), 210–39.

96. As Stan Apps and I argue in a forthcoming article about Reznikoff's memoir *Family Chronicle*, Reznikoff often figured clothing as a symbol of class critique. See Stan Apps and Tova Cooper, "Commercial Leases and Family Realities in Charles Reznikoff's *Family Chronicle*," forthcoming in *Studies in Law, Politics, and Society*.

97. Reznikoff, "Early History," 167.

98. Abrom Liessen, quoted in Fradle Pomerantz Freidenreich, *Passionate Pioneers: The Story of Yiddish Secular Education in North America, 1910–1960* (Teaneck, NJ: Holmes and Meier, 2010), 59.

99. Zalman Yefroikin, quoted in Freidenreich, *Passionate Pioneers*, 59.

100. Cahan, *Education of Abraham Cahan*, 241, 307. The socialist paper to which he refers here is *Di Neie Tzeit* (*The New Era*), which he began publishing in 1886.

101. See Jeffrey Mirel's fascinating discussion of foreign-language newspapers (Slovak, Polish, German, and others) that presented a merged vision of American and immigrant cultural ideals, particularly in their reporting on patriotic holidays and nationalist symbols; Jeffrey Mirel, *Patriotic Pluralism: Americanization Education and European Immigrants* (Cambridge, MA: Harvard University Press, 2010), 121–30.

102. Cahan, *Education of Abraham Cahan*, 237.

103. Ibid., 281.

104. Rischin, *Promised City*, 119.

105. In fact, after being accused of distancing the *Jewish Daily Forward* (*JDF*) from the socialist cause, Cahan announced in a March 1902 issue of the newspaper, "The *JDF* is not only a socialist organ, but also a socialist newspaper for the Yiddish speaking people as a whole. From now on news and articles will be written in plain Yiddish." Quoted in Ehud Manor, *Forward: The Jewish Daily Forward (Forverts) Newspaper: Immigrants, Socialism, and Jewish Politics in New York, 1890–1917* (Brighton: Sussex Academic Press, 2009), 27.

106. In an attempt to define American Yiddish cultural values, Fradle Pomerantz Freidenreich defines *Yiddishkayt* not in a religious sense (which would require Torah study, service, and good deeds) but rather in secular terms; citing Mervin Butovsky and Rabbi Harold Schulweis, she explains that it values an "ideal of humaneness, kindness, and decency" distilled "from the historic experience of an oppressed people"; Freidenreich, *Passionate Pioneers*, 16.

107. Abraham Cahan, *The Rise of David Levinsky* (New York: Penguin, 1993), 530. Subsequent page citations are to this edition and are given parenthetically in the text.

108. Bourdieu, *Logic of Practice*, 68. Discussing this issue in a different context, Sarah Wilson argues that Levinsky "attempts to incorporate" his life events into an evolutionary pattern or philosophy but ultimately fails to do so because his "old self" persists as an inescapable "inner identity" ("Evolution of Ethnicity," 263, 265; also, cf. n. 82).

109. Cahan, *Education of Abraham Cahan*, 221.

110. It is unclear whether Cahan was familiar with Oskar Panizza's 1893 story "The Operated Jew," the disturbing German-language tale of a man who unsuccessfully tries to remove the physical markers of his Jewishness through surgical intervention and physical therapy. This passage seems to invoke that story.

111. Cahan, *Education of Abraham Cahan*, 176, 180.

112. Ibid., 197.

113. The intertextuality between *Levinsky* and *Education* is evidenced by these scenes, which develop an amusing reversal; in the novel Levinsky cannot escape being identified as a yeshiva Jew, while in the autobiography Cahan ineffectually disguises himself as a yeshiva Jew.

114. Because foreign-born immigrants were more difficult to assimilate, most German Jewish educators focused their efforts on eastern European Jews who were born in America. Brumberg, *Going to America*, 135.

115. Phillip Barrish, "'The Genuine Article': Ethnicity, Capital, and *The Rise of David Levinsky*," *American Literary History* 5, no. 4 (Winter 1993): 646. Barrish also argues that "Bourdieu's model of cultural capital should be revised to take account of how individual subjects do not simply acquire a unitary 'disposition' associated with a single 'habitus,' but instead are structured by multiple, often conflicting, dispositions and social identifications (as well as by multiple habita)" (646).

116. In her analysis of *Levinsky*, Catherine Rottenberg describes identity in terms of the "competing norms" that exist alongside each other within a person. Catherine Rottenberg, *Performing Americanness: Race, Class, and Gender in Modern African-American and Jewish-American Literature* (Lebanon, NH: University Press of New England, 2008), 17. Though Rottenberg correctly notes that Levinsky encounters and performs competing ideals and behavioral norms, I argue that the ideas and behaviors he acquires upon arriving in the United States do not constitute as deep or complex a sense of self as the one he developed as a youngster in eastern Europe; this explains why this older self continually interrupts his experience of assimilation.

117. Apparently eastern European Jews had their own jokes about the German Jews they encountered in New York City. I heard the following joke from a German Jewish octogenarian in 2012: A German Jew traveling by train made sure to request a forward-facing seat when he purchased his ticket, as backward-facing seats made him ill. The man nonetheless was given a backward-facing seat, and suffered through the ride until a conductor passed. When the traveler complained about the seat, the surprised conductor asked why the man had not moved to the empty seat opposite him. The traveler, also surprised, replied that the seat was not the one he had reserved! This German Jew's rigid formality, the object of the joke's mockery, reveals the eastern European Jew's lighthearted critique of the German Jew, in particular because of his slavish submission to rules and official authority.

118. Cahan, *Education of Abraham Cahan*, 281, 242.

119. Ibid., 242, 243.

120. Paul Connerton argues that these two registers of knowledge result from embodied (or "incorporating") practice and linguistic (or "inscribing") practice. Connerton, *How Societies Remember*, 72–73.

121. Bernstein, "All Still!," 323.

122. Emanuel Weinstock, interviewed by Muriel Cadel, December 16, 1986 (American Jewish Committee Oral History Collection, Dorot Jewish Division, New York Public Library), Box 52, no. 3, pp. 5 and 7.

123. Ibid.

124. Ibid., 17.

125. Ibid., 50.

126. Ibid.

127. Supported by the Baron de Hirsch Fund, this school provided five-month training programs for eastern European Jews who wished to become carpenters, machinists, plumbers, and electricians.

128. Baron de Hirsch Trade School, Student Records, Correspondence of Superintendents, and Misc., American Jewish Historical Society, Box 37.

129. Ibid.

130. Student recollections from Carlisle similarly frame any critique of the institution with a positive account of the Americanization process, even when the critique indicates serious problems adapting to US life or achieving economic stability. In this sense, what these otherwise distinct programs share is their ability to teach students to internalize a narrative about their successful Americanization—one that shaped both their embodied experience and their perceptions—even when their experience did not justify this narrative.

5 / Emma Goldman, the Modern School, and the Politics of Reproduction

1. Emma Goldman, *Living My Life*, vol. 1 (New York: Dover Publications, 1970), 3. Subsequent page citations to this work are to this edition and are given parenthetically in the text.

2. Joseph Slaughter, *Human Rights, Inc.: The World Novel, Narrative Form, and International Law* (New York: Fordham University Press, 2007), 181.

3. A chain of events led Modern School educators to move the school to Stelton, New Jersey, in 1914. After three men at the Ferrer Center were killed by a bomb intended for the Rockefeller estate in Tarrytown, New York, the Ferrer Center was politicized and infiltrated by police informers and also lost some of its funding. Believing that the New York location was no longer a safe place to educate children, Modern School educators moved the school to Stelton. Fernanda Perrone, "The Move to New Jersey," in *History of the Modern School of Stelton*, accessed November 30, 2013, www.libraries. rutgers.edu/rul/libs/scua/modern_school/modern.shtml, sec. 3, para. 1.

4. As Paul Avrich—paraphrasing Harry Kelly—explains, it was mainly through the efforts of Emma Goldman that "the New York Ferrer School was opened." Paul Avrich, *The Modern School Movement: Anarchism and Education in the United States* (Edinburgh: AK Press, 2006), 75. This was one of many Modern Schools "administered by local branches of the Ferrer Association" (renamed the Modern School Association of America in 1916). The various Modern Schools shared a libertarian approach to education, promoted learning by doing, emphasized hygiene and physical health, and were committed to education for both children and adults. Avrich, *Modern School Movement*, 52.

5. Alice Wexler also explains that "after the Center was established . . . Goldman withdrew, playing a relatively minor role in its day-to-day operations and limiting her participation primarily to ceremonial occasions, fund-raising, and publicity." Alice Wexler, *Emma Goldman: An Intimate Life* (New York: Pantheon, 1984), 202.

6. According to Goldman, the Modern School originated with Paul Robin at Cempius, near Paris, after which it was "carried to Spain" by Ferrer. Emma Goldman, "Francisco Ferrer," in *Anarchy! An Anthology of Emma Goldman's Mother Earth*, ed. Peter Glassgold (Washington, DC: Counterpoint, 2001), 42. In the United States, however, the Modern School was shaped by the varying political and educational philosophies of its teachers, as this chapter illustrates.

7. The Ferrer Center also hosted evening classes where artists, intellectuals, and laborers could take art and English classes and attend lectures about political, philosophical, and literary subjects.

8. Carl Zigrosser edited the school's magazine from 1917 to 1920 and transformed it from a routine monthly newsletter into what both Hart Crane and Wallace Stevens praised as the most beautifully printed magazine to exist anywhere in the United States. Laurence R. Veysey, *The Communal Experience: Anarchist and Mystical Communities in Twentieth-Century America* (Chicago: University of Chicago Press, 1978), 96.

9. Leonard Abbot, "Symposium on Libertarian Education by the Board of Managers of the Modern School Association of North America," *Modern School Magazine* 5, no. 5 (October 1916): 105. From the Modern School Collection, Manuscript Collection 1055, Special Collections and University Archives, Rutgers University Libraries, Box 2, Folder 3.

10. William Thurston Brown, n. title, *Modern School Magazine* 3, no. 1, Special Anniversary Number (May 1916): 2, Modern School Collection, Box 2, Folder 3.

11. As Elizabeth Byrne Ferm—a longtime Modern School teacher—explains of Froebel (Pestalozzi's student): "Through his mathematical playthings—which he called 'Gifts and Occupations,' Froebel hoped to aid the child to develop according to the law of the child's own being." Elizabeth Byrne Ferm, "The Spirit of Freedom," *Modern School Magazine* 4, no. 4, 99, Modern School Archives, Rutgers Special Collections, Box B2, Folder 6.

12. William Shulman, "Symposium," 101.

13. M. Epstein, "Symposium," 108.

14. Francisco Ferrer, quoted in Brown, n. title, 12.

15. Ibid.

16. Brown, n. title, 13.

17. Emma Goldman, "The Social Importance of the Modern School," Emma Goldman Papers, Manuscripts and Archives Division, New York Public Library, Astor, Lenox, and Tilden Foundations, accessed February 13, 2013, http://dwardmac.pitzer .edu/Anarchist_Archives/goldman/socimportms.html, n.p.

18. As this book illustrates throughout, the US educational landscape at this time included public schools, trade schools, and citizenship education programs whose curricula often reproduced economic stratification in working-class communities of multiple racial, ethnic, and national origins. The founders, teachers, and parents of the Modern School, despite their differences (and there were many), sought to create an educational environment that simultaneously avoided the "deradicalizing influence" of such schools, public and otherwise, and the "oppressive paternalism" of the settlement house. Veysey, *Communal Experience*, 81, 79.

19. Goldman, "Social Importance," n.p., emphasis in original.

20. Harry Kelly, quoted in Avrich, *Modern School Movement*, 173.

21. Emma Goldman, quoted in Avrich, *Modern School Movement*, 41.

22. Mike Gold, "A Little Bit of Millennium," quoted in Victor Sacharoff et al., *Recollections from the Modern School Colony*, ed. Jon Thoreau Scott (Altamont, NY: Friends of the Modern School, 2007), 55.

23. John Dewey and Evelyn Dewey, *Schools of To-morrow* (New York: E. P. Dutton, 1915), Internet Archive, http://ia700300.us.archive.org/18/items/schoolsoftomorro0005826mbp/schoolsoftomorro0005826mbp.pdf, 70–71, 133.

24. Ibid., 176.

25. The Wirt system was discontinued as a model for the New York City public schools in 1917 as a result of a decade of opposition by "Jewish labor activists, socialists, and the mass of parents" who saw the vocational emphasis of Wirt's program "as reflecting a class bias on the part of reformers who were thought to be in league with the Rockefeller Trust." Stephan Brumberg, *Going to America, Going to School: The Jewish Immigrant Public School Encounter in Turn-of-the-Century New York City* (New York: Praeger, 1986), 145.

26. This comment was made by Laurence Veysey, a historian and former student at the Modern School. Veysey, *Communal Experience*, 152. Joseph J. Cohen—one of the school's co-founders—corroborates this view: "When Elizabeth Ferm set up her little neighborhood playhouse for the very young tots of the Colony in the old barn building in the summer of 1920 . . . we became convinced that here, at last, we had found the right people to introduce the proper method of libertarian education at our School." Joseph J. Cohen, "When Stelton Was Young," in *The Modern School of Stelton: A Sketch*, by Joseph J. Cohen and Alexis C. Ferm (1925; repr., San Diego: Factory School, 2006), 75.

27. Veysey, *Communal Experience*, 152.

28. Ana Koch-Riedel, "Basketry in the Modern School," *The Modern School: A Monthly Magazine Devoted to Libertarian Ideas in Education*, April 1921 (Stelton, NJ: Ferrer Modern School), 3, accessed January 8, 2013, www.talkinghistory.org/stelton/msmapr1921.pdf.

29. Ibid.

30. Elizabeth Ferm, quoted in Veysey, *Communal Experience*, 149–50.

31. Avrich, *Modern School Movement*, 250.

32. This and other photos of the Modern School may have been taken by Oscar Steckbardt (Steich), who, as Victor Sacharoff notes, was a "professional photographer . . . [and] unofficially, the photographer of colony personalities and events" who "took most of the old photos in the colony." Sacharoff et al., *Recollections*, 19. Cf. above, Introduction, note 112.

33. Dewey and Dewey, *Schools of To-morrow*, 191–92.

34. Ibid., 192.

35. Alexis C. Ferm, "Five Years of Creative Work," in Cohen and Ferm, *Modern School of Stelton*, 112.

36. Leonard Rico, "My Experiences at the Modern School," quoted in Sacharoff et al., *Recollections*, 99.

37. Quoted in Avrich, *Modern School Movement*, 111.

38. Avrich, *Modern School Movement*, 304.

39. Quoted in Avrich, *Modern School Movement*, 305.

40. This scene recalls Booker T. Washington's comments about a man he encounters in the Alabama countryside. Washington objects to the fact that, rather than cleaning house, this man is studying a French grammar book: "One of the saddest things I saw during the month of travel which I have described was a young man, who had attended some high school, sitting down in a one-room cabin, with grease on his clothing, filth all around him, and weeds in the yard and garden, engaged in studying a French grammar." Booker T. Washington, *Up from Slavery* (Boston: Bedford/St. Martin's, 2003), 96. Washington's unsympathetic portrayal of this man, in which the

evocation of "filth," "weeds," and "grease" overshadows the positive associations of "studying," exemplifies Washington's adoption of hands-on education to reproduce the economic status quo, despite his own history as a slave.

41. Later in the autobiography, Goldman offers a more analytical reason for rejecting the nuclear family when she writes, "Together with my own marital experiences [these experiences] had convinced me that binding people for life was wrong. The constant proximity in the same house, the same room, the same bed, revolted me." Goldman, *Living My Life*, 36.

42. Goldman, "Social Importance," n.p.

43. Ibid.

44. Goldman mentored Margaret Sanger, who was arrested twice for violating the 1873 Comstock Law; Goldman also smuggled contraceptives into the United States. See "Birth Control Pioneer," Emma Goldman Papers, Online Exhibition, http://sunsite.berkeley.edu/goldman/Exhibition/birthcontrol.html.

45. Mary Hansen recounts such messiness in her short history of the Living House. Describing the impact of the school's first group of educators—who "had an idea of making the child independent"—Hansen writes that the child "was to do everything for itself, regardless of age or sex, and by the end of the summer the thirty-two youngsters, having traveled over the colony on an average of once a day, each one carrying something for which he was responsible, left it wherever he got tired of the job. So tubs, basins, brushes, etc., were littered about the house, and the banks along the brook were dotted with mildewed clothing, while dishes and clothing could be found everywhere that they should not have been." Mary Hansen, "Facts and Theories at the Living House," *Modern School Magazine*, Convention Number, September 1921, p. 2, Modern School Archives, Box 4, Folder 4.

46. Charlotte Perkins Gilman, "The Collective Aspect of Education," *Modern School Magazine*, May 1918, 137, Modern School Archives, Box 2, Folder 9.

47. When the school was located in New York City, Goldman invited the Ferms to teach there, though at the time they declined because they "apparently thought the parents too vociferous and meddlesome to allow them to run the school without interference." Avrich, *Modern School Movement*, 296.

48. Sacharoff et al., *Recollections*, 37.

49. Avrich, *Modern School Movement*, 298.

50. Ibid., 291.

51. Rhya (Levine) Seligman, quoted in Sacharoff et al., *Recollections*, 83, emphasis in original. Seligman sent this recollection to the Rutgers Research Department on April 29, 2000.

52. Ferm, "Five Years," 113.

53. Cohen, "When Stelton Was Young," 40.

54. This type of isolation did not benefit everyone; as Leonard Rico recalls, "I was unaware of different kinds of people who might have been more violent or competitive. . . . It wasn't until I was thirteen that I became more aware of those influences and to some extent I suspect that my upbringing didn't provide an orientation to protect me from that broader culture." Quoted in Sacharoff et al., *Recollections*, 100.

55. Ray Porter Miller, "My Teachers at Stelton," in *Modern School of Stelton: Twenty-Fifth Anniversary, 1915–1940*, ed. L. D. Abbott, R. Rocker, and H. Havel (Stelton, NJ: Modern School of Stelton, 1940), 27.

56. Jon Thoreau Scott, Stelton Transcript, *Talking History* (Aural History Productions), www.talkinghistory.org/stelton/stelton_transcript.pdf, 4. Not only did other students in this documentary fondly remember these educational hikes, but the Modern School archives contain many recollections of hiking as a form of education at the school.

57. Jon Thoreau Scott, quoted in Sacharoff, *Recollections*, 33.

58. Francisco Ferrer, *L'école rénovée*, quoted in William Archer, *The Life, Trial, and Death of Francisco Ferrer* (New York: Moffat, Yard, 1911), 86.

59. Zachary Schwartz, "Not Just a School," in Abbott, Rocker, and Havel, *Modern School of Stelton*, 26.

60. Anna Cohen, "Girl Full of Wonder," *Voice of the Children* 6 (1924): n.p., Modern School Archives, Box 5, Folder 9.

61. Elizabeth Ferm, "Activity and Passivity of the Educator," *Mother Earth*, March 1907, 26.

62. A. Cohen, "Girl Full of Wonder," n.p.

63. Avrich writes, "There was no indoor toilet or furnace either in the house or dormitory. Ray Miller remembers waking up on winter mornings 'with my hair frozen to the pillow.' . . . The children kept warm 'by exercise or with the aid of bonfires' lighted nearby." Avrich, *Modern School Movement*, 260.

64. See ibid., chap. 7.

65. Wexler, *Emma Goldman*, 202.

66. Harry Kelly, ed., *The Modern School, A Monthly Bulletin Published by the Francisco Ferrer Association* 3 (Winter), n.d., n.p. Though this issue is not dated, it is probably from winter 1914, from before the school moved out to Stelton, New Jersey. Photos of this and other early issues of the bulletin are posted on the website of the Friends of the Modern School. Friends of the Modern School, "Photos."

67. One limitation of reading *Living My Life* as Goldman's self-representation is the fact, noted by Goldman's biographer Alice Wexler, that "the memoir was heavily edited by Alexander Berkman. . . . We know from Berkman's diaries the extent to which he changed, cut, and polished the manuscript." Wexler, *Emma Goldman*, xvii–xviii.

68. Elsewhere, Goldman attributes her anarchist sensibilities to her biology, announcing that she "was just born so." Quoted in Richard Drinnon, *Rebel in Paradise: A Biography of Emma Goldman* (Chicago: University of Chicago Press, 1961), 19.

69. When narrating her initial political awakening in 1887, Goldman writes of her shock at seeing policemen lining the walls at a socialist speech in which Johanna Greie demanded free speech and called the Haymarket trial a farce. Goldman, *Living My Life*, 8.

70. Whereas earlier in her career Goldman did not actively campaign for birth control, by 1916 she was sentenced to prison for speaking to the working poor about it; defending herself in court, she claimed her support of birth control was "not for personal gain or profit, but for the education of the working and professional classes who, harassed by economic conditions, by the high cost of living, by the terrible congestion of our large cities, cannot decently provide for a brood of children, as a result of which their children are born weak, are ill cared for and ill nourished." Leonard D. Abbott, "Reflections on Emma Goldman's Trial," in Glassgold, *Anarchy!*, 142.

71. Later in life, when Goldman was in her forties, she encountered similar demands to start a family from her longtime lover Ben Reitman, but this was twenty

years after she had already made the decision not to become a mother. Wexler, *Emma Goldman*, 159.

72. In a striking parallel, Jane Addams links her choice not to have children to her self-image as a maternal leader for the immigrant masses. As Heather Ostman argues in her comparison of Addams and Goldman, Addams rejected the normative assumption that the choice not to marry or have children is an "abnormal" one. Jane Addams, *Second Twenty Years at Hull-House* (1930), quoted in Heather Ostman, "Maternal Rhetoric in Jane Addams's *Twenty Years at Hull House*," *Philological Quarterly* 85, nos. 3–4 (Summer–Fall 2006): 363.

73. Alternately, other critics and biographers have explored Goldman's redirection of her motherliness into her editorship of *Mother Earth* and her relationships with various men. In particular, see Heather Ostman, "'The Most Dangerous Woman in America': Emma Goldman and the Rhetoric of Motherhood in *Living My Life*," *Prose Studies* 31, no. 1 (April 2009): 55–73. See also Wexler, *Emma Goldman*.

74. Alexander Berkman writes of his need to edit out the numerous passages in which Goldman describes her bodily pain at length. Drinnon, *Rebel in Paradise*, 20. Despite the symbolic import of Goldman's pain, it is also important to remember that she suffered from real illness throughout her life. Drinnon notes, "At one time or another [her physical distress] included consumption, varicose veins, a tendency to fall, and unknown to her, perhaps even diabetes" (20).

75. The simultaneous persistence of embodied memory and desperation to escape it may in part explain Goldman's continual movement—inside and outside the United States—throughout her life. It may also inadvertently have allowed her to reimagine home in terms of community, a view compatible with Goldman's lifestyle, and one that allowed her to find refuge in the like-minded people she encountered in the towns, cities, and countries to which she traveled.

76. The Kleinmans articulate their theory as part of a discussion about survivors from China's Cultural Revolution. Arthur Kleinman and Joan Kleinman, "How Bodies Remember: Social Memory and Bodily Experience of Criticism, Resistance, and Delegitimation Following China's Cultural Revolution," *New Literary History* 25, no. 3 (Summer 1994): 712.

77. Ibid., 715.

78. Ibid., 716.

79. Discussing Goldman's ambivalence about motherhood, Alice Wexler suggests that Goldman may have represented her choice not to have children as martyrdom because "she felt constrained to justify her untraditional choice in terms of traditional values." Wexler also suggests that Goldman's ambivalence might be a symptom of her "painful memories" of "her own cold, distant mother." Wexler, *Emma Goldman*, 73.

80. Kleinman and Kleinman, "How Bodies Remember," 716.

Conclusion

1. Joseph Slaughter, *Human Rights, Inc.: The World Novel, Narrative Form, and International Law* (New York: Fordham University Press, 2007), 94.

2. Ibid., 182.

3. A wide range of citizenship discourses has come to represent the cultural pluralist perspective, including feminist, cultural, reconstructionist, queer, and transnational discourses. For a thorough discussion of this development, see Kathleen Knight

Abowitz and Jason Harnish, "Contemporary Discourses of Citizenship," *Review of Educational Research* 76, no. 4 (Winter 2006): 653–90.

4. Bradley C. S. Watson, "Just as the Twig Is Bent: Civic Education in an Age of Doubt," in *Civic Education and Culture*, ed. Bradley C. S. Watson (Wilmington, DE: ISI Books, 2005), xxxiii. For example, Watson writes, "Today, of course, under the influence of various related ideologies that often go under the name 'multiculturalism,' both patriotism and education in Western or American ways is distinctly unfashionable" (xxxii).

5. Knight Abowitz and Harnish, "Contemporary Discourses," 658–59.

6. Ibid., 660. The presence of the Pledge of Allegiance in the public schools has long been a contested legal issue, examined in cases such as *Minersville School District v. Gobitis* (1940) and *Board of Education v. Barnette* (1943). In the first case, a Jehovah's Witness claimed that a Pennsylvania public school violated his child's religious freedom by expelling the child for refusing to stand and salute the flag while reciting the Pledge of Allegiance. Judge Felix Frankfurter—not surprisingly an assimilated German American Jew—ruled in favor of the school, arguing, "The ultimate foundation of a free society is the binding tie of cohesive sentiment," and further contended that the flag ceremony fostered a "unifying sentiment" on which democracy depended. *Minersville School District v. Gobitis*, 310 U.S. 586, 596–97 (1940), quoted in Anne Dailey, "Developing Citizens," *Iowa Law Review* 91 (February 2006): 443. *Gobitis* was overruled three years later in *Board of Education v. Barnette*; the ruling Justice Jackson decided in favor of the child, arguing that under the US Constitution "national unity" can be fostered "by persuasion and example" but not by "compulsion." *Board of Education v. Barnette*, 319 U.S. 624 (1943): 530. In his opinion, Jackson argues that he cannot allow the salute to be compulsory because of the possibility that children who go through the motions of the salute will become "unwilling converts." In other words, Jackson suggests, as I have in this book, that repeated action produces belief: saluting the flag does not involve a mere "[simulation of] assent by words without belief and by a gesture barren of meaning" (529).

7. Linda Bosniak, "Citizenship Denationalized," *Indiana Journal of Global Legal Studies* 7, no. 2 (Spring 2000): 491.

8. Ibid., 469 n. 81.

9. No Child Left Behind mandated math and reading tests throughout elementary and high school, supposedly to ensure that students of all races, classes, and geographical locations were being educated fairly. Because schools that did not meet their "performance targets" for two years ongoing were "subjected to sanctions," these schools "rolled out a relentless series of 'diagnostic' tests that were actually practice rounds for the high-stakes exams to come." "The Trouble with Testing Mania," *New York Times*, July 13, 2013, www.nytimes.com/2013/07/14/opinion/sunday/the-trouble-with-testing-mania.html.

10. Another development testifies to the influence of civic republican ideology on the field of standardized testing. In an ostensible attempt to close the "achievement gap" between black and Latino students who performed poorly in comparison with white and Asian students, the Virginia State Board of Education implemented a new system whereby passing rates on reading and math tests would be lower for blacks, Latinos, and students with disabilities. Claudio Sanchez, "Firestorm Erupts over Virginia's Education Goals," Northwest Public Radio, November 12, 2012, http://nwpr.

org/post/firestorm-erupts-over-virginias-education-goals. One might read this institutionalization of lower expectations for different racial groups as an expression of civic republican ideology: Virginia's actions suggest that it is trying to achieve racial equality, but in actuality it is using lower performance standards to justify a reduced quality of teaching.

11. The *New York Times* editorial "The Trouble with Testing Mania" states, "Some problems could be partly solved by the Common Core learning standards, an ambitious set of goals for what students should learn. The Common Core, adopted by all but a handful of states, could move the nation away from rote memorization—and those cheap, color-in-the-bubble tests—and toward a writing-intensive system that gives students the reasoning skills they need in the new economy." Forty-five states, the District of Columbia, four territories, and the Department of Defense Education Activity have adopted the Common Core State Standards. "In the States," Common Core State Standards Initiative, 2012, www.corestandards.org/in-the-states.

12. Even inclusion of written elements is limiting, because the test taker is constrained by the assumption that the test grader will be looking for answers that correspond to a limited range of predetermined possibilities.

13. "Is the Use of Standardized Tests Improving Education in America?" Standardized Tests, ProCon.org, 2013, http://standardizedtests.procon.org/. ProCon.org is a nonprofit, bipartisan organization.

14. On February 17, 2009, President Barack Obama's Race to the Top program was signed into law, inviting states to compete for $4.35 billion in extra funding on the basis of the strength of their student test scores (sec. 4, para. 2).

15. Eric Hanushek and Ludger Wößmann, "Impacts of Educational Quality on Individual Incomes—Developed Countries," World Bank Policy Research Working Paper 4122, February 2007, 7, https://openknowledge.worldbank.org/bitstream/handle/10986/7154/wps4122.pdf.

16. Ibid., 7–8.

17. It is interesting to note that China and Finland, while producing high-performing students, have very different approaches to testing.

18. "Non-traditional Mathematics Curriculum Results in Higher Standardized Test Scores," University of Missouri News Bureau, September 16, 2013, http://munews.missouri.edu/news-releases/2013/0916–non-traditional-mathematics-curriculum-results-in-higher-standardized-test-scores-mu-study-finds/.

19. "Trouble with Testing Mania."

20. Yong Zhao, "U-Turn to Prosperity," *Educational Leadership* 70, no. 5 (February 2013): 2, http://216.78.200.159/RandD/Educational%20Leadership/U-Turn%20to%20Prosperity%20-%20Zhao.pdf.

21. Zhao is the associate dean for global education at the University of Oregon, as well as a professor of technology and educational measurement.

22. Zhao, "U-Turn to Prosperity," 1.

23. Ibid.

24. Bosniak, "Citizenship Denationalized," 477.

25. Paul Wapner, quoted in Bosniak, "Citizenship Denationalized," 478.

26. Ibid., 449.

27. Ibid.

28. Richard Falk, quoted in Bosniak, "Citizenship Denationalized," 483–84 n. 156.

29. Evan Watkins, "World Bank Literacy and the Culture of Jobs," in *World Bank Education*, edited by Amitava Kumar (Minneapolis: University of Minnesota Press, 2003), 20.

30. Ibid., 20, 22.

31. Eric Liu, *The Accidental Asian: Notes of a Native Speaker* (New York: Vintage, 1999). This title seems to reference James Baldwin's book of autobiographical essays, *Notes of a Native Son*.

32. Ibid., 14.

33. William Boelhower, *Autobiographical Transactions in Modernist America: The Immigrant, the Architect, the Artist, the Citizen* (Udine: Del Bianco, 1992), 69.

34. Liu, *Accidental Asian*, 5.

35. Ibid., 7.

36. Ibid. "I never knew whether he, the son of a general, felt pressure to join the military. . . . I never knew what ambitions he packed with him when he sailed across the Pacific. . . . I never knew whether he was homesick when he cooked his first meal in America" (9).

37. Ibid., 15.

38. Ibid., 14.

39. Ibid., 19.

40. Jumpha Lahiri, "Nobody's Business," in *Unaccustomed Earth*, Kindle ed. (New York: Knopf, 2008), n.p.

41. Ibid.

42. Ibid.

43. Ibid.

44. Ibid.

45. Zhang Zhen, "The Jet Lag of a Migratory Bird: Border Crossings toward/from 'the Land That Is Not,'" in *Chinese Women Traversing Diaspora: Memoirs, Essays, and Poetry*, ed. Sharon K. Hom (New York: Routledge, 2013).

46. Ibid., 52.

47. Ibid.

48. Norma Field, quoted in Zhen, "Jet Lag," 53.

49. Zhen, "Jet Lag," 54.

50. Quoted in Sarah Wilson, "The Evolution of Ethnicity," *ELH* 76, no. 1 (Spring 2009): 267; Horace Kallen, "Democracy versus the Melting-Pot," in *Culture and Democracy in the United States* (New York: Boni and Liveright, 1924), 86.

51. Wilson, "Evolution of Ethnicity," 267.

Index

Bellow, Adam, 145, 243*n*62
Beloit College, 57
Bender, David E., 237*n*101
Benjamin, Walter, 239*n*9
Ben-Ur, Aviva, 238*n*1
Berch, Bettina, 72–73, 74–75, 88, 226*n*21, 226*n*28
Bercovitch, Sacvan, 21–23, 61–62, 223*n*141
Bergson, Henri, 12
Berkman, Alexander, 168, 179, 189, 251*n*67, 252*n*72
Bernstein, Maurice, 147, 148–49, 164
Bildung, 41–42
bildungsroman, 18, 19, 26, 214*n*4; antibildungsroman, 20–21; dissensual bildungsroman, 21, 101, 128, 135, 194; idealist bildungsroman, 56, 135, 199; realist bildungsroman, 21, 32, 68, 199
birth control, 167, 181, 186, 250*n*44, 251*n*70
Black, Charles, 211*n*73
The Black Atlantic (Gilroy), 111
Black Codes, 3
Blakesley, Betsey, 116, 235*n*75
Blaustein, David, 137
Boas, Franz, 15
Boeckmann, Cathy, 243*n*70
Boelhower, William, 55, 223*n*130
Booth, Charles, 231*n*2
Bosniak, Linda, 15, 195–96, 198, 207*n*9, 211*n*73
Bourdieu, Pierre, 12–13, 146–47
Boyesen, Bayard, 168
Boy Scouts' curriculum, 32, 47, 53, 92, 221*n*105
Boys' Life magazine, 50
Brown, Estelle Aubrey, 218*n*53
Brown, William Thurston, 169
Brownies' Book (Du Bois), 100, 115–19, 235*n*74, 236*n*83
Bruce, Blanche K., 119
Brumberg, Stephan, 242*n*42
Brumble, David, III, 214*n*7
Burgess, Marianna, 44, 66, 219*n*64
Burke Act of 1906, 215*n*14
Bush, George H. W., 196
Bush, George W., 196
By the Well of Living and Seeing (Reznikoff), 134

Cahan, Abraham, 5, 15, 16, 21, 27, 133–66, 193

Cahill, Cathleen, 213*n*2
Calloway, Thomas, 71, 225*n*11
Campfire Girls, 53, 221*n*105
capitalism, 12, 35, 46, 52, 59, 60
Carlisle Indian Industrial School, 5, 14, 25–26, 31, 43, 45, 71, 82, 219*n*58
Carnoy, Michael, 208*n*10
Casey, Edward, 12
Ceremony (Silko), 53
Chase, Hiram, 48
cheders (Jewish elementary schools), 138
Cherniavsky, Eva, 82
Cherokee Nation v. Georgia (1831), 38, 216*n*28
Child, Lydia Maria, 103
child-centered programs, 4
China, standardized testing in, 197
Chinese Americans, citizenship education geared toward, 208*n*16
Christianity, 55, 57, 59
citizenship, 13–17, 117
citizenship education, 2–4, 36–45, 67–98, 208*n*15, 208*n*16
Civic Education and Culture (Watson), 195
civic republicanism, 7, 13–17, 68, 100, 193, 194–95, 198
Civil Rights Act (1866), 38
civil sphere vs. private sphere, 208*n*9
Clifford, James, 236*n*91
clothing as symbol in American Indian assimilation, 40
Cloud, Henry Roe, 215*n*15
Cohen, Anna, 183
Cohen, Joseph, 170, 180–81, 249*n*26
Cohen, Ronald, 9
Columbian Guards, 120
Common Core standards, 196, 254*n*11
The Common School and the Negro American (Du Bois), 104
communal ownership of property, 46
communists, 184
compulsory education, 6
conformity required of American Indians, 32
Connerton, Paul, 246*n*120
Constitution, US, 207*n*3
consumerism, 12
Coolidge, Calvin, 3
Cora, Angel de, 49
corporal punishment, 42–43, 165
corporeal realism, 210–11*n*57

Race to the Top, 196, 254*n*14
racial intermarriage, 63–64, 228*n*63
racism, 3, 32. *See also* stereotypes
Ragged Dick (Alger), 24, 134
Rakosi, Carl, 244*n*95
realist bildungsroman, 21, 32, 68, 199
recapitulation theory, 121, 143
reconstructionist discourse, 17, 23, 102
Red Hunters and the Animal People (Eastman), 221*n*108
Red Matters (Krupat), 33
Reel, Estelle, 5, 68–69, 89–91, 218*n*47, 229*nn*76–77
Reform Judaism, 134, 139, 140, 159
Reitman, Ben, 251*n*71
repetitive practices used in education, 4
reproductive rights, 186. *See also* birth control
Reuben, Stephen, 94–95, 96, 97
Reznikoff, Charles, 134–35, 149–50, 200, 244*n*95
Rhodes, Chip, 208*n*14, 210*n*52
rhythmic and repetitive physical activities, 2, 134
Rico, Leonard, 176, 250*n*54
Riggs, Stephen, 215*n*13
Riis, Jacob, 25
Rischin, Moses, 240*n*12
The Rise of David Levinsky (Cahan), 5, 27, 134, 152–64
Robin, Paul, 247*n*6
Rodman, Henrietta, 178
Roe, Gilbert, 168
Rogers, Howard, 225*n*11
Rogin, Michael, 46
Roosevelt, Theodore, 3, 13, 142
Rosaldo, Renato, 15, 48
Ross, Edward Alsworth, 145, 210*n*48
Rottenberg, Catherine, 246*n*116
Rousseau, Jean-Jacques, 14, 51
Rulo, Zallie, 231*n*101
Runkle, John, 9
Rutgers Special Collections, 5

Sacharoff, Victor, 180, 249*n*32
Salazar, James, 142, 237*n*96, 237*n*100, 238*n*103, 244*n*85
Sanger, Margaret, 205, 250*n*44
Santee Normal School, 215*n*13
Santee Sioux, 34

savagery-barbarism-civilization continuum, 82–83, 108–9
Scenes in the Daily Life of an Orphan Child (HOA), 139
Schmidt, Peter, 80, 81
The School and the Immigrant (New York City Department of Education), 138
Schools of To-Morrow (Dewey & Dewey), 7, 171
Schwartz, Zachary, 182–83
Scott, Jon Thoreau, 181–82
secularism, 134, 139
secular jeremiads, 18, 21–23, 59, 61–62, 192
A Seed Lesson (Johnston), 78, 80
selfhood, 76
self-reflexivity, 32
self-regulation, 76
Selig, Diana, 236*n*86
Seligman, Rhya, 180
Sephardic Jews, 136, 240*n*20
September 11, 2001 terrorist attacks, 195
Seton, Ernest Thompson, 50
Shiels, Albert, 138
Shilling, Chris, 210*n*57
Shklar, Judith, 211*n*73
Shulman, William, 169
Silko, Leslie Marmon, 53
Simpson, Max, 118
Sinnette, Elinor, 235*n*74
Skrbis, Zlatko, 16, 119, 131, 212*n*81, 237*n*92
Slater Industrial School, 104
Slaughter, Joseph, 19, 20, 21, 41, 101, 135, 151, 168, 231*n*8
slavery, 106, 111, 116
Sloan, Thomas L., 220*n*80
Smith, Katharine Capshaw, 235*n*72
Smith, Rogers, 38, 39, 211*n*73, 216*n*26
Smith, Shawn, 73
Smith-Hughes Act of 1917, 227*n*41
social constructionists, 2
social Darwinism, 3, 4, 8, 10–13, 33, 57, 62, 68, 70–88, 119–32, 137
Society of American Indians (SAI), 47, 49
The Sociology of Cosmopolitanism (Kendall, Woodward, & Skrbis), 16, 131, 237*n*92
Solotaroff, A., 177, 189
The Soul of the Indian (Eastman), 58
The Souls of Black Folk (Du Bois), 115, 234*n*52, 235*n*70
Spack, Ruth, 72, 95, 230*n*89, 231*n*101

About the Author

Tova Cooper is an assistant professor of English at the University of South Florida. She is particularly interested in ethnic American literature and has published essays on American authors, photographers, and comic book artists in *Modern Fiction Studies, Paradoxa, Arizona Quarterly,* and *American Literature.* Tova is currently working on a book about US law and literature with the "poet lawyerate" Stan Apps; their article, "Commercial Leases and Family Realities in Charles Reznikoff's *Family Chronicle,*" is forthcoming in *Studies in Law, Politics, and Society.* Cooper is also writing an essay on the Aspergian literary hero and alternative ways of knowing in contemporary US fiction. In her spare time, Cooper works on her novel *Underwater Subdivision,* makes ceramic art, grows her own vegetables, and takes care of her two monkey-children, Leo and August.

CPSIA information can be obtained
at www.ICGtesting.com
Printed in the USA
FSOW02n0943130115
4473FS